Global Culture Industry

To the memory and the activity of Dede Boden, who was an integral participant in, and an inspiration to, this research

Global Culture Industry: The Mediation of Things

SCOTT LASH AND CELIA LURY

polity

First published in 2007 by Polity Press

Polity Press
65 Bridge Street
Cambridge CB2 1UR, UK

Polity Press
350 Main Street
Malden, MA 02148, USA

ISBN-13: 978-07456-2482-2
ISBN-13: 978-07456-2483-9 (pb)

A catalogue record for this book is available from the British Library.

Designed and Typeset in FF Swift 9.25pt on 11.75pt
by Peter Ducker MISTD
Printed and bound in Great Britain by MPG Books Ltd, Bodmin, Cornwall

For further information on Polity, visit our website: www.polity.co.uk

Contents

Acknowledgements

The project on which this book is based was proposed in 1995. The authors developed the proposal for an empirical study of 'The global biography of cultural products' with their then colleagues Deirdre Boden and Dan Shapiro at Lancaster University. The proposal was to the Economic and Social Research Council (ESRC) as part of the Media Economics and Media Cultures Programme. Simon Frith was Director of the Programme and we would like to thank him for his support. In addition to our colleagues, Dan Shapiro and Deirdre Boden, the research officers on the project, Jeremy Valentine and Vince Miller, also contributed greatly to this book. Nicholas Abercrombie had been a central member of earlier group projects and his contribution stayed with us.

The following trademarks are included in the book – they are either referred to in the text or featured in the photographs. The extent of the list is itself testament to the ubiquity of branding in the contemporary world. We acknowledge that these are all registered trademarks, and stress that they are being used solely for academic purposes.

90 Minutes	Bugs Bunny	Daimler-Benz
Aardman	Burger King	Daimler-Chrysler
Abril	Buzz Lightyear	Daily Express
Adidas	Canal Plus	Daily Telegraph
Air Jordan	Canary Wharf Ltd	Disney
Air Max	Canon	Disneyworld
AMFA	Carlsberg	Domestos
Amstel	Casio	Donald Duck
Angel Delight	CBS	Drastona
Antiques Roadshow	Channel 4	EBU
Apple	Christies	Eeyore
BBC	Cinemax	Elsevier
Boots	Clinton Cards	Embratel
BOSS	Clothes Show Live	EMI
Blue Ribbon Sports	CNN	Energizer
British Museum	Coca-Cola	ESPN
BSkyB	Comme des Garçons	Euro '96
Buena Vista	Daffy Duck	Euro Channel

EuroDisney
FA
FIFA
Five Nations
Ford
Four Four Two
Fox
France Telecom
French Connection
Fujifilm
General Electric
General Motors
Gillette
Globo
Goal
Guardian
Happy Meal
HBO
iBook
iMac
IMG
Intel
IPC
iPod
ISL
ITV
James Bond
Just do it
JVC
Kellogg's
Loaded
L'Oréal
Lumière
Manchester City
Manchester United
MasterCard
McCann-Erickson
McDonald's
Mercedes-Benz
Mickey Mouse
Microsoft
MIFED
Miramax
Mirror
Motorola

Music Media
   Productions
Naspers
National Express
NBC
Netscape
New Musical Express
Nike
Nike Town
Nintendo
NME
Observer
Olympics
Omega
Onitsuka Tiger
Opal
Oscar
Our Price
Pandora
Paper Tree
Pepsi-Cola
Philips
Pixar
PlayStation
Polygram
Popeye
Portugal Telecom
Prada
Radio 1
Radio 5
Random House
RCA
Reebok
Reed International
Sainsbury's
Seagram
Selecão
Shaun the Sheep
Shoot
Simply Red
Smash Hits
Snickers
Sony
Sotherby's
So What Arts

Sunday Mirror
Sunkist
SWATCH
Swoosh
Teenage Mutant Ninja
   Turtles
Telecom Italia
Telefónica
Televisa
Telmex
Tesco
The Face
The Matrix
Time-Warner
Timex
Top of the Pops
Total Football
Toyota
Toy Story
Typhoo
UEFA
Umbro
Unibanco
Universal
Virginia Slims
Wallace and Gromit
Warner
Woolworths
Young & Rubicam
Zone

① Introduction: Theory – Some Signposts

Dialectic of Enlightenment

It is now some sixty years since Max Horkheimer and Theodor Adorno first published *Dialectic of Enlightenment*, the book that was to be the handbook of critical theory. Critical theory's classic dialectic grew from the study of the *ancien regime*: of feudalism, absolutism, of *gemeinschaftlich* social relations. The dialectic developed from the analysis of a regime in which social position was fixed by birth; in which serfs were tied to the soil; in which an absolutist monarch ruled through the mediation of aristocracy and Church; in which men fought and died for King and religion. From this medieval darkness of necessity arose *Les Lumières*, bringing light and transparency to what was darkness and obscurity, bringing the rationally established rights of man into a space where previously there were only obligations, legitimated not by reason but by tradition. From this darkness of necessity rose the freedom of possibilities of social mobility, so that birth did not fix social position generation after generation. Breaking with the cyclical time of peasants' crops and nobles' migration from country house to court emerged a temporality of progress and possibility. Killing off a vengeful God and putting the potential of humanity in his place, Enlightenment arose dialectically out of

1

darkness also in markets, in freedom of expression, in burgeoning citizenship, in the emergence of *le peuple*, opening up a space of autonomy, of emancipation, where once there had been chains. This was Enlightenment. Enlightenment for critical theorists was an emancipation of outer nature, of inner nature and of social nature.

But Enlightenment contained within itself a contradictory logic: a logic in which its core values turned into their opposites. Enlightenment here for Horkheimer and Adorno becomes a new darkness of myth – as quality turns to quantity, freedom to necessity, autonomy to determinacy and emancipation to new chains. With the removal of Church and King, man himself took on powers to realize his potential in a number of arenas. With Enlightenment and the demythification of outer nature, science – Galileo, Newton – took on the ability, the power, to know nature. Human inner nature was emancipated from the Church's teachings on morality and original sin. For its part, social nature was liberated from the unholy trinity of kings, priests and nobles. Indeed, with the rise of the social contract, natural rights and the people, the very meaning of society changed. Previously associated with gatherings of the upper classes at balls and banquets and other exclusive settings, society came to mean the people, the rights-bearing citizens of the newly emergent public realm. But Enlightenment's dialectic turned emancipation into domination. Enlightenment's enabling power was changed into a new darkness of power as domination. *Savoir*, or knowledge, became linked to *pouvoir*. This was not emancipatory knowledge. Man's power to explore nature became his power to use nature as an instrument, to commodify and deplete it. The emancipation of man's inner nature was transformed into institutional power over inner nature as the clinic, the prison, the school and the factory normalized and disciplined. In social nature this reversal was the most extreme, as bureaucratic and authoritarian power allied to a new brutality in racial ideologies underscored the rise of fascism.

One major sphere in which the dialectic of Enlightenment played out perniciously for Horkheimer and Adorno was in the realm of the *culture industry*. The point for critical theorists was that a previously autonomous or relatively autonomous sphere now itself came under the industrial principle. This meant that culture, once a space of freedom, came under the principle of instrumental rationality, became instrumental in the hands of Hollywood and the emergent monopoly concentration of capital in publishing, recording and advertising. It meant that culture, previously a source of edification, the *Bildung* of human potential, turned into a machinery of control, whose main goal was the expenditure of resources in the interests of the financial profitability of corporate oligopolies. Culture took on the same principle of accumulation already widespread in the capitalist economy. Now the logic of the factory colonized the dream factories of the culture industry.[1] Now culture, previously associated with the development of human subjectivity, became objective like any other commodity.[2] The implication for Horkheimer and Adorno was that culture, previously a site for critique and a place of non-identity, became subsumed under capitalism's logic of identity. In this identity-logic, the heterogeneity – the grain of the art-work – is reduced to identical units of utility; the qualitative, internal values of things are reduced to identical units of exchange-value and quantities of money. Industrialized culture, for Horkheimer and Adorno, is homogenized culture. In homogenized culture one unit is like every other. One unit, in its nature as commodity and instrumentality, is identical to any other. This was the principle of identity that Horkheimer and Adorno deplored. It was the principle against which critique was to be launched. For critical theory, with the proletariat incorporated into the newly 'organized capitalism' from the First World War, the only place for critique had been culture, which was autonomous from the principle of identity, from the atomism and normalization of the economy. But now, with the rise of the culture industry, this atomization also invaded culture, creating what Marcuse (1991) later called 'one-dimensional man'.

Horkheimer and Adorno's theory of culture industry is one of the founding sources of what later has become known as cultural studies. Its resonance has been of course much wider, throughout the human sciences. In this book – on *global* culture industry – we argue that things have moved on since the time at which Horkheimer and Adorno were writing. This is a book not about culture industry but about *global* culture industry. This is a book that follows, or tracks or traces seven cultural objects – *Toy Story*, the Wallace and Gromit short feature films, Nike, Swatch, *Trainspotting*, Euro '96 and young British artists (YBA) – as they move through a great number of transformations in a great number of countries. This book disagrees with Horkheimer and Adorno's thesis. This is nothing new. Indeed, classical cultural studies, that is the British, Birmingham tradition (Hall 1980; Hall and Jefferson 1993), was born out of disagreement with critical theory, in the sense that culture – and the media – was argued to be a site for resistance as much as it was for domination. But we disagree with Horkheimer and Adorno not so much to argue that the social uses of cultural objects and media representations can be used for resistance as well as for domination. Our disagreement with Horkheimer and Adorno is not so much that they were wrong, but that things have moved on. Indeed, we think that theories of both domination through, and resistance to, the culture industry were right. We think however that – since the time of critical theory *and* since the emergence of the Birmingham tradition in the middle 1970s – things have changed.

We think that culture has taken on another, a different logic with the transition from culture industry to *global* culture industry; that globalization has given culture industry a fundamentally different mode of operation.[3] Our point is that in 1945 and in 1975 culture was still fundamentally a superstructure. As a superstructure, both domination and resistance took place in and through superstructures – through ideology, through symbols, through representation. When culture was primarily superstructural, cultural entities were still exceptional. What was mostly encountered in everyday life were material objects (goods), from the economic infrastructure. This was true in 1945 and still so in 1975. But in 2005, cultural objects are everywhere; as information, as communications, as branded products, as financial services, as media products, as transport and leisure services, cultural entities are no longer the exception: they are the rule. Culture is so ubiquitous that it, as it were, seeps out of the superstructure and comes to infiltrate, and then take over, the infrastructure itself. It comes to dominate both the economy and experience in everyday life.[4] Culture no longer works – in regard to resistance or domination – primarily as a superstructure. It no longer works primarily as hegemonic ideology, as symbols, as representations. In our emergent age of global culture industry, where culture starts to dominate both the economy and the everyday, culture, which was previously a question of representation, becomes *thingified*. In classical culture industry – both in terms of domination and resistance – mediation was primarily by means of representation. In global culture industry instead is the *mediation of things*. And this is the central thesis of this book. The book is thus an exploration of global culture industry in terms of a mediation of things.

Towards Global Culture Industry

Let us outline how we think things have changed – how global culture industry differs from culture industry – in a set of theses. In doing this, we do not want to claim that classical culture industry has disappeared. Indeed, in most situations there are impure admixtures of the global and the classical or 'national' culture industry, of the mediation of representations and the mediation of things. This book's focus though is on the emergent. So let us list some changes in a set of theses and then – in the following chapter – address the method that we have tried to follow in the research and the book. The method itself is inseparable from the emergence of global culture industry: from the emergence of things become media, of media become things.

From identity to difference

In Horkheimer and Adorno's culture industry the assumption was that cultural products, once fabricated, would circulate as commodities, as identical objects, and in their movement would contribute to capital accumulation. As people purchased the objects, they would atomize them, constituting them as the atomized subjects necessary to the reproduction of capitalism. In global culture industry this changes. Products no longer circulate as identical objects, already fixed, static and discrete, determined by the intentions of their producers. Instead, cultural entities spin out of the control of their makers: in their circulation they move and change through transposition and translation, transformation and transmogrification. In this culture of circulation (Lee and LiPuma 2002), cultural entities take on a dynamic of their own; *in this movement*, value is added. In global culture industry, products move as much through accident as through design, as much by virtue of their unintended consequences as through planned design or intention. In changing, cultural entities themselves become reflexive in their self-modification over a range of territories, a range of environments.

The products, the objects of Horkheimer and Adorno's culture industry, were determinate, that is, determined. The objects of global culture industry are indeterminate. To be reflexive (or reflective) is to be indeterminate (Beck 1992; Beck et al. 1994). The objects of culture industry were determinate, not just in being determined, but in their effects. They had determinate effects on social subjects. In determining their audience, they slotted those subjects into the reproductive cycle of capitalism, the nuclear family, the proper place of the home. The objects of global culture industry are also indeterminate in this second sense. We, as social subjects, relate to them in an indeterminate mode. This does not mean that capitalism is not reproducing on a global scale now. It only means that it is reproducing differently. Now the much less determinate objects of global culture industry encounter the characteristically reflexive individuals of today's informational capitalism (Castells 1996; Kwinter 2001; Adkins 2002; Lash 2002; Urry 2003; Thrift 2004). Determinacy, in Horkheimer and Adorno's sense, is a question of 'identity'. Indeterminacy is a question of 'difference'. In global culture industry, production and consumption are processes of the construction of *difference*. In culture industry, production takes place in the Fordist and labour-intensive production of identity. In global culture industry, it takes place in the post-Fordist and design-intensive production of difference. Yet the paradigm of indeterminacy and difference in global culture industry is less a question of resistance than a way in which capital successfully accumulates.

Commodity to brand

The way in which global culture industry operates through brands is a central theme of this book. If culture industry worked largely through the commodity, global culture industry works through brands. The commodity and the brand are largely sources of domination, of power. The commodity works via a logic of identity, the brand via a logic of difference. How is this the case? A good is a commodity to the extent that it is characterized by exchange-value. The exchange-value of a good is an abstraction from its use-value. A good's exchange-value is expressed in abstract equivalents, in money. Exchange-value is thus a question of quantity, use-value of quality. Commodities have value in units of abstract equivalence. Goods are commodities to the extent that they exchange, not for other goods, but for money, for units of abstract equivalence on markets. But as a consumer you cannot go to a market and buy a brand. Brands do not typically exchange at all. They are only for sale on capital markets, where their value is a function of the expected future profits above those contributed by all other assets (those that produce the commodity) (Interbrand et al. 1997).

The commodity is produced. The brand is a source of production. The commodity is a single, discrete, fixed product. The brand instantiates itself in a range of products, is generated across a range of products. The commodity has no history; the brand does. The commodity has no relationships; the brand is constituted in and as relations (see Lury 2004 for the argument that the brand is a set of relations between products). The commodity has no memory at all; the brand has memory. The products in which a brand instantiates itself, indeed actualizes itself, must somehow flow from the brand's memory, which is the brand's identity. The Nike brand, for example, has largely succeeded in actualizing itself in football (soccer) products; it has done less well in golf products. Football seems to relate more easily to Nike brand identity and memory than does golf.

Goods as commodities are all alike. They are distinguishable only by the quantities of money for which they exchange. Brands are not alike. Brands have value only in their difference – their distinctiveness – from other brands. Commodities only have value in the way they resemble every other commodity. Brands only have value in their difference. Brands thus are singular or singularities: commodities are homogeneities. The commodity has only exchange-value in Marx's *Capital*: it is abstract and homogenous, expressed in units of equivalence. Marxian use-value is concrete, singular and qualitative. Thus your personal laptop computer or your private copy of Marx's *Capital* is a use-value, dog-eared, with your own marginal scribblings. The brand, like the use-value, is also a singularity. But it is not a concrete, but an abstract, singularity. The brand – say Boss, Nike or Sony – is not the same as my suit, my trainers or my laptop. But your relations with the brand are part of its value.

The commodity is dead; the brand is alive: it comes into being (it becomes) through the generation of a series or range of goods. The brand, constituted in its difference, generates goods, diversified ranges of products. The commodity is determined from outside: it is mechanistic. The brand is like an organism, self-modifying, with a memory. Thus the commodity is characteristically 'Fordist' and works through the production of large numbers of the same product. Brands work through, not generalized Fordist consumption, but through specialized consumption, and the production of many different goods. Commodity production is labour-intensive; branded goods production is design-intensive (Lash and

Urry 1994). The commodity works through reproduction of identity; the brand through evermore production of difference.

What kind of *value* is at stake? A good has use-value as a concrete singularity. It has exchange-value (is a commodity) as an abstract universal, or homogeneity. It works as a (part of a) brand, it has, in Baudrillard's sense, 'sign-value'. A good works for me through my hands-on use of it. It works as a commodity in terms of how much money I bought or will sell it for. The brand functions as a sign-value through its and my difference. This difference is generated by (my relation to) a brand. Use-value and the commodity are qualities of products. Sign-value and the brand are not qualities of products: they are qualities of *experience*. This experience is situated at the interface – or surface – of communication (Moor 2003; Lury 2004) of the consumer and the brand. It is a part of events; it is eventive (Malik 2005).

In brief, commodities work through a mechanistic principle of identity, brands through the animated production of difference (Fraser et al. 2005). Thus processes of invention are of necessity central to the brand. Yet the brand's cosmology of difference and invention is at the same time the source of a reassembled system of domination. Global culture industry's emergent regime of power results in inequalities, disparities and deception rarely encountered in Horkheimer and Adorno's classical age.

From representations to things

For Horkheimer and Adorno, culture, though 'industrialized', was still in the superstructure. Horkheimer and Adorno were writing in the heyday of manufacturing capitalism. The principles of the economy, that is, of utility and exchange, had invaded and colonized the cultural superstructure. In this context, culture no longer represented the unique, was no longer autonomous, an end-in-itself. It instead became subsumed in homogenous units, each one identical to the next. Culture had become a utility, a means for something else; it was administered. Culture had become subsumed in the means—end rationality of the commodity. But global culture industry and informational capitalism is less a matter of the base determining the superstructure than the cultural superstructure collapsing, as it were, into the material base. Hence goods become informational, work becomes affective, property becomes intellectual and the economy more generally becomes cultural.[5] Culture, once in the base, takes on a certain materiality itself. Media become things. Images and other cultural forms from the superstructure collapse into the materiality of the infrastructure. The image, previously separated in the superstructure, is thingified, it becomes *matter-image* (Deleuze 1986).

In Horkheimer and Adorno's culture industry, mediation was predominantly through representation. In global culture industry, we have the *mediation of things*. Horkheimer and Adorno's culture was commodified. But these were commodified representations and not cultural things.

Mediation by representation is quite other to the mediation of things. The object of art is different from an object like a hammer in that we engage with the former primarily in terms of meaning, while the latter is a matter of doing or 'operationality'. Painting and sculpture are media or mediums, as writers like Rosalind Krauss (1999) insist. They are media before the age of the mass media of communications. But they are media only insofar as their value is primarily cultural: only insofar as their value has to do with meaning. When media become things, however, they no longer exclusively have cultural value. They come very importantly to have use-value and exchange-value.

There is such a thingification of media when, for example, movies become computer games; when brands become brand environments, taking over airport terminal space and restructuring department stores, road billboards and city centres; when cartoon characters become collectibles and costumes; when music is played in lifts, part of a mobile soundscape (Hosokawa 1984; Bull and Back 2004). Media objects in everyday life come to rival manufactured objects. We deal with media as representations – painting, sculpture, poetry, the novel – in terms of meaning. When media become things, we enter a world of operationality, a world not of interpretation but of navigation. We do not 'read' them so much as 'do' them ('Just Do It'), or do with them. This was already incipiently the case with the 'mass media', newspapers, radio and television. Their ubiquity, and the fact that they were not confined to a separate space, as was art, the museum, cinema or indeed the university, meant that they were already encountered as things. They were much more ready-to-hand already than are mediums such as painting or sculpture. What was incipient with the emergence of mass media has become the axial principle of global culture industry. In global culture industry, what were previously media become things. But also, what were things become media.

This book is about seven products in the global culture industry. Four of these cultural objects – Wallace and Gromit, *Toy Story*, (the movement of) young British art(ists), *Trainspotting* – are media become thing-like. Young British art, for example, comprises in part installations, or multimedia spaces. The typical representational space of the picture frame has won only one Turner Prize in the past decade. The dress styles, merchandise and toys for *Trainspotting*, Wallace and Gromit and *Toy Story* have come to rival the films in their visibility. And Disney, Warners and Universal are incorporated in the object spaces of retail outlets and theme parks, parallel to the branded object spaces in airports, shops and department stores. In the case of our three other objects – Nike, Swatch and global football – things, or thing-events, become mediated. When, for instance, Nike's Swoosh logo appears on the (media images of the) cap that Tiger Woods wears in golf competitions,[6] Nike trades on a whole series of mediated connections. These connections help make the space and time, the flows, in which Nike products (and people) move. In spaces such as Niketowns, Nike's logos – including the word 'Nike' and associated words, symbols and acronyms, including 'Swoosh', 'AirJordan', 'Total Body Conditioning', the tag line 'Just Do It' and the graphic mark that is known as 'Jumpman', among others – do not only mark a line of products, they are also built into the very architecture and fittings of the building. But at the same time, as Jarvis, an assistant in the Los Angeles Niketown, and himself owner of numerous pairs of Nike shoes, said to us, Niketown isn't a store at all; it is 'an experience'. In other words, the physical environment is the setting for immersion in a highly mediated brand experience; very concretely, it is the installation of sensation.

Four of our cultural objects have thus 'descended', as it were, halfway from the superstructure, and the other three have 'ascended' halfway from the base. They meet in the middle in something like a 'media-environment'. In this in-between zone a material environment (such as a football stadium) has become mediatized. And mediums (the films and art) have descended into the environment, as merchandise, as installations. Image has become matter and matter has become image: media-things and thing-media. At stake is a true industrialization of culture. What Horkheimer and Adorno called industrialization was only in fact commodification. It was the commodification of representation. It is the thingification of media that brings the principle not just of the commodity but also of industry into the heart of culture itself. This runs in parallel with the 'culture-ification' of what previously was industry. The above-mentioned design-intensivity and ubiquitous research and design is the culturification of industry: the mediation of things. Thus culture industry entails thing-mediation. And the flux and flow of globalization is what is created by the movements of things-become-media and media-become-things. As we will see in the course of this book, the properties of such movement, such flux and flow (Appadurai 1996), are just as central to global culture industry as the coming together of media and things.

From the symbolic to the real

In *The Matrix*, Keanu Reeves is, by day, Thomas A. Anderson, a software writer in Metacortex, a software firm in turn of the twenty-first-century Chicago. Anderson 'pays taxes', he 'has a social security number'. By night he is hacker-alias 'Neo', developer of myriad illegal applications, of countless 'computer crimes', which he sells to gangs of cyber-punks, hidden on discs stored in his copy of *Simulations and Simulacra* (Baudrillard 1994). Neo, already uncertain which of his two worlds is dream and which is reality, is contacted by Carrie Anne Moss's Trinity. She proposes to him that his night-time obsession is her life-long project, that both of them are searching for the answer to the question, 'What is the Matrix'? 'The answer', she says to him, 'is out there. It's looking for you and it will find you.' Next day, at work, Neo receives a recorded-delivery mobile phone, on whose other end is Trinity's mentor (and virtual father), Laurence Fishburne's Morpheus. Morpheus tells Neo not only, 'I've been looking for you', but also that 'they're coming for you'. 'They' are the Matrix and their agents, especially their special agent, Smith. Hugo Weaving's agent Smith, together with the Chicago police, capture Anderson/Neo. Smith knows Morpheus is on to Neo, and he knows why. Morpheus knows that Neo is 'the One', who will lead the battle against the Matrix and save the besieged city of Zion. Smith is a machine in the Matrix's future age of the machines. Zion is the last bastion of humanity. Smith and the Matrix want to use Neo to get at Morpheus, 'the most dangerous man alive', a 'known terrorist', and 'help bring him to justice'. They know Neo will soon be with Morpheus. Smith thus inserts a bug, a spidery machine, in Neo through his navel.

Neo wakes up from this 'dream', is phoned by Morpheus and is instructed to wait under Chicago's Adams Street Bridge. Trinity and friends collect him in a car and extract the spider bug from his stomach. Neo remarks, 'Jesus Christ. This thing is real', and is taken to meet Morpheus, who greets him with the words: 'Welcome to the real world.' Neo asks Morpheus, 'Where are we?' Morpheus responds, 'The question is not where, but when.' The answer is that 'we', and the real world, are somewhere in 2199. In contrast, the world of 1999 is a dream, is what social and cultural theorists call *the symbolic,* the world of representations, of ideology (Zizek 1997). The Matrix, the machines, in the real of 2199 are pulling the strings in the dream world of the symbolic of 1999. But this symbolic has extraordinary powers. Though it is 'only a neural interactive simulacrum, a dream-world', 'It is everywhere', intones Morpheus to Neo. The Matrix pulls a world 'over your eyes to blind you'. 'You are a slave, born into bondage.' In the first half of the twenty-first century, Morpheus continues, the humans celebrated their achievements with the full development of AI. But the machines gained their autonomy and the war between the humans and the machines was begun. In this war, it was 'we [the humans] who scorched the sky', destroying the sun, to deprive the machines of solar energy. But the machines switched their energy source to the heat generation of human bodies and, by the end of the twenty-second century, have come to devise ways of growing human beings in fields. The Matrix's goal is to reduce human beings into batteries for machines. The triumph of the machines is the triumph of the Matrix, who, via the special agents, who are 'sentient programmes', want to close down the last bastion of resistance in Zion. Zion is the 'last human city', underground, near the earth's core, where there is still – in the absence of the sun – sufficient heat to sustain human life. The Matrix's plan is to tap into the access codes of Zion's mainframe computers. Zion is served by a number of hovercraft-like ships, which 'broadcast pirate signals'.

Smith lectures the captured Morpheus: the development from 'your (human) civilization to our (machine) civilization' is a question of 'evolution, Morpheus, evolution'. But Neo, 'the One', is even further evolved than Smith. On entering what Morpheus calls 'the desert of the real', he is trained through a set of programs to enter 'replication'. As 'the One', he is on the side of the humans, but is more than a human, and more than a machine. He can do all of Smith's moves and transformations – indeed, he destroys Smith at the end of the film by entering his body, as in Cronenberg's *Scanners* – exploding him from the inside. The Matrix's agents, though they are self-organizing, are 'still based on rules'. There is still an irreducible element of mechanism in the machines. 'The One', in contrast, is a rule finder. He is guided by Morpheus, and by the Oracle, who prophesized his coming. But he must 'walk the path'.

In its entirety, *Matrix* plays off an opposition of the symbolic and the real. The symbolic is above ground. There is still sun. It is Chicago in 1999. The real is underground, in the bowels of the earth: there is no sun. The main characters have a double existence: in Chicago's sunny twentieth-century symbolic and in the darkness of the real, Morpheus, Tank, Dozer, Cypher, Neo and Trinity exist in the real, strapped in chairs in Morpheus's ship, unconscious, connected to electrical terminals. The connections between the symbolic and the real, the 'exits', are in Chicago's subway stations. Connection to the real from the symbolic is by mobile phone, but the truth, the real, is in the mind. The real is not extensive, but intensive. The appearance(s of the symbolic) 'are a mental projection of a digital self', which is where the real action is. Zion rangers like Morpheus and Trinity, 'unplug people' from the (symbolic) matrix to join the struggle in the real. The symbolic is the place of the sense-world, of 'electrical signals interpreted by the brain'. In the real, humans eat tasteless gruel with all necessary vitamins and minerals for the brutal struggles of its sunless desert.

Horkheimer and Adorno's classical culture industry worked through the symbolic, through daylight, the light of Enlightenment and other ideology, through the pleasure of the text, and of representation. Global culture industry is a descent of culture into the real: a descent into the bowels, the brutality, the desert of the real. The real is more evolved than the symbolic. It is brutal, but a question less of body than of mind: bodies are merely energy sources for the mind's real. The inner and under-ground space in which the human hacker-ships operate is the 'service and waste systems of cities that once spanned hundreds of miles' trans-muted into 'sewers' at the turn of the twenty-first century. The real is brutal, a desert, a sewer, a waste-and-service system, below the subways, under the underground. The cosmology of waste and sewage is also that which structures Don DeLillo's *Underworld* (1998). DeLillo's protagonist works in the waste industry and sees the world in terms of a cosmology, a metaphysics of flows of waste. DeLillo's real is this 'underworld' of waste.

Classical culture industry occupied the space of the symbolic: global culture industry the space of the real. Culture industry is Hollywood's dream-machine, global culture industry brute reality. Global culture industry deals in simulations, but these escape the symbolic, escape representation, and as intensity, as hyperreality, enter a real in which media become things. The symbolic is superstructural: it is a set of ideological and cultural structures that interpellate subjects in order to reproduce the capitalist economy and the (Oedipal) nuclear family. The real is not superstructural; it is not even structural. The real is base. It is in excess of the symbolic. This excess is abjected, spewed out downward through exit-holes into the desert of the real. For Georges Bataille (2000), the abjected was Marx's lumpenproletariat, who made no contribution to the reproduction of capital. To be abjected into the real was to be ejected – out of the bottom (Bataille's 'solar anus') of the symbolic space of form into the *informe*, the formlessness of the real. Global culture industry operates in this space of the real. In the symbolic, signification works through structures to produce meaning. In the desert of the real, signification works through brute force and immediacy. Meaning is no longer hermeneutic; it is operational, as in computer games – that is, meaning is not interpretative; it is doing, it is impact.

Things come alive: bio-power

Culture industry for Horkheimer and Adorno worked through the logic of the commodity. In global culture industry we deal with *singularities* (Appadurai 1986). Singularities are very much the opposite of Horkheimer and Adorno's atomized and atomizing cultural goods. Such atoms work on a principle of Newtonian *mechanism*. For Newton and Descartes, simple bodily substance was atomistic: atoms are identical to each other, they are externally caused. Opposed to the atom were the *monads* of Leibniz (1992). Adorno's commodities are atomistic; the global culture industry singularities are monads. The monad presumes that simple substance is difference. Monads are all different from each other because each carries its own trace. This trace is a monad's memory, its path dependency.[7] Atoms are the stuff of simplicity; monads are the stuff of complexity. Monads are self-organizing and, in this sense, reflexive. The atomized products of Horkheimer and Adorno's classic culture industry worked like mechanism. The self-transforming and self-energizing monads of global culture industry are not mechanistic, but vitalistic. Thus, Arjun Appadurai can speak of a social *life* of things (1986). In global culture industry, things come alive, take on a life of their own. Cultural objects as commodities, as atoms, are mechanisms. Singularities for their part are alive.[8]

Horkheimer and Adorno's culture industry is a locus of power, a power that works mechanistically, through external determination of subjects. In global culture industry, power works vitalistically. Vitalist power is *bio-power* (Foucault 1976). Mechanistic power works through the fixity of being. Vitalist or bio-power operates through becoming and movement.

Thus power leaves structures and enters flows. Bio-power, as opposed to 'mechano-power', works through the becoming of self-organization. Not only do resistance or invention operate through movement and becoming in the global age, so too does power. Mechano-power ensures the reproduction of capitalist relations, the family and the proper place (of privacy, propriety and property). As a guarantor of reproduction, mechano-power works through a principle of identity. Bio-power, as Foucault insisted, works through production. It is chronically productive. If reproduction is tied to identity, production is tied to difference, to invention. Bio-power does not stop subjects from producing difference. It is effective through the production of difference by subjects. Brands are not in an ideological or representational (or symbolic) superstructure; they work not transcendentally, but immanently, in the arteries of society. Bio-power, in working through arteries, is less mechanistic than physiological.

Bio-power of the global culture industry works on subjects as if it were monads. But there are two types of monads. There are Leibniz's monads which were closed systems: systems, as he noted, with no windows, no doors. These monads are self-causing, self-determined by their own traces. There are, on the other hand, singularities, which are monads with windows and doors. They are doubly open systems, abstract machines, rhizomes, multiplicities (Deleuze and Guattari 1999; Lazzarato 2002). Global cultural products and subjects can operate either as closed systems or as singularities. Brands are often operationally closed; that is, they work through a kind of exclusion. For example, BSkyB in Britain has used premiership football in this way. You incorporate the object (football). You mediate and brand it. You achieve a monopoly. You exclude others. And you make the viewers pay. But brands can sometimes take on windows and doors. As closed systems, they incorporate aspects of the environment, but they do not form syntheses or connect with other systems. Once they have windows and doors, and form such doubly open systems, they become singularities.[9]

Extensity to intensity

Cultural goods in Horkheimer and Adorno's classical culture industry were commodities, equivalent atoms. These were subject to the laws of Newtonian mechanism. Such goods take on the shape of what Descartes understood as *res extensa*. For Descartes, body and mechanism were a matter of *res extensa* and mind of *res cogitans*. Here we have extensive substance on the one hand and thinking substance on the other. For Descartes, extensive substance was atomistic, and thinking substance monadological. The Latin *res* is a question of substance but also of property. Thus property in manufacturing capitalism (and culture industry) comes largely under the heading of *res extensa*, but in information capitalism and global culture industry, property – that is, intellectual property, – comes under the heading of *res cogitans* (Castells 1996). In this sense, the information economy is based on the materialization of *res cog-itans*. Intellectual property is its legal expression and regulation. Once materialized, *res cogitans* is no longer inside us. As the materialized immaterial, it becomes *res intensiva*. Now extensity is counterposed, not to *cogitans*, but to *intensity*. The point is that the products of the classical culture industry functioned as extensities; those of the global culture industry function as intensities.

For Marshall McLuhan (1997) the intensive was not just thinking sub-stance, but the entire human sensorium, a multimodal notion of sense. For him, the global network, or 'village', of media and communications was the 'outering' of the sensorium. It was the extension of intensity, or of matter-image. In this view, subjects encounter not a signifying struc-ture, or even the materiality of the signified, but the signified or sense itself as it is materialized. This is communication. This is information. The media environment, or mediascape, is a forest of extended intensi-ties, of material signifieds around which subjects find their way, orient themselves via signposts.[10] Thus Horkheimer and Adorno's culture indus-try recalled the extensity of a landscape; today's global culture industry has the intensity of a mediascape, is a scape of flows (Appadurai 1996). The information economy is an intensive economy, an economy of inten-sities (Thrift 2004); the media environment is an intensive environment.

The rise of the virtual

The brand experience is a feeling, though not a concrete perception. Thus Walter Benjamin talks about the colour of experience (Caygill 1998). What Benjamin is saying is that you may perceive the painting, say, as an object, but what you *experience* is non-objectual – that is, colour. This is the experience of an intensity. Brands may embrace a number of extensities, but they are themselves intensities. Brands are in this sense *virtuals*. As virtuals, they may be actualized in any number of products. Yet the feeling, the brand experience, is the same. Brands typically involve trademarks. The trademark in intellectual property law must be in the public domain. Thus David Beckham as brand is in the public domain. But though they are in the public domain, brands themselves are not perceived. As virtuals, they are ineffable. In semiologist Peirce's sense, brands may be icons. Peirce (1978) understood signification in three modes, via symbol, index and icon. Symbols signify in a Saussurean manner, through the differences among signifiers in a signifying struc-ture. An index signifies much more immediately. Signals are very much motivated by the thing they signify. Thus a baby's cry is an index, as is a train signal, or the thud a punch in the jaw makes. Icons do not for Peirce signify through resemblance, as is commonly held; instead, the sign denotes the object by being like it, and the interpretant represents the sign as a sign of *qualitative possibility*. Symbols are mediatedly attached to objects, and signals quite immediately attached. But icons need not be attached to objects at all.[11] Brands, working through the intensities of their iconography, are one way in which contemporary power works.

In global culture industry, not only the mediascape, but also the cityscape takes on intensive qualities. Architecture and urbanism become less a question of objects and volumes. Urban space becomes a space of intensities. These intensities, which are virtual, describe a certain topology. They describe a space of multimodal experience, not just that of vision, a space of virtualities and intensities that actualize themselves not as objects but as events. Thus Bernard Tschumi speaks of 'event-architecture' (2005), while in Rem Koolhaas's *Harvard Guide to Shopping* (2001) architecture becomes increasingly surfaces of communication, intensities, events. Global culture industry is a matter in this sense of object-events. Our cultural objects are self-organizing systems, sometimes operationally closed, at other points emergent, singularities forming connective syntheses, at many points actualizing themselves in events. Contemporary culture – unlike that of the classical culture industry – is 'event-culture'.

Horkheimer and Adorno's culture industry was dialectical. We are today, perhaps, less dialectical than *metaphysical*. Dialectics presumes ontological difference: between spirit and matter, being and beings, superstructure and base, same and other, friend and foe. Metaphysics is instead a monism, an immanence of spirit-matter, of superstructure-base. The ontological difference of dialectics is displaced by metaphysics' ontology of difference. In this ontology of difference, simple substance itself is difference. This simple substance as matter-image, as difference, is the stuff of global culture industry. The *Weltanschauung*, the *episteme* of global culture industry, is no longer that of dialectical but of metaphysical materialism, based on the materiality of the monad, the reality, as in *Matrix*, of mind. This is matter as multiplicity, matter not as identity but as difference.

 Method: Ontology,
Movement, Mapping

Introduction

The method adopted from the start of this project was to 'follow the objects'. We were self-consciously developing a sociology of the object. The seven objects we chose to follow are a subset of those produced by the global culture industry. They were chosen both for their relatively high visibility in the contemporary landscape and for their potentially long and varied trajectories. They are: the films *Trainspotting* (Miramax, 1996) and *Toy Story* (Pixar/Disney, 1995); the Wallace and Gromit animated film series from Aardman Productions; Euro '96, the European football championship held in 1996; the art movement YBA or (a group of) young British artists; and two global retail brands, Swatch and Nike. In each case, we were concerned with the life-course of the object. If, for instance, we follow a particular film back in time and forward along its biographical trajectory: what are the key components of the story? Who are the central figures? What are the key moments? How are pivotal transactions managed? Where is the film released, successfully or otherwise? What apparently tangential issues divert, recast and redirect the initial project? Throughout, how is the object transformed – and how does it transform – from stage to stage, context to context?

The collection of research materials was concentrated in the three years 1996, 1997 and 1998, but since then our objects have proliferated in a variety of other ways and we can present more selective data here. The branding of Euro '96 spawned an even more focused Euro 2000 and features of Euro '96's branding were also refracted through the World Cup in 1998 in France. The very different animation styles in *Toy Story* and Wallace and Gromit have won Oscars for their respective producers over the past ten years and have now resulted in follow-up feature films, *Toy Story 2* and Wallace and Gromit in *The Curse of the Were-Rabbit*, and big contracts with Disney and Spielberg respectively. *Toy Story 2* in turn appeared on ice in London in 2004. The plastic fashion watch from Swatch has resulted, on the one hand, in a now-waning, but once intense, global wave of collector frenzy and, on the other, in related design and marketing principles being used to create a 'micro' car in joint venture with Daimler-Benz. Nike continues to expand.

There were a number of influences on our understanding of objects. The first was the anthropology of material culture (Miller 1987, 2005), especially the material culture of moving objects, as proposed by Arjun Appadurai (1986) and Igor Kopytoff (1986). As the study went on, during the years of writing, we were influenced by Alfred Gell's anthropology of art (1998). Another major influence came from the sociology of science and technology (Serres 1980; Latour 1993; Callon 1998). We were already familiar with what is now sometimes known as 'media theory' (Lash 2002), specifically with Jean Baudrillard's theory of the object (1996), and with Paul Virilio's analysis of vision and objects in movement (1994). None of the above notions of the object comes from classical subject-object thinking. None of them sees the object as volumetric and mechanical or in terms of *res extensa*, and the external cause and effect of positivism. All these writers understand instead the object as a sort of singularity. In this sense, Appadurai and Kopytoff's 'singularities' resemble 'quasi-objects' as well as the hyper-real object.

A third influence came from taking seriously the notion of biography (which we initially found in Kopytoff 1986), and a consideration of the anthropologist Alfred Gell's claim that it is the study of the life-cycle that defines the anthropological approach (1998: 10–11). Gell argues that it is biographical depth of focus that characterizes anthropology – that is, the attempt to replicate the time perspective of social agents or actants themselves. This way of thinking contributed to our adoption of an understanding of time in which it is not external to (natural or social) objects or agents, but is rather internal to the object, or, to use another vocabulary, may be understood as a process of differentiation. Tracking the movements of our objects thus meant that we began to consider not only the temporal sequencing of production, distribution and consumption, but also to consider our objects in terms of duration or differentiation (Bergson 1991; Deleuze 1991). This enabled us to consider our objects not as existing ideally in a steady state or condition, but as a set of relations, that is, as always coming into existence (Whitehead 1978; Barry 2001; Fraser et al. 2005).

A fourth influence was the work of Gilles Deleuze (1994) on multiplicity, especially insofar as he presents it in *Difference and Repetition*. Multiplicity was helpful in thinking about an object as always coming into existence as a set of relations. Deleuze writes of multiplicity that it 'must not designate a combination of the many and the one, but rather an organization belonging to the many as such, which has no need whatsoever of unity in order to form a system' (quoted in DeLanda 2002: 12). What attracted us to this way of thinking was the attention it draws to the variable number of dimensions of multiplicity, and the absence of a supplementary (higher) dimension imposing an extrinsic positionality (or coordinatization), and hence an extrinsically defined unity (ibid.). This Deleuzian notion of multiplicity is informed by mathematical thinking about the manifold and theories of dynamical systems, in which a geometric object such as a curved line or a surface can be modelled as trajectories in a space of possible states (ibid.: 13–14). The relevance of such thinking for the study of the objects of the global culture industry may not be immediately apparent, but the points we took were relatively straightforward: that an individual object may be many or manifold, without having a unity of its parts; that its movements are not to be understood in relation to an external dimension or extrinsic force, but are rather immanent; and that the object's state is embedded in a complex space and cannot be separated from it. As we shall see, the relevance of thinking about geometric objects such as *surfaces* was also greater than might initially have been imagined.

A final influence, from the subdiscipline of economic sociology, was that of Karin Knorr Cetina's work on what she calls global microstructures (Knorr Cetina and Bruegger 2002). Many analysts assume that global flows of (cultural) products are organized in *networks*. But are they? Networks typically have hubs, perhaps terminals, and weak ties. At issue in our biographies, we came to think, was something else. As Knorr Cetina puts it: 'Networks are sparse social structures and it is difficult to see how they can incorporate the patterns of intense and dynamic conversational interaction, the knowledge flows, and the temporal structuration that we observe in the area studied' (ibid.: 910). In Knorr Cetina's terms, global microstructures are forms of market coordination in which participants, although not in a situation of face-to-face interaction, are oriented, above all, towards one another. Global microstructures involve actors who are geographically distant to each other, but nonetheless observe one another in relation to an object. What we took from this was the possibility of investigating the organization of markets in the global culture industry via a study of the organization of markets *by the objects themselves*. This is to consider the markets of the global culture industry as neither pre-given nor static, as neither simply global nor as merely local, but as dynamically constituted in the movements, the biographies, of objects. What we wanted to investigate is how it is that the objects of the global culture industry may come to act as life-forms, give faces to and animate the markets of the global culture industry.

Methodology

Our methodology of 'following the object' comes principally from Appadurai (1986). As we understand it, this approach does not privilege or focus exclusively on one moment in an object's life: its production, or its circulation in, for example, publicity and advertising, or its reception. It is tempting either to run these three moments together or to give undue prominence to one of them so that one of production, distribution or reception becomes the 'determining instance' which dictates the meaning of the product in every other context. In either case, the result is more or less the same: a delicately balanced sequence of relations is obscured to be replaced by a simplistic set of reductions, ignoring the changes in objects as they circulate through networks, trajectories, cycles or 'lives' of production, promotion and reception (Lury 1993). In contrast, the notion of the biography makes it possible for us to avoid seeing the object as the outcome by which one structure out of a set of predefined forms acquires reality. Instead, it ensured that our concern was with how things actually move, how they 'transition' between many states, how they are (self-)organized as temporal, rhythmic morphologies or coherent behaviours (Kwinter 1998).

A second advantage of the approach is that it avoids an opposition between the local and the global (Tsing 2005). In locating and following the biography of specific objects, our research was designed as a grounded yet globally oriented analysis. In Gell's terms, the field we were concerned with was the spaces traversed by our objects in the course of their biographies. One of the initial aims of the study was to explore the extent of globalization in the culture industry. At a simple level, we found that there was considerably greater reach and penetration for many of these objects than we had suspected. But exploring the object in terms of its biography makes it possible to highlight the limitations of an approach to globalization in terms of extensity, that is, of distance travelled. It makes it possible to show how while local events and contingencies may have global aspects and consequences, these effects and results are also local – somewhere else. But more than this, the Deleuzian differential geometry outlined earlier also makes it possible to hold open the question of the coordination of the rationality – the processes of rationalization – at work in the global culture industry. We tried not to assume a fixed relation – or ratio – between time and space in the global culture industry markets we were studying, but instead saw this relationship as potentially variable, produced in part by the object themselves and as

such something to be empirically investigated. What our findings suggest is that the production of locality by globalization is neither simply a
question of reach and penetration or even motility, not merely processes
of dis- and re-embedding, but rather of *a changed relationship to context*
(Strathern 1999). It is a question of both extensity *and* intensity.

A third advantage of the biographical approach is that it draws upon
the historical tendency of anthropology towards what Gell describes as 'a
radical defamiliarization and relativization of the notion of "persons"'
(1998: 9). Gell suggests that there is a long-standing anthropological preoccupation with the 'ostensibly peculiar relations between persons and
things [in] which [things] somehow "appear as" or do duty as, persons'.
This preoccupation may be found in anthropological studies of 'primi-
tive cultures' (Tylor 1964), magic (Frazer 1993) and exchange (Malinowski
1984; Mauss 1976; Bourdieu 1977), and is further developed by Gell himself in his own theory of art which 'considers art objects as persons'. In
the work of sociologist of science and technology Bruno Latour (1987),
there is a similar concern with the agency of objects or 'actants', as he
describes them. As the study developed, we too came to think of our
objects as having a life. We were using an anti-positivist, a *humanist*
method: but what was involved was a humanism of the inhuman. We
were involved in a mobile ethnography (in the very broadest sense), in
which the ethnos was a community of things.[1]

But how do you follow objects? Very simply, you find out as much
about them in as many places in time and space from as many points of
view as possible. To do this, we decided to employ not only situational
observation, but also processes of observation that were attentive to the
temporality of the (subjects and) objects concerned. Our assumption was
that an object only makes sense if it is experienced (Crary 1992). And it
must be experienced from a point of view. So we tried to proliferate the
points of view we adopted. We went to many cities and spoke to 130 or so
'experts' in regard to our objects in detailed interviews – with journalists, curators, festival organizers, intellectual property lawyers, advertisers, designers, distributors, retailers and audiences or users of the
objects. However, the excerpts of interviews included in this book are
intended neither as records of subjective opinions nor as documentary
records of fact, but as fragments of (shifting) points of view. We also collected and consulted trade magazines and newspaper articles. We pho-
tographed and filmed the objects, using also the point of view of the
camera lens. The visual materials used here are not intended as illustration though, but as non-verbal, non-discursive accounts. This is especially
important to the argument being made here because of the focus on the
movements of objects. For a visual sociology (Becker 1986; Taylor 1994;
Knowles and Sweetman 2004), images compose a moving hypothesis of
lines, of shapes, of volumes and images, of things-in-motion; in these
visual records of practice, then, the properties or qualities of objects-as-

persons are revealed. A further reason for the use of both the still image of the photograph and the moving image of the video (although of course in this book this image too has been stilled) is that it calls attention to the time of seeing, of the editing of seeing, of movement in points of view. In these ways then, we tried to build a rich description of the objects from a great number of points of view and in many time-places, though these were nevertheless limited (see Bhatt 2004 for a critique of 'flow').

Finally, we also want to reflect, briefly, on the writing of this book. We have deliberately made use of different styles and genres of writing within this single text (and this is not only because the text has more than one author). The intention here is to find some way of representing the multiple temporalities that intersect or converge in a single biography; the different spatio-temporalities at issue here have different intensities, and are, we think, best represented in different ways. So in what follows, scenarios are described, personal biographies recorded, multiple trajectories are juxtaposed and discontinuous temporalities are set alongside one another. In the discussion of the use of interviews and visual materials above, we suggested that the stories and images presented in this book are not intended as illustrations, but as devices by which the situatedness of points of view can be made explicit. In addition, we have made use of different ways of representing the arguments of the book in the layout and design not only of the images, but also of the written text, with the aim of drawing attention to internal differences in register and tone. One of the arguments developed in this book is that the global culture industry is animated, and with this argument in mind, we have chosen to try to animate the text itself. Thus we decided to make a small move towards making the letters of the text into 'characters' (see chapter 5 for a brief discussion of the history of animation), putting lines of argument alongside each other, cutting and editing thoughts, using intervals in space to make associations within and between chapters, and draw the reader into the thesis we are developing. In the biographies that follow, we provide some preliminary examples of this experiment.

BIOGRAPHY I

In tracking the movement of *Trainspotting*, we were able to identify a sequential object biography, in which the object followed a relatively linear path of transformation and dispersion from short story to novel, to film, to poster, to film soundtrack, marketing tie-in products and stage performance. We traced the movement of the object, conducting interviews in theatre and literary scenes in Edinburgh, with literary publishers and Film Four in London, and distributors, exhibitors and journalists in São Paulo and Rio de Janeiro. We documented the film's reception in advertisements, posters, newspaper reviews and conversations in the USA, Switzerland, Austria, Germany and France. What became clear in collecting this material

was that mapping a biography had to include not only the extensive movements of the object, but also its intensive transformation.

In our interviews, the origins of the film *Trainspotting* were typically
located in a literary short story circulated in Edinburgh in the very early
1990s in the context of the New Scottish Writing explosion, 'Trainspotting
at Leith Central Station'. Encouraged by Jonathan Cape's Deputy
Publishing Director, the author Irvine Welsh extended the story to novel
length. The manuscript circulated in Cape's parent firm, Random House,
and 3,000 copies were published as a Secker paperback in 1993. Positive
reviews encouraged republication as a Minerva paperback. The book
obtained a cult following, spawning a series of imitators. For Random
House, an unreadable book had been adopted by a post-literate generation
(Valentine 1999). In 1994 the book sold 300,000 copies. And then, in
1996, this book about 1980s Scottish heroin culture (it was set in the mid-
1980s, the film in the late 1980s) was translated into a hallucinogenic visual
style and Britpop soundtrack for a late 1990s cinema audience.[2] The film
was shot in four weeks in May and June 1995 in Glasgow, and marketed
(but not screened) at the Cannes Film Festival in 1995. Cannes director
Gilles Jacob 'loathed the film' and would not have it in the 1996 competition, but a 'Special Screening Out of Competition' was negotiated. This is
one of the moments in the biography at which the integration of the object
is such that it came to be recognized as separate, discrete and external. Or
to put this another way, it is a moment at which the object acquired a sufficient density of internal relations to emerge from its context; indeed, to be
sufficiently robust so as to produce its own context, its own past, its own
origin. This is the moment in which the object acquired integrity as the
artistic work, *Trainspotting*. But this integration should not be seen to produce a static object. Rather, in terms of its biography, the dynamic, integrated object, the film *Trainspotting* continues to be organized, or organizes itself, in a series of sequenced movements.

Optioned to Figment Films, and like *Shallow Grave* co-produced with
Channel 4, the cinema distribution rights to *Trainspotting* were bought by
Polygram Filmed Entertainment and released in all the territories they then
owned: Australia, Belgium, Holland, Canada, France, Germany, Ireland
and Spain. Initially shown on 57 screens in the UK – principally in the West
End and Scotland – distribution of *Trainspotting* was extended to 248
screens nationwide by March. The film then went on to successful runs in
Europe, the USA (in which territories it had been sold to Miramax)[3] and
some territories elsewhere, including Brazil (see chapter 8). In the UK, the
promotion of the film property – which, as is now common in the film
industry, cost more than the production of the film itself (£1.5 million) –
negotiated potential conflict between controversial content and the desired
mass audience through careful deployment of PR and advertising. Making
use of the considerable number of images taken by a photographer who
they had arranged to be on set everyday, Polygram was initially able to

manage the appearance of a promotional package in a very controlled way. As Julia Short of Polygram said, when interviewed in January 1998:

So in fact what we did was to choose loads of different sets of photography and said right the first set of photography we are going to let out are these shots, then to the women's mags we're gonna give out this set of photography, to the men's mags we're gonna give this set of photography, to the national press we're gonna keep this set and nobody but the national press can use it, then we're gonna have a special set of photography of Ewan McGregor, a special set of Robert Carlisle and we were absolutely rigid in our strategy and then everybody had a completely different photograph to the media that had broken before.

Additionally, a 'teaser trailer' was shot on a day taken out of shooting; its release was planned to coincide with both the release of a video of *Shallow Grave* and the occasion of university students' Freshers' fairs. The timing of the distribution of the film itself was decided by Polygram on the basis of an analysis (internally conducted) of when in any year '18' films were historically most successful (which, they found, is just after Christmas). Television advertising was not agreed until the film was showing, and broadcasting was then linked to the results of weekly exit polls, and used strategically to boost falling attendance.

Most notable in these movements, however, was the poster. This made use of a graphic interpretation, not of the film, but of the literal connotations of trainspotting, the hobby: so, for example the poster reproduced some aspects of the look of a train timetable, as did much of the associated merchandise and publicity. For some people, the poster eclipsed the film. Julia Short says: 'And, in fact, we created the campaign for the world. We didn't realize it at the time, 'cos we just thought it's a film about drugs, about heroin, whose gonna go and see it?' Or, as one newspaper report put it, '[*Trainspotting*] has become a film, and two soundtrack albums and a play in several versions, and a poster so recognizable that newspaper cartoonists parodied it' (Beckett 1998: 6). However, while many aspects of the PR campaign could be rigidly controlled, Polygram could only monitor a fraction of the resulting copies of and improvisations on the design template of the poster that proliferated at this time (and still continue). These

included, among numerous others, an accountancy recruitment promotion advertisement, an advertisement for Adidas trainers, the Clothes Show Live exhibition and National Express, window displays in the fashion chain store French Connection, and home-produced posters advertising student housing, among many others. The film thus drew on popular culture and fed back into it. Some of the companies

that appropriated features of the poster design were threatened with legal action by Polygram for breach of copyright. For most, however, the only financial penalty was to make a 'voluntary' financial payment in the form of sponsorship of the football team that is part of a Drug Rehabilitation Unit featured in the film. But in any case, in some kind of happy ending, the owners of the copyrighted literary property were able to capitalize on these illicit appropriations as the cover of the novel was redesigned according to the same template, helping lift sales to 800,000 in 1996 alone.

What is significant about this account in relation to the notion of biography that we are proposing is that some of the movements of the object *Trainspotting* described here, while still sustaining its integration, no longer required (or helped produce) its integrity as an artistic work (cf. Adorno 1991). Instead, it is specific intensive features of the object, rather than any kind of aesthetic unity, which enables some of its movements. To put this another way, certain features become the intensive ordinates of movement. Furthermore, this movement does not occur in relation to a fixed origin. Let us give some examples to illustrate this. The elements of the poster that were most frequently reproduced by the many imitators included: the colour orange, chosen "cos we knew orange was gonna be the fashion colour, where-ever-you-looked lipstick'; the timetable layout; and the use of photographic portraits, a device whose initial rationale was described by Julia Short in the following terms:

We went through the script and we identified all the characters and the key characteristics of each of the characters, so you know the aggressive one had to be fairly in your face, Sick Boy was obsessed by James Bond, we decided to have a girl on the posters 'cos we didn't want five blokes 'cos we thought we'd alienate the women audience and in fact she wasn't a really major part of the film, but for us it was critical to have a girl on it.

Other features of the object *Trainspotting* that enabled movement included a style of T-shirt, worn by the character played by Ewan McGregor, which became fashionable and was linked to the film (even though the style long pre-existed the film). Wearing such a T-shirt – with the intention of recalling the film or not – could be taken to indicate a participation in the film. Additionally, the second album of *Trainspotting* music included not only songs featured in the film alongside tracks mentioned in the book but not featured in the film, but also songs that had been considered but not included in the film and not even mentioned in the book. Here then the object's movements have multiple origins, some actual, some virtual.

In mapping even this apparently simple biography, it became clear that there were elements of complexity and at least two general principles of transformation, or coordination, at work (Lury 2004). The first might be described as *translation*, an organizational process in which the product moves in a linear, sequential fashion as a short story to a book to a film to video to television and so on. In these movements, while there are significant translations in cultural form, the object develops and maintains an aesthetic integrity, a discursive unity of sorts, and moves within and across relatively fixed, stable territories. This movement – in which integration results in the integrity of an artistic work – occurs in an indexical or motivated relation to an origin typically understood in terms of authorship, creativity, regional or national culture. It is representational and ownership of the property is secured by the laws of copyright. The second process – in which object integration does not require artistic integrity – may be described as one of *transposition*. This is a process in which it is the intensive features of the object, rather than any kind of aesthetic unity, that enable movement. It is a process of the mediation of things and the thingification of media. The organized movement enabled by transposition is not linear, but is instead characterized by multiplicity, and an intensive, associative series of events, merchandise promotion and publicity, organized in part by the laws of trademark and passing off. And while the movement transposition affords is defined by territorial boundaries, it is not so much a matter of the overcoming of distance from an origin, but rather of the multiplication of origins. As the author of the novel puts it, '*Trainspotting* has been appropriated so much it's like a Richard Branson product. A zone of identity that's used to sell products' (quoted in Beckett 1998: 6).

BIOGRAPHY II

We traced the phenomenon of Young British Art (YBA), a group of young British artists, through exhibitions in London, New York, Paris and Chicago and via curators, collectors, museum directors and art journalists in London, New York, São Paulo, Rio de Janeiro and Tokyo. The phenomenon originated in journalistic commentaries that anticipated the impact of an elastic group of artists created by a self-promotional curatorial community in a series of exhibitions during the late 1980s and early 1990s. Famously, the artist Damien Hirst curated an exhibition of his own and other artists' work in a show titled 'Freeze' in 1988 (including the artists Mat Collishaw, Ian Davenport, Sarah Lucas, Gary Hume, Fiona Rae, Angus Fairhurst, Anya Gallaccio and Simon Patterson). In 1990 many of the

artists who came to comprise YBA had their work shown at the ICA in London in the New Contemporaries show. International momentum began to acquire velocity with 'General Release: Young British Artists at Scuola di San Pasquale' at the 1995 Venice Biennale, and was assisted by 'Brilliant! New Art From London' later in the same year at public galleries in Minneapolis and Houston. The British Council was involved in both of these events, in the first case as site owners, in the second as brokers

between artists and dealers, and the galleries' curators. The Council also brokered touring YBA shows in Scandinavia and Eastern Europe. Pictura Britannica, featuring YBA, was also the Council's contribution to the seven-yearly exhibitions of British art in Australia in 1997.

Significantly, however, the object that circulated abroad was not just fine or visual art, but spaces, microcosms of turn-of-the-millennium ('Cool Britannia') British cultural life. In the 'Life/Live' show in Paris in 1996 curators moved (or created) not just the art, but also the art scene or art spaces to Paris. The exhibition physically reconstructed 'Independent Art Spaces'. These were, at the same time, artwork, gallery and commercial spaces. In this and other instances, the artworks and their immediate context of production were merged. In this instance, the artwork is no longer understood in an indexical relation to an origin or source, an author or national culture, but simultaneously with that context, indeed as that context, as a dynamic media environment. There is a contrapuntal relationship between a definite bounded work and an indefinite bounded space, a relationship that works the edge between a specific frame (or artwork) and the distributed system or flow of production of which it is a part (Frow 2002; Lury 2004). In the space, the self-presentation of the artwork requires not interpretation and decoding, but instead invites the perceptual practices of distraction, operationalization, and de- and recontextualization.

In both this and the previous biographical example, significant alteration occurs in the process of transposition across media, including transformations in the object's internal organization. The biographies suggest that elements such as catch-phrases, gestures and graphic details circulate as intensities of sensation or affect. In terms of the process of transposition, they suggest that flow should not be understood in terms of, or at least not only in terms of, the movement of discrete objects with a relatively fixed internal organization, but also as affect, intensity and sensation in or as a series of open-ended object-events.

And such characteristics need to be put alongside the defining characteristics of variability, speed and the miscellaneous identified by Raymond Williams (1974) in his study of television if some sense of the *experience* of global flow is to be captured.

BIOGRAPHY III

We[4] sit and watch people. Some cycling, some roller-skating, some roller-blading; the insignia on their clothes are usually too small to see until they have passed us by. As Rob Shields (1997: 4) comments of his observation in Rodeo Street, Seoul: 'So much happens, so quickly that 180 degree vision would be necessary to begin to "observe" such a scene.' Shields goes on to say that he needs to be 'dazed' to see, since it is only when the observer's body is set 'onto its own auto-pilot of balance and inertial drift ... [that he or she can] concentrate on "taking in" events' (ibid.). Here, by Manhattan Beach in LA, you have to be on the move to see whether it is Adidas or Nike. If we were on blades too, we could move up behind people, overtake, hang back, or turn around to get a second look. Imagining this movement, the placing of insignia on the back of clothing suddenly seems to make sense: you still have a face, even when your back is turned. The insignia are communication in movement, moving communication; not turn-taking, but turn and turn about, as fronts and backs of people move past and around each other.

Earlier, when sitting on the beach, we had seen two boys playing in the waves, both wearing Nike shorts, the letters, NI and KE on each leg of their matching shorts. One is bigger, one is smaller: the shorts are what unite them; the boys are larger and smaller versions of each other. Their shorts gave a flickering message as they ran in and out of the water. This was a visual message, but it also had an aural accompaniment: a bit like a football chant, or at least a crowd chant. NI-KE, NI-KE. This is not face-to-face communication then, but involves the whole body; it involves the use of profiles, of sound, of silhouettes and shapes, and most of all of passing by, of the body in movement.

In shopping malls, we observe how the careful positioning of Nike logos situates the wearer's body in a Cartesian three-dimensional space; the marks or logos are often at right angles to each other. This is most obvious when we observe someone sitting down, with one leg at a right angle to the other, the ankle of one leg resting on the top of the knee of the other. There is a Swoosh in a contrasting colour on the sole of the shoe, looking out at us. This proper, perpendicular space is also apparent as we watch people walking by, wearing shorts and socks, the Swoosh riding high on the side of their ankles. Yet although their legs move in sequential time, while they are clearly in three-dimensional space, they are simultaneously repositioned by the logos or marks. It is as if the mark of the brand collapses the foreground into the background, and slides now into then; these Sunday morning window-shoppers are moving into and out of multiple planes in space and frames of time. The mark – as a conceptual outline or trace of movement – is seemingly pressed against an enveloping surround of space and time which can simultaneously seem far away *and* near, right here *and* already gone, over there. In short, the mark functions as a recalibration machine in time and space.

A week or so later, one of us is in Portland, sitting outside a coffeeshop, watching a group of young people messing around on a street corner. Not many of them were wearing Nike, although most were wearing trainers, many with built-up soles. They were wearing very wide trousers, sometimes almost down to the ground, the trainers just peeping out, sometimes one leg of the trousers rolled up, the other down to and over the shoe, or wearing long shorts that come down below the knee. They reminded me of Popeye, cartoon characters, what Norman Klein (1993) calls hose-pipe characters. The width of their trousers carries the perceptual and physical width and bounciness of the shoe up through the legs, giving them an apparent elasticity or bendiness. These 'kids' were dancing and fooling around to music. They walk up to, around, by the side of each other; their trainers elevating them just that little bit.

Methodology Revisited

These biographcal scenes indicate how the goal of the study – to follow the chosen objects globally – determined the methodology we adopted. The methodology is not objective but 'objectual'. It is neither positivist nor phenomenological. A positivist method is objective; a phenomenological method is more subjective or constructivist. The objects of study – seven mobile cultural objects – carried with them the method. With this recognition came a number of other understandings. A method that follows cultural objects needs to presume the existence of something like a 'mediascape' (Appadurai 1996) or media environment. In such an environment, the people who make, circulate and use objects are *not external* to such an environment. To put this differently, our method does not assume a distinction between media and society; our assumption is instead that we live in a media-society, and that the users, producers and circulators of media are not on a separate level to others.

In our methodological assumption that media are objects is also implicit the understanding that media are *not texts*. Perhaps media did work at one point predominantly as texts – that is, as if they were narratives, or as if they were discursive in their effects – but to investigate media as objects assumes that they are no longer texts. You *interpret* texts. You *use* objects. Texts, it seems to us, are always outside the interpreter. We disagree with Jacques Derrida's assertion that '*il n'y a pas un dehors du texte*'. By definition, our relation with a text is via a *dehors*: the 'ontological difference' presumed by Derrida entails such a *dehors*. Our point is that media have come to act less as texts and more as things, as platforms or as environments (Kittler 1999). And corresponding to the shift from texts to objects is a shift in how we encounter culture: from reading and interpretation to perception, experience and operationality. As a consequence, we are concerned less with symbolic communication as such than with agency, affect, effect and transformation (Gell 1998: 6). Empirically, of course, producers and audiences or users are at many points both inside and outside of media, but our belief is that there is a tendency for the 'mediascape' and the 'socioscape' to come together. The study maps this cutting (and spreading) edge or surface of our selected objects rather than a representative sample of the contemporary culture industry.

To follow, to track, objects means the investigator must descend into the world with the objects and be on the move with them. Thus the investigator is at once ontologized and mobile. To be in the world with the objects means a shift in knowledge relations, a shift that might be described as one from epistemology to ontology. In 'epistemology' the investigator is, as it were, on a different plane from the object and thus is only able to know it as 'appearance', that is, as form in the Newtonian-Kantian manner adopted by social science positivism. In this perspective, the objects we know are variables or functions. To descend into the world with the objects (and subjects) is to encounter them not epistemologically but ontologically. Hans-Georg Gadamer (1976) traced the rise of phenomenology in terms of such a move from epistemology to ontology. In ontology we are in the world with objects and have an 'attitude' towards them. An objective epistemology presumes the absence of attitude, interest or intentionality. As consciousness descends into the world with the things, it comes to know them as more than appearances. It starts to begin to come to grips with things-themselves. To encounter something epistemologically, for Kant, is to enter into instrumental or utilitarian relations with it. It is to be a self-enclosed subject encountering it as a self-enclosed object. Knowledge here is from the outside as appearance. And the subject will engage the object as a utility. This sort of epistemological relation – encountering objects as utilities – is what Georg Simmel (1990) described as calculation and what Marcel Mauss (1976) understood as a part of market exchange. It is in contrast to gift exchange, in which subjects encounter objects as very much the opposite of utilities. In gift exchange the subject opens up. He or she is not a universal, a closed universal, the individual, but a singularity. The object too opens up. It is not closed, as a utility. The object is no longer a particular: it too is a singularity. Subjects and objects as singularities are in the world with one another. Subjects enter directly into the logic of objects. The ontological gaze penetrates. As the object moves out of the epistemological space of extensity, it enters a space of discontinuity, fluidity and excess; it becomes ec-static as an intensity. So this kind of research means getting ontological with things.

But it presumes more than this. It presumes that the investigator does not have a fundamentally different status from the things. Phenomenology does not allow this. In phenomenology, though we move into the world with things, we at the same time make a transcendental move. The phenomenologist wants somehow to know the thing-itself. He or she wants to grasp its ontological structure. There needs to be a transcendental move for this. Phenomenology thus grants consciousness a different ontological status from things. Phenomenology foregrounds perception and experience but still wants to give a different ontological status to consciousness (presuming a difference in kind rather than a difference in degree between objects and subjects). Deleuze makes a distinction between phenomenology and more vitalist assumptions, such as those informing the present study (see also Lash 2005; Fraser et al. 2005). In positivism, consciousness has no attitude: so it is an effect *of* nothing (it is, in Kracauer's terms, a 'senseless amassing of material' (1995: 213)). In phenomenology, consciousness is *of* something. For vitalism, consciousness *is* something. So for us, both ourselves as investigators and the people we study *are* something. The investigators, the subjects and the objects occupy the same world. Investigators, and teams – or project-networks of investigators that may include theorists and practitioners, alongside the subjects and the objects studied – all perceive. The objects in this study are also worlds. They are worlds that are both relational and microcosmic (in Leibniz's (1992) sense). Our objects not only comprise relational worlds, but they perceive relational worlds. Thus investigators, subjects and objects all are engaged in relations of perception with one another.[5] All three know, in their fashion, all reflect, all more or less communicate, all have relations with one another, all are possessed with memory and specific path dependencies (Urry 2003).

All three of subjects, objects and investigators are involved as perceivers and knowers and affect-givers and affect-takers and believers.[6] All three are engaged in sense-making of this world. The way that the investigators make sense is called method. The subjects and objects that we make sense of as human (and post-human) scientists are then not beings, but becomings. And they are making sense of us as we are making sense of them. Investigators, subjects and objects are, in this view, singularities. They are – through their memory traces and anticipated futures – self-organizing. Yet they are – or may be – in their intensive communications, in their connectivity, operationally open.[7]

These singularities, these becomings, are not only ever changing: they are literally moving in global media space. And the only way for the investigator to keep up with and perceive their transformation is to be mobile too. In each case, in this sociology of objects, we track the object as it moves and transforms through a media environment. At points, these environments transform into assemblages of connectivity and communication. By definition, when objects close (operationally), they encounter other objects and subjects as environments. When they open, environments are transformed into webs of connectivity – what Deleuze and Guattari (1983) call machinic conjunctions and assemblages. At moments in global media space, our objects undergo partial disintegration, a partial descent into entropy. At moments they are discrete, at other points they are indistinct, blurred with their own pasts and futures, overlapping and only partly distinguishable from other objects. Classical sociological methodology tells us that variables must be discrete and mutually exclusive. Our objects are often (but not always) indiscrete and (often but not always) mutually inclusive. They are events (Barry 2001), happening facts (Whitehead 1970; Fraser et al. 2005).

The method at stake here is clearly somehow geographical, or cartographic. At issue is topology, mapping. Sense-making through mapping (as a method) breaks with both the predominant methods in the human sciences: those of positivism and hermeneutics (phenomenology). In positivism, sense-making is achieved by understanding the world in terms of causal determination and classification.[8] In phenomenology it is established in meaning and narrative. In, let us call it cartography[9] – or should it be 'cartology'? – sense-making happens through some sort of navigation. This is thinking not through analysis, in which the complex is broken down into simple components, and reconstituted. It is also not sense-making through interpretation or the construction of narratives. It is, instead, knowing through ways of doing, some sort of orientation or navigation.

But navigation as it is understood here is not the mapping of volumetric and extensive space. The ideas of mental cartography in Kevin Lynch's (1960) and Fredric Jameson's (1991) 'cognitive mapping' and Situationism's 'psychogeography' (Debord 1997) come closer to this book's method. Lynch spoke of the importance of developing mental images of the city. He saw legibility as a guide to the 'good city' in his work as a theorist of planning. In this he drew on five urban elements, including the square, the node and the street. In his description of the disorienting interior of the Bonaventura Hotel in Los Angeles, Jameson also argues that a new kind of mapping is necessary in the postmodern age. But what we are proposing, in contrast to Lynch and Jameson, is a mapping that is not primarily cognitive. Situationism's psychogeography is in many ways just such an anti-cognitive mapping. Against legibility, Debord (1981) preferred disorientation, insisting that 'life can never be too disorienting'.[10] The Situationist strategy was one not so much of legibility as of *détournement*, in which legible objects were made illegible. Situationism's *dérive* or drift was inspired by the organized urban expeditions of Dadaism. For the Dadaists, the contourless indistinctions encountered in the meanderings of urban space open up possibilities of invention that are inaccessible to the closed psychoanalytic subjectivity of surrealist *écriture automatique*. Psychogeographical *dérive* also puts the focus on movement. It is a mobile method, but, unlike cognitive mapping, *dérive* is locomotion without a goal. *Dérive*'s mobility opens up possibilities in space for constructing situations. It is further understood by Situationism as a method, as 'psychogeographical research' or 'psychogeographical experiments'. *Dérive* is 'a situation-creating technique' (Plant 1992).

The cartographic method we are proffering in this book dovetails with Situationist psychogeography. It is a research technique that presumes a mobile investigator. Its objects are not clear and distinct, but often unclear and indistinct; they are not concrete but more or less abstract. They may contract into clearness and distinctiveness, into legal, economic and cultural closure, yet they are somehow also open to both *détournement* and to entropic drift. The goal of intensive capital accumulation at junctures dissipates into a spectacular and aleatory goallessness. Finally, our space is rather like an experimental, a laboratory, space. It is not inclusive of most of the world's population of subjects and objects, but yet is expanding, intensively.

But our method departs from psychogeography in a number of ways. First, we address not urban space but the spectacular world on a global scale. Second, where we go is determined by the objects we follow. This is not an aleatory experiment such as, for example, the use of a map of London by the Situationists to explore the mountains of the Harz in Germany. For us, the objects are out there ahead of us in their own *dérive*, their own drift: we are following the spectacle/situation rather than creating it. Third, much of psychogeography addresses the effects of urban space on the emotions of the individual. We are not concerned with the effects of urban extensity on the psychology of the individual. We are operating in a world in which the psyche and indeed the sensorium have, in McLuhan's sense, been already 'outered' as the flows, fluxes and neuronal switching points of global cultural networks. So our method is less an urban psychogeography than a global geography of intensities, or an intensive geography (Thrift 2004). Finally, if cognitive mapping deals with subjects and objects as legible and closed systems, we would endorse what might be a more *tactile* mapping of singularities, as described in, for example, de Certeau (1998). At stake for us is a more tactile or, better, a multimodal and proprioceptive mapping.

To what extent is this sort of cartography also a search or a research of the virtual? This, of course Deleuzian, method is developing in the study of cinema.[11] Here the search is for the outlines of a film's or a director's 'time-image' when all we have explicit access to is the shots in a film. But analysis can lead to discussion of a time-image, which is a virtual (although of course every virtual is only so from a certain point of view). In some ways this book is a sort of search into the virtual of the global culture industry. This said, we fear that too much of a focus on the virtual can lead to neglect of the actual. It is often fused with the assumption that the actual is a Euclidean or mechanistic obstacle to the virtual. We think that the (post-)human sciences in mapping mode or cartography must be sciences as much of the actual as the virtual, since for us 'events' are as much actual as virtual. Extensive space is volumetric,[12] while intensive space is some sort of event-space. Communications are not objects. Communications are not volumetric. They are intensities. But communications and, for that matter, units of information are also not only virtuals. They are not systems, but are the actualizations of systems. They are what systems, what self-organizing systems, produce. This book's seven cultural objects are sometimes open, sometimes closed, yet always reflexive systems.[13] In following objects, we are tracking a whole series of object-events, of actualizations.

The Chapters

The chapters of this book look at the global culture industry via the biographies of seven cultural objects from a number of different points of view, in relation to multiple trajectories and at different speeds. As we noted above, we have experimented with the presentation of these biographies by adopting different genres, styles and registers at different moments. Each chapter has a different organization to capture the heterogeneity we seek to describe.

Chapter 3 focuses on one cultural object:[14] Euro '96 – the 1996 European Championship.[15] The game of football is a 'thing' that has become mediated. At stake is the commodification and mediation of play. Football of course has for a long time been commodified, but it has more recently become doubly mediated, first, through branding and association with brands like Nike and Adidas, and second through worldwide broadcasting, especially on pay television.[16] The biography of a cultural product, we argue, may be seen in terms of a 'value-chain' (Miller 2000), in which one side of each link in the chain partakes of the material economy and the other side, of a desiring or libidinal economy, an economy of affect and intensity. In chapter 3, we focus on culture-industry practitioners in recorded music and sports marketing all of whom consistently referred to the tournament as a 'property'. It is a property that can gain or lose value when it comes together with other 'properties', and those properties can gain or lose value in their attachments.

The chapter opens in the offices of the company East-West Records, whose recording artists are also called 'properties'. Indeed, the company is described as worth little more 'than the sum of its properties'. One of East-West's properties, the adult-oriented pop group Simply Red, was to be promoted via an attachment of their music to Euro '96. East-West was thus to use the tournament as a 'communications platform' to prop up the 'brand value' of Simply Red. This was part of an effort to brand the event, an effort that was not confined to East-West, but was simultaneously, but not always harmoniously, undertaken by UEFA (the Union of European Football Associations), the FA (the (British) Football Association) and others. Thus, the chapter also considers the activities of Music Media Partnerships, whose client is the FA, and whose efforts were in part directed to detaching Simply Red from the Championship in order that the latter would not lose its brand value.

The chapter also considers the role of football magazines in the object-event Euro '96 and again documents the attachment of popular music and popular culture in general to football. Many journalists, from magazines such as *Goal, Total Football, Match, Shoot, When Saturday Comes* and *World Soccer*, had at points in their biographies worked as pop music journalists. They think of football in terms of popular culture. In conversations they propose that football was still very territorialized and local at a point when British pop music was already opening up a global and liminal space in the 1960s. It is only at the very end of the 1980s, starting in Manchester (with Manchester United) that football starts to become liminal: that football lifestyle and clubbing culture come together. It is at this juncture that football also becomes big business and goes global with the massive media deals of BSkyB, the beginning of the Premier League and high-priced sponsorship.[17] Some thirty years later, football and pop come to occupy similar spaces in the flows of the global culture industry, although not easily. Chapter 3 considers here the implications of the way in which the championship comes to be associated with pop music and a shifting sense of English national identity.

Chapter 4 looks at art in the context of global culture industry, holding parallel two discontinuous temporalities: one internal to 'art history', the other opening out onto local places and global flows. One line maps conceptual art in its broadest sense. Here we see a distinction between first- and second-wave conceptualism, both with lineages from the work of Marcel Duchamp. Both first- and second-wave conceptualism break with formalism, the logic of the aesthetic materials and the flatness of the picture plane as found classically in Picasso, Matisse and Abstract Expressionism. In both, the concept has priority over form or matter. First-wave conceptualism in this context embraces both Minimalism and more literal conceptualism. This supposes a break with

the verticality of the flat picture plane for the horizontality of phenomenology (Krauss 1999). At stake is the horizontality of the ray of perception
of the phenomenological vector, the ray of intentionality from viewer to
the art object. Here the viewer is situated in a phenomenological field in
which he or she must make sense in relation to the artwork. First-wave
conceptualism also entails a critique of the institutions of art. Young
British Art, we suggest, is part of a *second* wave of conceptualism. This pro-
ceeds again from Duchamp, but it does not pass through Minimalism,
but instead through pop art: through Andy Warhol and, for example,
Richard Hamilton. Whereas first-wave conceptualism is based on propositional thinking or the intentionality of phenomenological consciousness, second-wave conceptualism is pervaded by the popular media. Its
'ideas' are those of the mediascape, of the information economy. If first-
wave conceptualism is based on the 'light-on' of the proposition or the
phenomenological vector, then second-wave conceptualism is based on
the 'light-through' of contemporary media (McLuhan 1997). Taught
Minimalism in art college, Damien Hirst, for example, resituates the aesthetic value of artworks from the perception of Minimalist volumes onto
communicational surfaces. These artists, as 'Thatcher's children', also
were at home in the decomposition of the social and its reordering as
both market and media. Second-wave conceptualism is in a very broad
sense 'media art', drawing on the more general and vulgar visual culture
in a way that the first wave could not. Young British Art does not involve
a critique of the institutions of art; it is, instead, a way out of the institutions of art altogether. It breaks with both institutions and critique.

A second trajectory in the biography mapped in this chapter is the
meltdown of London's institutions of art. In the aftermath of the Second
World War, British art was based more or less on a set of institutions
structured around Empire, the tradition of Cork Street, the British
Museum and the National Gallery, on the one hand, and the social-polit-
ical institutions of the industrial working class, radical proletarian local
councils and the classical welfare state, on the other. We describe the
emptying out of these institutions. This is a literal emptying out and
refilling of spaces such as disused warehouses of Canary Wharf and a disused power station in Southwark: the initial YBA exhibitions were in the
former, the building of Tate Modern in the latter. The first were created
with the demise of radical Labour councils and their displacement by
Thatcher-created Development Corporations over the course of the
1980s. One of Thatcher's most famous casualties was the Greater London
Council (the GLC) and its leader Ken Livingstone. The second phase of
this dislocation and relocation of cultural and political power is marked
by the symbolic date of May 2000, when Livingstone came back to power
as the first elected mayor of London and the Tate Modern opened its
doors. The ex-industrial spaces became not heritage sites, but spaces of
flows. In documenting this line (of flight), we look at London as art-

space. London, much more than Paris or New York, is to a large extent such a space of flows. Paris, with its volumetric architecture, its Haussmann structures, its planning, its bars to capital and labour, is much more a space of structure. London has more than twice the level of immigrants per thousand inhabitants than New York. In New York, finance enters from abroad to move into American firms. In London there is financial throughput, from outside, through the City of London, to another outside. New York, since Mayor Rudi Giuliani and especially 9/11, is cleaned up, cleaned out. London is dirty and cluttered. London is the space of flows of migrants, of media, of art, of finance. This supports a popular, or 'street', visual culture that in a number of ways comes to blend with the fuzzy dimensions of visual art.

Chapters 5, 6 and 7 describe and outline two processes: one in which media – that were formerly representations – become things, and another in which things that formerly were more exclusively material objects become media. Thus at stake is a certain thingification of media, on the one hand, and, on the other, the media-ification of things. The focus in chapter 5 is on the first of these. The chapter presents the biographies of the three Wallace and Gromit short animated films and *Toy Story*. What we document is the conversion of a film-media object into the things of merchandising. There is in the first instance something extraordinarily thing-like in the animation of both *Toy Story* and Nick Park's shorts in comparison to other cartoons. Historically, most animated cartoons used drawing, whereas *Toy Story* and Wallace and Gromit use computer digitalization and clay-mation. In both cases, things – digital objects and clay models – rather than drawing are at centre stage. Whereas Mickey Mouse and Bugs Bunny (Klein 1993) were (hand-)drawn animation that subsequently become merchandising, in Wallace and Gromit, but especially in *Toy Story*, it is as if the toys (the figures or merchandising) were already there in the film. It is as if they never needed to be converted.

Chapter 6 takes us in the other direction: the mediation of things. Three of our cultural objects – Nike, Swatch and football – were, at one point, things that were not yet media. In chapter 6 we see how the material economic objects of what may have been Marx's industrial capitalist economic base become the mediatic quasi-objects of what is now a more McLuhanite communication. An economy that mostly produced objects in its focus on the means of production now mostly produces quasi-objects in its foregrounding of the means of communication. Here, we are at a halfway point between base and superstructure. Whereas films such as *Trainspotting* and Wallace and Gromit descend part way from superstructure of spirit and subjective culture into the base, our other products, Nike, Swatch and football, ascend part way from the base. The focus in this chapter is empirically on Nike and Swatch. In both cases, products communicate as parts of an abstract object, the brand. The brands Nike and Swatch operate as if they were *interfaces* or surfaces of communication. As surfaces of communication (Moor 2003), they open up space for intensities of affect. They become what we call abstract objects through the centrality of design and distribution in their production. Cinema and the recording industry always had such a pre-eminence of the design process. In these cases, more value was produced in bringing out new 'prototypes' than was involved in the reproduction of existing prototypes, that is, making say fifty or two hundred copies of a film for distribution or pressing one million records. With the centrality of the design process, Nike and Swatch, classical industry makes its entry into the culture industry.

Chapter 7 looks at how the movements in time and in space of cultural objects produce an ebb and flow of pattern and randomness. Here we look at the entanglement of subjects in the global flows of the culture industry, drawing on observations, interviews and visits to end-users of the products. Among the things mentioned here, a number were initially received as mementoes or gifts, sometimes as 'free gifts', or promotionals, while others were acquired as commodities. Think for example of the flooding of households with the branded toys enclosed in every Happy Meal at McDonald's or their Burger King equivalent. Not just these gifts, but the ubiquity of unpaid-for web advertisements, muzak, music from other people's car boom boxes, the proliferation of television channels, junk email, junk fax and junk text-messaging means that the flow of capital these days is also a flow of waste. This is not necessarily an overload, but such a co-presence of a multiplicity of event-communications continually threatens to explode into entropy, into pure randomness. Such too is the junk space that architect Rem Koolhaas (2001) has described: spaces of communication, and signage always threatening a descent – and in fact often descending – into junk, into entropy. Yet what seems like an entropic overload of cultural signs finds new value through the distinctive configurations of the brand. The logo, say McDonald's golden arches, repeated in the central zones of all major global cities, serves as stabilizer, as an orientation point in a seemingly chaotic urban space. Such stabilizations through repetition create pattern out of the randomness of junk capital, and lay the bases for new rounds of capital accumulation. Through its very ubiquity, and especially its repetition, the brand creates patterns for the recognition of distinctiveness in the public domain.

Chapter 8 shifts the point of view to Latin America and in particular to Brazil. It starts with an overview of culture industry and especially what are effectively new media – extra-terrestrial television, internet, brands, mobile phones – in Latin America, and then focuses on the movements of *Trainspotting* and to a lesser extent Wallace and Gromit, into and through Brazil. In Britain, the classical national culture juxtaposition of institutions was a question of Empire, the organized working-class and social

policy institutions of the state. In Brazil, the meltdown that characterized the rise of global culture industry was otherwise. There was, to
begin with, a dictatorship from 1964 to 1985. At the same time, a disaf-
fected intellectual youth, sometimes in prison and finding politics
impossible, went into cultural collectives such as the cine-clubs as an
alternative form of politics. After the dictatorship, the personnel of the
cine-clubs went into distribution, circulation and production in the
global culture industry. We trace these figures and speak to them. We
look at the importance of what Knorr Cetina calls 'global microstructures' in this context, as our objects become the locus of a global interaction order. Yet at the same time, the prime Brazilian genres of culture are
not cinema or the novel, but dance, football, music, carnival. If the
global culture industry can find a place in London's intensity, then it is
more fully at home in São Paulo's hyper-intensity, and full out-of-control-
ness, its (un)control. Global culture industry in the future may be much
less the thing of Paris, New York, London or even Los Angeles than of São
Paulo, Mexico City, Shanghai, Mumbai and Lagos. National culture
industry gave us linear, extensive culture on a national manufacturing
model: it described what was fully a culture of extensity. Global culture
industry, involving an informational culture of intensity, may one day
soon be most at home in these fast-mutating and mega-cities, in these
(still) emergent economies.

   In the context of the above, chapter 9 constitutes a theoretical reprise
and a view towards possible futures of the global culture industry.

3 Football Biography: Branding the Event

In this chapter, the biography of the football championship Euro '96 is presented in terms of the intersection of a set of trajectories: of pop music and stars, of newspapers and magazines, of television and radio, of lifestyles, of global branded sponsors, of English and European football histories, of governing bodies and of a host of small, medium sized and large commercial companies. All of these trajectories intersect in a time–space conjunction, an intensive month, the very brief existence of Euro '96. What we are suggesting is that the biography of a single object combines the paths of such value chains (Miller 2000; Fine 2002) in an event.

Simply Red

It is 1996. Elyce Taylor works in the London office of East-West Records, a label owned by Time-Warner with branch offices throughout Europe. Simply Red is an East-West recording band. East-West was founded in 1990. Simply Red is an East-West 'property'. A record company, if it is itself in the background and thoroughly unbranded,[1] is worth not a lot more than the sum of its constituent properties. In this case, the properties also include the artists Jimmy Nail, Chris Rea and Phil Collins.

Simply Red is a music property, one type of cultural object which was for a while attached to Euro '96, another cultural object. Elyce Taylor's company is in the business of marketing its properties.[2] In this particular case she works in close alliance with another company called So What Arts Ltd., a Manchester-based firm run by Elliot Rushman. So What Arts is Simply Red's agency. East-West market Simply Red in all sorts of ways. They have been very successful, for example, in retail promotion: their sales presenters have positioned Simply Red in very prominent places in the most important British retail record sellers, into 'Our Price, Woolworths, everywhere'. To attach Simply Red to Euro '96 was sought after by Taylor and Rushman, since they believed it was bound to be 'good for the long-term Mick Hucknall image'. Hucknall – the lead singer of Simply Red – would be more 'than just a bird on the arm'.

Enter a third player: Music Media Partnership (MMP), a firm run by Rick Blastley. MMP was involved in the approach of the FA, the (English) Football Association, to Simply Red. Blastley's client was not Simply Red, but the FA. Blastley specializes in helping organizations and companies promote their brand value: that is, the brand value of the event they are organizing through the attachment of music to the event.[3] He is a 'cultural intermediary' (Featherstone 1996), mediating between the organizing body the FA, the music industry and thxe media. Blastley's clients include not only sport governing bodies such as the FA or Rugby Football Union, but also commercial manufacturing companies such as Sunkist. But he sees himself as close to bands and to the music industry, having previously worked at EMI. He says that bands can use 'events like Euro '96 as a communications platform'. Similarly, he believes, the FA can use the bands and the music as a communications platform (see Interbrand et al. 1997 for a marketing discussion of co-branding).

MMP was involved with the organization of the music used by sports events, such as the Rugby Football Union World Cup in 1991 and 1995. The Rugby World Cup was first launched in 1987. Previously, international rugby had been confined to the Five Nations championship. The first Rugby World Cup attracted scant attention. 'ITV inherited the 1991 Cup and thought, "Help! How can this be promoted?"' ITV 'hyped' the 1991 Cup as 'the biggest sporting event here since 1966'. They brought in Blastley and MMP, who put together a version of 'Swing Low Sweet Chariot' as the official England song for the event. Now Mark McCormack's IMG (International Marketing Group) has become promoter of the Rugby World Cup. The 1995 Cup in South Africa became for the first time a world media event, a branded event. Following in the wake of the success of the soccer football World Cup USA '94, the Rugby World Cup caught the public imagination. The South African Rugby Union organizing committee, now working with IMG, had approached Blastley and MMP to do the official music, not for the England team, but for the Cup as a whole. The result was the 'World in Union' song, performed 'African-style' by Blaze, the 'biggest act at the time in South Africa'. The music, Blastley noted, was produced to a tight timetable and needed to be completed six months before the opening ceremony in order that it could be 'choreographed'.

IMG and the South African organizers had 'really created an event'. IMG often works by creating events for sponsors, like the Virginia Slims tennis tournament or the Toyota World Matchplay Golf. The force behind the European Championship were their competitors, ISL (International Sports Leisure and Culture Marketing). ISL usually works with the organizers of an already created event such as the Olympics and the World Cup. These are already branded events for which ISL's job is to strengthen the brand profile. The European Championship had also been around for a long time, but it was very low profile, almost unbranded. In 1992, it consisted of only eight teams and fifteen matches, in contrast to the World Cup France '98™ fanfare of thirty-two teams and sixty-four matches, or even the Italia '90™ and USA '94™ World Cups of twenty-four teams and fifty-two matches. The first tournament to be branded in the European Football Championship was England's Euro '96. In this sense, UEFA, ISL, the FA, eleven official sponsors and many others created the European Football Championship as a 'cultural property'. The biography of this particular cultural product is thus its transformation from a sporting occasion into a *cultural property*, from a tournament into a brand.

Already a player in the British and global sport field, MMP was a natural go-between for the FA and music marketing. MMP opted for Simply Red, 'the biggest English band ever in Europe'. Red's previous 1993 *Stars* album was the decade's best-selling English LP on the European Continent. When approached, Simply Red themselves put forward 'We're In This Together', a track from their new 1995 album, *Life*. The BBC and ITV were sounded out and they 'went for it'. Radio 5 said 'perfect: overseas broadcasters would use it too'. The governing bodies, the FA and UEFA, also assented, and thought 'maybe the sponsors will use it. It could work well for the opening and closing ceremonies.' So a contract was signed between the FA and Simply Red, the single was released and the video of 'We're in This Together' was cut to the beat with football footage.

Euro '96 involved, Blastley noted, both 'brand repositioning' and 'brand extensions'. Brand extensions include, for example, the organization of spin-off events from the tournament: for example MMP's staging of a concert for Pepsi-Cola featuring the band East 17. Again, there was the trio of the footballing event, the music and the commercial product (in this case Pepsi-Cola). Blastley's speciality is exploiting this sort of triumvirate, or using music 'for an event to brand'. In such a context, it is not always clear who is being exploited by whom. In the example above, Pepsi-Cola was not an official sponsor of the event but was 'ambushing' it at the expense of *Coca-Cola*, which was an official sponsor.[4] And while Simply

Red's involvement was legitimate, they also had something to gain, as well as to sell. Their audience was shrinking. Their previous *Stars* album had sold 3 million copies, while *This Life* struggled to sell 1.4 million. The band's sales were increasingly limited to the market category of adult rock. Attachment to Euro '96 was part of an attempt to reposition Simply Red as a brand, to broaden their market. But this exercise was itself dependent on the repositioning of Euro '96, of football itself. The ambition was to reposition football as not exclusively of interest to British lower-working-class male youths. 'We're In This Together' was also a 'communications plat-

form' for the FA. As the tournament's official song, it was saying 'no' to terrace violence and British nationalism. It was saying, 'we are European'; more specifically, it was also saying football 'is the "beautiful game" as played in Europe'. Blastley also helped produce an album called *The Beautiful Game*.

A secondary theme for Euro '96 was of 'football coming home', a reference to the origins of football in England as well as to the English World Cup victory in 1966. (In 2004, the phrase was rewritten as 'Football's coming Homer' on the front page of the Guardian (5 July), to mark Greece's victory in the Euro 2004 competition, an ironic testimony to the enduring resonance of the motto.) MMP thus approached the Lightning Seeds, knowing that lead singer Ian Broudie was a 'huge fan of football, a Liverpool season ticket holder'. It was Broudie who decided to bring in comedians Frank Skinner and David Baddiel from the television programme *Fantasy Football*, a show particularly popular with the BritPop generation of fans, then aged 13–20. Broudie wrote the music, Baddiel and Skinner wrote the lyrics, and the song, 'The Three

Lions', caught the mood of the tournament. Terry Venables, the England manager, and the national team appeared in the video. This song – and not 'We're In This Together' – became the official England team song. The album was released by RCA, 'because they're soccer nuts and it was almost how do we not do it with them'. And 'everybody wanted to be a part of this album. Bands like Black Grape wrote a brand new song for the album, which went into the Top Ten. The only band missing was Oasis, and that's only because they submitted the day after we cut the album' (interview, Blastley). The single – because Lightning Seeds were under contract – was released by Sony. The part in the lyrics about 'three lions on your chest', along with the England team presence in the video, 'helped shift hundreds of thousands of Umbro shirts'. (Umbro, an official UEFA tournament sponsor, have their logo on the England team shirts alongside the England heraldic device of three lions.)

The album was sponsored by Coca-Cola, the world's most successful brand, according to Interbrand et al. (2004). Coca-Cola is among the companies – Microsoft, General Electric, Intel, Netscape – that have most increased their market capitalization over the past decade, to a greater value than, for example, General Motors. Integral to Coca-Cola's strategy is to sponsor football, to get access to promote their product to football fans. 'All brands go for football today because today it's fashionable to like football.' The Coke strategy is 'going for the local, for the fan, not global, but we are like the lad next door, of the people'.[5] It was for this reason that while Pepsi-Cola chose to have pictures of global stars such as Claudia Schiffer, Andre Agassi and Cindy Crawford in their advertisements, Coca-Cola chose to feature fans, face-painted fans in the stands, fans who, as the ad goes, 'eat football, sleep football and drink Coca-Cola'.

For their part, the music artists were using Coca-Cola as a communications platform. The company made an agreement to distribute an offer of tracks from *The Beautiful Game* on '180 million cans of coke'. Here Coca-Cola is not just a manufactured object, it is not just an identity or cultural object: it is also a medium. It is a means of communication, a communications technology or a (distributed) surface in which other cultural products, in this case a music artist and a sporting event, can be communicated. Signifiers might communicate, but they are not media of communication. Media are surfaces or waves or spaces or signals in which various contents may be communicated. The Coca-Cola can is such a medium. Older media worked from a principle of (attempted) separation of the content, of the message from the medium or technology (see the discussion of Adorno in chapter 6). Now the message – or content – is a combination of signifier and signified and referent, and the medium is a space or surface of communication. This is true not just of the Coca-Cola can, but also of football itself (they mediate each other). Football is something that is most frequently watched on television. But the content, the football match itself, is a medium, a three dimensional space of quasi-mass communication (the football ground) in which players, referees and managers communicate to perhaps 50,000 fans. The fans are enthusiasts, literally fanatics, almost specialists, and as such are part of the 'football field' themselves (in Bourdieu's (1993) sense. The message, the content that the television broadcast watcher receives, is thus a content that is already a communications medium. That is, the content is a combination of the match and its reception by a highly interactive audience – an audience (the crowd) which is so interactive as to be part of the spectacle itself. Indeed it is so much a part of the spectacle as to be the content of the Coca-Cola advertising.

East-West Records activated the sponsorship, that is, the association of the property Simply Red with the event, through a £250,000 advertising campaign. So What Arts worked with Nigel Tweeney, whose company specializes in promoting bands and had previously negotiated Radio 1 airplay for Simply Red. 'We're In This Together' got only B-list airplay, however: fifteen plays per week, in contrast to the twenty-five plays per week of A-listed records. Rushman convinced another official sponsor, MasterCard, to activate their sponsorship of the Championship by promoting a concert with Simply Red and the band M People, which was itself to receive television coverage. There was extended coverage of 'We're In This Together' at the opening and closing ceremonies of the tournament. A BBC Euro '96 highlights feature showed an entire three-minute section of clips of play from the previous Wednesday night's matches to the tune of the single, much of it 'in glorious and marvellous slow motion'. This 'semi-turned the single around that week', as it moved into the charts at number eleven, and was played on 'Top Of The Pops'. And the album 'muscled up to number three' on the album charts.[6]

But it slowly became clear that Simply Red was not going to be an asset to the Championship, that it might even subtract value from the sporting property rather than adding to it. MMP did not include Simply Red in *The Beautiful Game* album. 'If the BBC had pushed it, the sky would have been the limit'. But there was a new head of sport at the BBC, who 'didn't like the record' and 'relegated it to the play-out tune', some 'eight seconds at the end of every show'. The FA for their part was 'unhelpful', but 'because of contractual obligation they kind of tolerated it and fulfilled the minimal obligation they had to'. The FA was obliged to help secure the participation of European footballers in the video, but none participated in the end. The FA did not press the BBC to give the single sustained coverage. In the event, the album 'got some football fan purchases', but did not really reach the fans, even in Continental Europe. For example, in Germany, East-West Records managed to secure some television coverage for the single, but the German fans did not take to the music: 'everyone wanted BritPop-like stuff'.[7]

This just described moment in the life of Euro '96 connects the tournament with two pop records ('We're In This Together' and 'The Three Lions'), three official sponsors (MasterCard, Coca-Cola and Umbro), several media players including BBC Radio 1, BBC Sport and a host of other cultural intermediaries, including a manager, a music event marketing firm and a record company. The footballing event was marketed through the music and the music was marketed through the footballing event. And both were marketed through the media of the sponsors, the commercial brands. The commercial product brands for their part are marketed through both the footballing event and the music. But to be marketed in conjunction with another cultural product is not enough. The important thing is to be marketed with the *right* other cultural objects; in the end, the FA and the organizers of the tournament simply did not want to be attached to Simply Red.

The Passion and the Fashion: Magazines

IPC is in 2006 Britain's largest magazine group, owned until November 1997 by Reed Elsevier. Reed International, a British company, which previously sold the Mirror group to Robert Maxwell, purchased IPC prior to their merger with the Dutch publishers Elsevier. The selling of IPC is consistent with the more recent logic of Reed Elsevier's focus on publishing scientific journals, electronic publishing and professional database-building. In 2003 IPC was owned by Time-Warner.

As you enter the IPC Media building – in the King's Reach Tower in Stamford Street, poised between Tate Modern and the South Bank Complex in London – you are queried about your appointment and upon proof of identity given a badge and told to take the lift to the sixth floor. There you find the floor occupied by IPC's sports magazines. *90 Minutes* occupies a few cubby-holes and one of these is the desk of Andy Strickland, who provides a considerable portion of the copy for the football weekly. Like many of his football magazine colleagues, Strickland's background is in music journalism. He was the main freelancer for the *Record Mirror*, edited by Eleanor Levy, which was shut down and sold off in 1991. *90 Minutes*' other senior staff writer also has a background in the music press; he came to the magazine with experience of the *Record*

Mirror and four years at *New Musical Express. 90 Minutes* began in 1990, published by Paul Haultsby 'and a mate', and ran as a home publishing operation until it built up debts and was taken over by Dennis Publishers. This company paid the debts, shifted the magazine to a colour format and sold it to IPC in 1992–3. In-between times, Haultsby had brought in Levy as production editor and Strickland as a writer. With the acquisition by IPC, Levy became editor of *90 Minutes*, and Haultsby director of all five of IPC's football titles. This included *Goal*, a pricier, glossy monthly, started in 1995, which for Strickland's tastes was 'really not different enough from *90 Minutes*'.[8]

90 Minutes, like *Goal*, was not just about football: it covered some pop music too. For example, the magazine took some Manchester City players to an Oasis concert to meet the group, famous supporters of the then downwardly mobile club, and conducted an interview with players and group members together. In July 1996 the magazine's staff went to the Phoenix Pop Festival, at which they 'actually play[ed] football. There's a big Five-a-Side tournament ... You've got actors, TV actors, film actors, musicians, journalists, comedians, everyone ... there and playing football, having a good time, listening to music and stuff.' The 'cross-over phenomenon', Strickland notes, 'began with the rise of Smash Hits in the early eighties.' There were a few precursors of this in punk itself: for example, 'the cover of a Lurkers punk album in '78. There's a picture on the cover of him – "Bag for Fulham". This album, called *Fulham Fallout* by the Lurkers, the cover shot is like a gig and one of the guys down front is Stuart Pearce [a one-time England defender and in 2006 Manchester City manager], aged 16 or something.' More recently, at an awards dinner, the staff of *90 Minutes* shared a table with Ruud Gullit and Damon Albarn from Blur. Successful football players have become much better paid, and some have become stars much like the popular musicians, whose fame (and wealth) preceded them some twenty years earlier. As stars they are 'better at expressing themselves and relating to other stars'. 'When you get musicians and footballers together, the musicians just want to talk about football, and the footballers about music.'[9]

The three (male) main senior figures at *90 Minutes* all have a music journalist background, are in their mid- to late thirties, and have a background in punk culture. Their younger staff writer, Julia, has a football fanzine writing background. So has Michael Hodges, an editor of *Goal*, previously a freelancer doing 'some music journalism, but mostly sports'. 'There has been lots of cross-over in England between music and football journalism. Once football achieved a certain hip-ness and footballers and pop stars started hanging out together', like Oasis and the Manchester City players, Posh Spice and David Beckham, Danny Behr and Ryan Giggs, Liverpool's Robbie Fowler and Phil Redmond's (of soap-opera *Brookside*) daughter. 'Football is embedded in the consciousness of certain young English people pretty much in the way that punk rock was. It's been repossessed by them: in a way it's changed their cultural identity.'[10]

As a 5- or 6-year-old child going to matches with his father in the early 1970s, Hodges experienced a scene 'more like the '50s: lots of men in scarves and flat caps'. This began to change in the heyday of football violence from the mid- to late '70s, which is when the 'yob thing' started. Punks, for the most part, avoided football, but skins and other 'yobs', some famous for being racist, flooded into the grounds. According to analysts of football violence, such as Dunning (1999) and Williams (1989), these were the excluded, by many standards anomic, lower-working class youth coming to watch football. Football, previously 'territorialized' in solid skilled working-class culture and intact working-class families, had become 'deterritorialized'.

The change that concerns us, however, came in a second moment of football's deterritorialization in the early 1980s. Now the character of football violence changed. Football became not just liminal, but stylish. This coincided with the emergence of the 'casuals' as a youth subculture. The casuals were, according to Gavin Hills of the England and Manchester United magazines, 'hooligans' but not 'yobs'.[11] The casuals came after the 'skins'. They were not scruffy. Hills, born at the end of the 1960s, was a casual. 'When I was at school in the late '70s and early '80s the thing to do was to be a casual. Skinheads had gone out and the thing to do was to wear smart clothing and go to football and cause trouble.'[12] 'There was an air of violence in the late '70s and there were guaranteed fights in the stands. For a 14-year-old that's incredibly exciting. If you actually talk to the lot at *Goal* and the others about their early memories of football, if truth be told, winning cups and matches and particularly good performances from players would not be the key moments. They'd actually talk about the time Tottenham played Arsenal and everybody was on the pitch throwing chairs. It was kind of a bonding experience. If you wanted a bit of a kick you'd go with "the firm" and run down the streets and maybe rob a few shops and hit somebody.'[13] Lots of the 'intelligentsia' at the time thought 'football hooligans were racist', 'but a lot of them were black, for God's sake'. The casuals/hooligans were 'more from a mod background. It was all about being clean-cut and listening to black music and soul weekenders. A lot of them were black, the "top boys" so to speak. There's people like ... who's (now) a very successful DJ. He was a very naughty boy with Spurs in the early '80s, very trendy and fashionable "top lad" type thing. Like the "Sting" figure in *Quadrophenia*; a hooligan not a yob. Always smart, a bell boy during the week.'[14] The casuals, born at the end of the '60s, dressing smart, listening to black music, fighting at games, reading the new magazine *Smash Hits*, were also the roots of many who wrote in and published the football fanzines that appeared in the mid- and late '80s.

The rise of the fanzines, started by ex-casuals among others, was also tied to the rise of dance culture in Manchester and elsewhere, where they were joined by yet another generation of youth, who rejected the seriousness of the punk tradition and crossed independent music over into dance. They went to the Manchester club, the Hacienda, and listened to the Happy Mondays and the Stone Roses. The club was owned by Tony Wilson and members of New Order who were from the older generation punk scene but who were part of the transition into a more dance-like electronic, cooler sound. The clubs were 'a large space like football grounds'. Previously, the middle classes, who 'were distinctly into rock, turned their noses up at football, and had serious discussions as to what the latest Clash single meant for humanity. But suddenly in the late '80s all hell broke loose'. There was a 'straight progress from punk fanzines of the late '70s like *Sniffin' Glue* to the football fanzines' a decade later. But it wasn't the same people. 'Adrian Thrills, who got his name in 1977 because he was in a punk band – he was really called Earl something from an Irish background' – was on one of the famous punk fanzines before moving on to the *Daily Express* as deputy football editor.[15]

There is another history to the glossy football magazines: the monthlies. *New Musical Express* was a weekly music paper, begun at the end of the '60s at the same time as the decidedly untrendy *Shoot*, also a newspaper and a weekly, but about football. The first monthly popular culture glossy was *The Face*, published by Nick Logan, former editor of NME, in the mid-'80s. A decade later the football glossy monthlies such as *Total Football*, *Goal* and *Four Four Two* were published. These popular culture and sport glossies were expensive. They were explicitly commercial, and drew considerable revenues from national and global brand advertisers. For *Total Football* and *Goal* the paradigm was set not so much by *The Face*, but instead by the '90s lads' magazine *Loaded*. It was *Loaded* that 'changed all the rules'.[16] More acceptable, especially to an older generation, is the mild, 'adult new laddism' associated with Nick Hornby. All of which brings us back to his contemporaries Frank Skinner and David Baddiel: 'The Three Lions' and 'Football's Coming Home'. 'There was a point' (in Euro '96), Hodges notes, 'where Skinner and Baddiel at Wembley were near the Royal Box. It's like they were the Queen. It was the Scotland match. We beat the Scots and the whole crowd except for the Scots was singing "Football's Coming Home". They were all turning to Skinner and Baddiel and it's all like some sort of homage. It's frightening really. It was like Berlin in 1936. Skinner was a stand-up comic and knows how to milk an audience. This is the total cultural cross-over – football, music, TV, comedy, the lot. Skinner is the traditional, chirpy working-class lad with a bit of the cheeky lad in class, being very popular you know. That will be popular with Mums, Grannies, with the stylish element, with people with cultural agendas, with children. He's got a particular kind of English style. And it's connected to football which is the national game.'[17]

Europe '96

In June 1996, just before the quarter-final between England and Spain, the *Sunday Mirror* showed a British Beefeater beheading a Spanish matador on its front page. The headline, 'Achtung! Surrender!', appeared on another day in June with photos of Paul Gascoigne and Stuart Pearce in First World War helmets, with the caption: 'For you Fritz, ze Euro '96 Championship is over.' Other tabloid treatment of 'the Spanish, calling them "dagoes" and saying "their mothers have moustaches"' provoked a series of letters to the editors.[18] Philip Cornwall of the low-budget magazine *When Saturday Comes* (who, along with founder editor Andy Lines, has a degree in European History from London University), was relieved that the strategy 'backfired'. Cornwall connects it with the more general 'Europhobia' of the tabloid press, including the description of civil servants in Brussels as 'Gauleiters' in the *Express* and *Mail*, and the routine portrayal of Chancellor Kohl in tabloid cartoons in First World War uniform.[19] If the FA had one big worry for Euro '96, it was English fan violence.

As late as 1978, it was not allowed for English clubs in the Football League to field foreign players: Ossie Ardiles and Ricky Villa's appearance at Tottenham that year finally put paid to that rule. So the behaviour of England away fans was more consistent than inconsistent with the behaviour of the country's football institutions. England away fans – sometimes with connections to the British National Party (BNP) and later Combat 18 – labelled publicly as not 'true' football supporters, have often been in the news for violence (Back et al. 2001). 'The Nazi element', Gavin Hills notes, was 'rarely there at league grounds.' Millwall, Leeds and Chelsea were exceptions, with Chelsea drawing 'lots of its support from very white suburban areas'. At the 1988 European Championship in Germany, in which England qualified but lost all three of its group games, there was a 'Nazi rally on the steps in Stuttgart. There was BNP printed on the Union Jack flags of about fifty fans [who were] singing, "There ain't no black in the Union Jack" and handing out "No Pope" stickers.'[20]

'No Pope': English football racism also takes an anti-Irish form. Chelsea fans were not atypical: in some games Irish players were 'getting booed as "balaclava cunts" ... like because they were Irish they must be IRA. They're still out there.' In 'Chelsea matches in Europe ... there's still an element of this thing called "True Blues" and songs like "Do you want a chicken supper Bobby Sands?" "Do you want a chicken supper you dirty Fenian fucker?".' (True Blues refers to the 'Protestant' sides of Chelsea, Rangers and the Belfast Protestant Club Linfield.)[21] This racism was allowed to continue until just a year before the onset of Euro '96 in the 'friendly' away match versus the Irish in Dublin, which had to be stopped because of the violence of England fans. Andy Strickland, covering the match for *90 Minutes*, observed: 'the fighters are all guys from tiny little places in Lancashire, Stockport, Mansfield. They are never Leeds, Man U, Tottenham, Arsenal. You look at the flags. If you look at the pictures of English away fans, they are all from those small towns. They take the Union Jack which obviously shows they don't know what they are doing anyway because it's the Union Jack and not the Cross of St George, and across it says almost always Mansfield or Stockport.'

The continuation of this violent racism was the real worry of the FA organizers going into the tournament. Hence when Media Communications Workshop (MCW) entered, and subsequently won, a competition set up by the FA to design a logo for Euro '96, there were a number of 'don'ts' and 'do's'. The 'don'ts' in 'creating an identity for Euro '96' were to be 'not British, not aggressive', but to be 'modern, European'. To quote chief designer Ralph Robinson, 'we wanted Euro '96 to be a celebration rather than an actual sports competition. We wanted it to be more European: a family occasion, almost like going on a holiday, and a cultural experience because you would be meeting all different people from all over Europe.'[22] The FA similarly brokered the publishing of the England magazine, starting some fifteen months before the tournament, at about the time of the

Dublin match. Publisher James Friedman, son of Edward Friedman, then Director of Manchester United merchandising, purchased rights from the FA to use the England logo. Editor Gavin Hills pursued an active anti-racism campaign. He felt, 'slightly responsible for the fact that you didn't see too many Union Jacks at Wembley. We did the Cross of St George and we made some effort to change the national anthem. We did "drop the Union Jack" articles.' Like the three lions logo, the 'official England badge is dating from Richard the Lion Heart. Singer Billy Bragg has always said, "if you give the flag to the right you're just giving in". The point is to redefine national identity. There's an English radical tradition going back to Blake who was always multicultural. In fact they're having a St George day next year. It's being elevated in the English Church to a proper Saint's day.'[23] Strickland says: 'One of the greatest things about Euro '96, we talked about it in the [*90 Minutes*] office, is that it made it quite comfortable going to watch England sitting in the crowd wearing an England shirt. It's almost like the decent fans have reclaimed the England shirt. Before if you're in an England shirt you automatically thought, "steer clear, a bit dodgy". Especially someone my age.'

There were nevertheless incidents during the 1996 Championship, including violence at Trafalgar Square after the semi-final defeat by Germany. Some 'Germany supporters with Scotland flags and "Fuck England" banners at Wembley, singing a song that [in translation] went something like "You've got mad cow disease. Because you eat the beef. You're all mad because you eat the beef".' But the level of racist activity was seen to be much less than it might have been. Strickland says: 'One of the greatest things of the whole tournament was coming back to London after games on trains and there was such a fantastic mixture of not just England but other fans. I was on a train coming back from Portugal-Croatia. It started off in Leeds, so there were Danish fans in there and they'd just basically been knocked out of the tournament but it was a fantastic atmosphere on the train. I stood up all the way from Birmingham, from Scotland to Holland and there was just no vicious-ness at all.' For Cornwall, 'We are heading towards a situation where, at the sort of cultural level, not a political level, the split with the Continent is broken down. There is a famous *Daily Telegraph* headline, "Fog in Channel: Continent Cut Off" which expressed perfectly the insu-larity of the predominant English culture. It was as if the whole of Continental Europe was cut adrift from civilization by the fog in the Channel. Now we are seeing a much more positive view at every level, partly through football. In the same way, the role of black players and the breakdown of racism in this country has been crucial. The fact that we are now going to have players from the whole of Europe competing in England. And everyone will have their own Continental player if they are a football fan.'[24]

It is hard to separate out the biography of an object from its context, an event from the relations in which it occurs. The biography of the intensive event, Euro '96, with a very slow lead-in of about a year, a month of inten-sity and a very short aftermath, cannot really be separated out from the biography of European football. The European Championship, in Euro '96, increased the number of teams competing for the first time from eight to sixteen, from fifteen to thirty-one matches. It became a systemat-ically sponsored event for the first time. The European Cup negotiated a similar sponsorship deal through the sports-marketing firm Team.[25] This comprised many of the same sponsors – only Ford instead of GM, PlayStation (Sony) in place of Philips, Amstel in place of Carlsberg, as the Cup has developed from a knock-out competition into the fully fledged Champions League. In 1992 a team – which had to be top of its domestic league to qualify – could win the European Cup playing six matches. By 2002–3 even a team that came fourth in the domestic league could play a two-leg qualifying round to enter. This is followed by six matches in a group of four, followed by six more matches in another group of four, followed by two-legged quarter- and semi-finals and a final – that is, seven-teen to nineteen matches in all. This was a dramatic expansion in time and space of the European network, a highly mediated, highly sponsored, elite network of teams, promoters, sponsors and brands. This has been seen by some to be at the expense of the individual national divisions, which – it is UEFA policy to cut to eighteen teams – will play some thirty-four games per year. In 2002–3 a team could play half as many games in Europe as in England's domestic league. Finally, there is the World Cup, which is European-dominated. Seven of eight seeded teams in France '98, for example, were European, as was the huge mass of viewing audience with purchasing power. By 2006, with the continued expansion of interest in football and in purchasing power in the Far East, this had dramatically changed. Since 1996, football as a culture industry has become truly global.

The Media Field

This account raises the question, at which points are cultural object and medium separate? How do they interrelate? Which dimensions of object and media are undifferentiated? Here, Manuel Castells, in *The Rise of the Network Society* (1996), might be instructive in his distinction of a first media age of mass communications, of a 'McLuhan Galaxy' from a previous 'Gutenberg Galaxy' of print communication. For Castells, the Gutenberg Galaxy was organized along the lines of craft production: not really mass broadcasting, as it was, but print narrow-casting. This was communication from 'the one to the many' (Thompson 1995) to be sure, but not to the very many. The Gutenberg Galaxy presumed the active receiver: the reader. In the McLuhan Galaxy, there is mass communication: the image takes over from the printed word, and the receiver is now a member of the 'audience'. Castells suggests that the indiscriminate nature of communication meant that the message was not to be attended to any more. Thus the message lost in importance with respect to the medium. For Castells, however, it is the information age in which the message is truly the medium. By this he means that the message determines the form of the medium. In this way of thinking, the cross-over, intermediated message of football and pop determined the form of *Goal* and *Total Football* as media. Being, say, a Manchester United fan determines the medium of pay-per-view digital satellite television in order to be able to watch United home games. What this means is a greater selectivity, a return to narrow-casting, that, at least to the extent that it is selected, is interactive.

And it is these narrow-cast sources that have emerged on a grand scale. This began at the end of the 1960s with the publication of *Shoot*, also published by IPC, with considerable information on matches but 'really aimed at 14–15 year olds', with a circulation of 100,000 and the market leader in 1997 for IPC football. *World Soccer* began at about the same time, not as a journalist's magazine with a house style, but more of an information magazine, putting together articles from newspapers in Europe and to a lesser extent elsewhere. Its 60,000 readers were adult, predominantly Continental European fans resident in England and British fans living abroad. The readers of both *Shoot* and *World Soccer* were committed fans, junior and not so junior players, coaches, enthusiasts. A rather different genre began in the late '80s with the fanzines, including *90 Minutes* and *When Saturday Comes* (WSC). The latter began as a fanzine, with fifty copies produced in March 1986 on a copier in the Bethnal Green library. Started by Andy Lines and Mike Pitcher, it took off at the same time as the Football Supporters Association (FSA) in the late '80s. It became a national magazine, peaking in 1993 at a circulation of 39,000, dropping to 30,000 by July 1996, but increasing again between 1997 and 2006.

The glossy monthlies, beginning in the mid-'90s, really opened up the market for football magazines. *Four Four Two* 'invented the market', appearing in 1994, and two years later selling 75–85,000 copies per month. But *Four Four Two* is focused on 'reliable information: for your figures and serious assessments of players'. *Goal* has been called the *Loaded* of football. It has more 'gutsiness' than *Four Four Two*, is 'more humorous, more anti-establishment'. In an early 1996 issue *Goal* did the 'Sex Files', where 'there's a bit about gay football. They wouldn't show men kissing in *Four Four Two*.' Unlike *Loaded*, *Goal* has 'no naked girls', but shares 'an informed irreverence'.[26] *Loaded* and *Goal* will look, for example, 'at footballers in sex scandals', while *Total Football* has brought 'twenty something' working-class males who 'wouldn't have ever bought before' into the shops.[27]

The new cross-over – football and lifestyle – glossy monthlies recruited an audience far wider than the specialist readership of *90 Minutes* and *WSC*. A much wider readership still, though, is reached by the traditional tabloid press, seemingly 'on a different planet' from the magazines. 'I think', Strickland notes, 'we are different from the dailies. I think if you spoke to the guys at *Shoot* that's very much their career path. But we are much more magazine people. I mean I've not thought at all about going to work for a daily paper. Those guys distrust us. We come across them a lot and there's a real barrier between us. [The dailies] are completely reactive and have just a completely different way of working. They are creating their own news, pissing people off.' Strickland and Philip Cornwall of *When Saturday Comes* do not see themselves as having a future in newspapers. This is in contrast to Gavin Hamilton, in his late twenties, at *World Soccer*, with a journalism degree from Bristol, who describes it as, 'much more a job I suppose, I suppose less a passion. You need to write for a very broad range of people: you're not writing for people who have a certain range of knowledge already.'

Consider also, though, the career path of another Gavin – Gavin Hills, editor of the *England* magazine. Hills, an art college student in the late '80s, wrote for fanzines from 1988, where he was noticed and given assignments by Cynthia Rose, then editor of *City Limits*. In the mid-1990s, Hills was a writer for *The Face* and wrote for the *Guardian/Observer*. He did not just cover sports but also 'foreign coverage too, Bosnia, the Angolan War, El Salvador'. He 'went with a Labour MP to Somalia'. In 1996 he was working two days a week at the *Guardian* and three at *Zone*, which was started in 1993 by Jack James (aka James Friedman), Hills and a third partner, and which by 1996 had become a multi-purpose establishment with some fifteen employees.[28] Through Friedman's father, *Zone* became publisher of the official Manchester United monthly magazine. The magazine sells well with teenagers, and especially girls, 'research on the market' shows, 'who buy it because of Ryan Giggs, David Beckham'. It resembles a pop star magazine, 'a bit like the NBA in the States', very photography oriented – unlike other sports papers – hiring the top photographers. The magazine outsells any of the IPC magazines, indeed any football magazine: it is 'the biggest sports monthly in the country' at 140,000 per month. Zone also produces video magazines, bi-monthly, for Liverpool and Everton. They publish the England magazine. They produce junior calendars for Manchester United and books for the club, such as for example the Alex Ferguson biography. It is 'completely a commercial process, the videos of Man. U always go platinum.'[29]

The media is the key actor in this biography of Euro '96. It is not so much the 'spin' they put on the game, as that most people experience football in the media. They experience football, first and traditionally, in the mass circulation newspapers. They experience football, only much more recently, in league matches on television. While international games have been broadcast on television for a long time, league football came very late to broadcasting, almost at the time that the McLuhan Galaxy came to shift to what Mark Poster (1995) called 'the second media age'. This is the age of, first, satellite and cable and, second, of the subscription club Internet website. This has been partly a movement from broadcasting to narrow-casting, described above, but in the second media age with the cross-overs or intermediation of football, pop music and lifestyle, comedy and fashion, there has been a double movement. There is, on the one hand, a shift towards narrow-casting, towards selectivity and interactivity, and, on the other, a movement towards the global extension of networks. Hence the World Cup and the European Championship are the second and third most widely viewed sports events in the world. This is a shift from the national Fordist mass communication press to the global 'Fordism' of international TV football, and the network expands and mutates further through its attachment to music, lifestyle and consumer brands. This is the double movement of communication in the global information society. To the extent that it is informational, there is a greater selectivity and interactivity. The father's generation saw football on television. The son's generation (and it is still largely sons, not daughters) experiences football through the computer game FIFA '97 and all the other PlayStation, Nintendo and PC games. They read specialist news about their clubs on the Internet, which also gives them the option of paying further for more specialist information via club mobile phone messages. They keep up with latest events and discussions, and participate in club competitions via official and unofficial team home pages on the Web; on email they may also receive now and again JPEG and MPEG files, pictures of players that a friend or colleague scans in at the other end. As an object of the global culture industry, football extends its network through media outreach, translation and transposition, through the recruitment of other objects. Perhaps most apposite is not so much the 'message is the medium' (Castells) but the 'medium is the medium', or better, 'the medium is on the medium'.

Traders in Rights

ISL are traders in rights. They are rights merchants: they buy rights and they sold rights. Insofar as anyone ever 'owned' the object-event that was Euro '96, it was ISL. They had 'ownership of the image' (Edelman 1979), and insofar as they licensed that image, Euro '96 went into circulation. ISL bought those rights, not from a private profit-making firm, but from a quasi-public, not-for-profit international organization, UEFA, the Union of European Football Associations. This quasi-public yet highly profitable relationship of UEFA with ISL is complex and, we shall argue below, characteristically European. It is inscribed in a cultural economy that is a public–private mixture, with strong dimensions of neocorporatism. This suggests a mode in which cultural and economic capital accumulates in Europe – and Britain here is also European – that is vastly different than other modes of cultural economy, notably the purer market model in the United States and what we will see to be the more anarchic 'speed' capitalism of Brazil.[30]

ISL acquired Euro '96 as a bundle of rights and sold them in bits. In the selling of these rights, the cultural object moves. It moves to television screens in front, to take another object-event, of a cumulative World Cup audience of some 32 billion.[31] It takes on mobility through attachment to the icons of the official sponsors: Canon, Carlsberg, Coca-Cola, Fujifilm, JVC, MasterCard®, McDonalds®, Opal, Philips, Snickers® and Umbro®, whose names appear on the back of match tickets, on hoardings, on buses, taxis and television. It moves long distances intensively inside Europe, but also outside

Europe on Coca-Cola cans, inside McDonald's restaurants, stamped onto MasterCards and plastered on the wrappers of countless Snickers bars. In this regard, it makes sense to speak not just of the brand environment, which is primarily a space, but also of the brand*scape*, which is spatial and temporal, extensive and intensive. And the European Championship is also inscribed in the movements of an ethnoscape: in the case of Euro '96, routes in real space of some 11,000 Germans, 12,000 Dutch people, 7,000 Danes, 4,000 French, 4,000 Italians and the Russians, Czechs and many others who made their way into England to see the event live. This movement within the ethnoscape, that – painted faces or not – made Euro '96 'European', also depended on rights. This was not so much the buying and selling of rights, but the relinquishing of rights by UEFA to the English FA

(in exchange for a set of obligations) to print and sell tickets to the real event. The multinational ethnoscape of the real event then becomes part of the object itself as it circulates in the mediascape.

ISL stands for International Sports, Leisure and Culture Marketing. On the façade of the firm's grey building in the centre of Lucerne, Switzerland ('for tax reasons' – far both from Geneva and Zurich), you see a sign with the firm's full name as you enter the building. Its founder, Horst Dassler, son of Adi Dassler of Adidas, saw the company as a new concept in sports marketing. Typically, marketing firms, like advertising firms, are business services: they have clients and hold accounts to run campaigns for a fixed sum of money, usually a proportion of media costs. However, ISL is not a normal marketing firm. It is, according to Fraser Peet who previously worked for the London advertising agency Collet, Dickenson and Pearce, a firm oriented around 'legal contracts. We buy rights and then we sell rights'.[32] At one point ISL did the marketing for the International Olympic Committee (IOC); in 1996 their main 'partners' were FIFA and UEFA. Most of their 90–100 employees work on the marketing of the World Cup and European Championships.

UEFA owned two types of rights – broadcasting rights and marketing rights – to the European championships. The broadcasting rights had historically been bought by the EBU, the European Broadcasting Union. ISL has had these broadcasting rights since 1995, and it sells them on to various European and non-European television broadcasters.[33] The marketing rights are usually sold to a range of different companies. The top tier of rights are linked to the right to be named as a sponsor of the event. These include the right to put a logo and company name on the perimeter boards of the stadium to be seen by the viewing millions and the right to use the event's own trademarks, such as the trademarked name (Euro '96™) and logo (the little man in the football) in association with the sponsor's product or service. They were sold, in this instance, to the eleven companies listed above. There are about twenty-five global brands which typically purchase this most expensive set of marketing rights. A governing body such as FIFA, UEFA or the IOC can either sell these rights in-house or use a middle-man company such as ISL to buy and sell them on. The IOC used ISL for the Olympics from 1988 to 1996 to do this, but have since then carried this out in-house. FIFA and UEFA, acting in concert, continued to use ISL for this.

A second set of rights goes to the event's organizing committee. This might be a national governing body, like the FA in England, which was the local organizing committee for Euro '96. (For World Cup '94 USA™, the US Soccer Federation set up a separate legal entity as organizing committee called World Cup USA 94 Marketing. There was also a separate – from the French Football Association – organizing committee for the World Cup held in France in 1998.) The local organizing committee prints and distributes tickets and has rights to the revenue from these; in addition, they can sell off second-tier marketing rights usually to national or more local firms. A third important source of revenues is licensing, in which trademarked title and logo are used on products such as shirts and computer games like PlayStation's (an official sponsor) FIFA '98. At issue in such distribution of rights are regimes of public and private rights in the image (Lury 1993). In conjunction with the internationalization of football described above, there has been a shift in the UK and much of Europe from a public rights regime to a private one – that is, a shift to a system governed by private rights in what are still largely public goods (Garnham 1990).

According to Peet, 'we create a set of marks (emblems) exclusively for sponsors, which are an incredibly powerful sales tool'. The founding myth of the company, perhaps apocryphal, tells of Horst Dassler approaching the International Olympic Committee in Lausanne and saying he wants to buy the marketing (trademark) rights to the Olympic rings. The IOC replies, 'They're worthless, they're everywhere', but he buys them anyway. Then, 'He gets lawyers – at some expense – to prosecute everyone that is using them. He cleanses the world of the Olympic rings.' And suddenly they are a very 'popular property'. 'He sells the rings [to sponsors]. He gets his money back.' Until the 1994 Trade Mark Act, it was only possible to obtain rights of trademark for marks (words or logos) that were already recognized in the public domain – for example Superman or Mickey Mouse. This was the case with Dassler obtaining rights to the Olympic rings, but in the case of the logo and the name Euro '96™, the 'property' was legally entitled to be – and was in fact – 'trademarked in advance of selling'.[34]

Originally, the marketing rights of official sponsors included just the perimeter boards. 'All you had to do was to plant into the world's consciousness your brand name and subsequently back it up with traditional forms of advertising, but the important thing was to say "Canon". Just play the name "Canon" into the people's awareness, so that when they went into a store to buy a camera and the name that is top of your consciousness is "Canon". And then confronted with the guy in the store, the expert in the store he can start telling you about Canon cameras.' Planting the 'corporate name', the 'brand name', 'is all you can do anyway on this board which is a 6.5m by 90cm sign. All you can do is to plant the name, your corporate name which is uniform around the world in the minds of the TV audience and which is around the world.' 'The 1982 World Cup in Spain was the turning point for systematic sponsorship.' Here, 'ground advertising was 95 per cent of the interest of the sponsors.' It was the 'global village idea. '[35]

Keith Cooper is a top official in FIFA. Along with Federation Secretary Sepp Blatter, he presided over the television draw for World Cup France '98 in December 1997. He was one of four founding members of ISL and worked there until 1992. According to Cooper, the first global media sports event with the ISL package was the 1982 World Cup. Of the nine original official sponsors, four were Japanese companies – Fuji, Canon, JVC and Seiko. It was after the 1978 World Cup in Argentina that Dassler 'conceived of the global sports advertising concept'. In 1978 Dassler co-founded the British-based sports marketing company West Nally with Patrick Nally, in partnership with Peter West, the former television cricket commentator. Nally and Dassler fell out subsequently. Dassler founded ISL in 1982 specifically as a firm that would 'deliver rights' to sponsors. The operative idea was 'sectoral exclusivity', to give competitive advantage to one brand in a sector by excluding their competitors. This often meant excluding them from sports sponsorship altogether. Coca-Cola used a particularly intense activation of such sponsorship – in the World Cup and Olympics – in its struggle against Pepsi. If a firm manages to acquire sectoral exclusivity in the sponsorship of the World Cup, the Olympics, the European Championship and the Champions League, there is not much space otherwise for meaningful mass global event sports sponsorship. It helped Coca-Cola 'achieve their global ambitions far more easily, even if expensively, than traditional forms of advertising'. 'If you can say you're Coca-Cola and you are sponsor of the Olympic

Games and World Cup and Pepsi Cola is not, that actually means something and the public actually does identify with companies who are sponsors.'[36]

ISL put together a systematic sponsorship package complete with rights delivery for the World Cups in Spain in 1982 and Mexico in 1986, as well as Italia '90, World Cup USA '94 and France '98.[37] The first European Championship to have the sponsorship package was Euro '96. For the sponsors, the World Cup and European Championship are part of the same four-year 'Intersoccer' package. Nine of the eleven World Cup sponsors – Canon, Coca-Cola, Fujifilm, General Motors (Opal), JVC, MasterCard, McDonald's, Philips and Snickers – were also Euro '96 sponsors. Umbro and Carlsberg were solely European Championship sponsors, Gillette and Energizer solely World Cup official sponsors. The total 'Intersoccer' rights package cost about 30 million Swiss francs (US$21 million) for the maximum package of four perimeter boards for both World Cup and Europeans, reduced to 20 million Swiss francs (US$14 million) for just two perimeter boards and only World Cup exposure. The eleven sponsors yielded about US$180 million for ISL, from which they had to subtract the amount they paid to FIFA and UEFA to procure those rights. This money is spent by the football governing bodies on youth training programmes, football development programmes in poorer nations and other activities.

None of this package is worth anything at all to the sponsors, however, without effective rights delivery. FIFA and UEFA would be bereft of sponsor revenues, and the sponsors would not have access to direct marketing of the event, unless there is effective 'rights delivery', which includes effective 'policing of the brand environment'.[38] This is largely done through the regulation of this environment in relation to the implications of trademark law. Thus a considerable proportion of ISL's resources were spent on legal advice to ensure 'trademark protection': it is 'complicated and expensive'. 'The "World Cup"', for example, Fraser Peet notes, 'is a generic' (and generic signs cannot be trademarked in law). 'But "WC '98", "FIFA WC '98", "France '98", "Coupe du Monde '98" are real trademarks.' Thus 'we have protection of that mark, including the box, including the ball [pointing to Felix the little mascot of World Cup France '98]. We have trademarked a huge ring fence around there to make sure that when people come anywhere close to it, we can skin them.'[39] Once the lawyers establish that ring-fence, it then becomes a matter of enforcement, of keeping people off your intellectual property. And that is a matter for the 'brand police'. The brand police – or brand sheriffs – prevent three types of 'ambush'. The first of these is the ambushing of an official sponsor by another sponsor in the same sector, violating the principle of sectoral exclusivity – for example the ambushing of Umbro by Nike or Coca-Cola by Pepsi. The second is the ambushing of some official sponsors by others. For example, Coca-Cola may spend some seven times that of the other sponsors in activating their sponsorship. The third is the ambushing the event itself, by making it look too commercial.

Marc Butterman was the ISL representative for Euro '96 day-to-day operations. Butterman, in his mid-thirties, was born in Germany and moved to the USA with his parents as a young child. He is an American who knows soccer like a European. A few months after the event, Glen Kirton, who was Public Relations Director at the FA and the main person responsible for running Euro '96 at the FA, moved to preside over the football department at ISL.[40] The Football Department divides into three sections: Operations, which Butterman heads and which deals directly with the local organizing committee and with the international governing bodies; Client Services, which deal with the sponsors; and Marketing Services, which deal with the outside world, the general public and the media. Peet is responsible for this last section. This is the de jure organization, but de facto, Butterman stresses, 'all three sections really service the clients, service the account'. UEFA, FIFA and the FA are 'partners of ISL', and the sponsors are the clients or the accounts. In direct contact with the clients are 'account representatives'. Thus 'Coca-Cola will deal with one person physically at ISL'. In terms of delivery, each client has 'binders and binders full of correspondence'. 'We sell these companies a bill of goods', a 'bill of rights', 'and

then we need to administer or deliver these rights, a delivery of anywhere from 2 to 4 years'. 'It took', Butterman notes, 'one guy to sell it [the sponsorship] basically, one guy and a lawyer, but 'it took twenty-two to administer it', referring to the twenty-two people at ISL entrusted with overseeing rights delivery. 'We guarantee that, or we end up in court.' 'We end up in court, or not get renewed, or get complained about to FIFA or not get paid' (sponsors pay their US$10 million over four years in instalments). But in fact, 'the rights have never not been delivered. One of ISL's strengths which isn't exactly seen that much is rights delivery.'[41] This is the 'after-care service we offer to customers: like they've bought a very expensive car'.[42] It is really after the selling of a sponsorship 'that work begins, doing the servicing of the sponsors, maintaining the relationship, delivering what you sold to them, and renewal'.[43]

This service entails policing the image environment and regulating the brand environment. It means the graphics office at ISL must approve all promotions by Coca-Cola and others to ensure they are in line with the contract. It means 'dealing with civic authorities on their land to prevent ambush'. For example, 'we went right across from the Sir Matt Busby statue at Old Trafford in the VIP parking lot. There's like five billboards in a row. We go to the stadium many months in advance and say, "That's an ambush opportunity", but we also talk to the organizers and say, "Are those signs on Manchester United [their] property? In fact they own ... the street, but they don't own the strip of grass where the signs are.' Smartly dressed figures with ISL badges and mobile phones could be spotted during the tournament walking around the perimeter of Anfield before the Czechoslovakia versus Italy Euro '96 match. They were there, says Butterman, 'to make sure that people from Nike didn't walk on and put up Nike signs. Or bunches of Italian fans weren't there with Nike hats or flags.' But they were there 'also to ensure that the official sponsors didn't abuse their rights. You can't just come inside and put up signs everywhere. You have the right to put up a controlled and limited number of signs.' We 'know the contracts' and 'we are basically the mouth, the eyes and ears of the sponsors'.[44] 'We are taking companies to court.'

Nike clearly worried ISL and the sponsors with the expensive television advertisement they ran concurrently with Euro '96 in which Eric Cantona kicked a ball through the belly of a satanic monster. But Nike 'do not know football' and made mistakes on their billboards by featuring players such as Cantona, Les Ferdinand and David Ginola, who were not playing in the tournament. 'Kids will say, "I'm not gonna wear your boot. You guys don't even know who's playing in this thing. I don't even know if you guys can do up your shoelaces." You questioned why Nike was in football. They're American. You think their shoes are made in Japan. And what do they know about football? They have no tradition. Umbro, Adidas, OK. But Nike – football?! Adidas has a reputation and you don't really question Adidas shoes. Like Umbro says, "We know football." And Nike can't say we know football, we don't even know who's playing.'[45]

Public Goods, Public Rights: The European Model

The official sponsors of Euro '96 listed above were typically partners in the sponsorship of a particular event for the long term: they 'think the property is so valuable that they won't go anywhere'. This long-term relationship is reminiscent of the long-term national collective bargains between the partners of capital and labour in Europe and the UK in the 1960s and 1970s – that is, of the institutions of neocorporatism. This bargaining was dependent on the belief in a positive sum game: wage restraint on the part of unions in return for welfare benefits and investment and price restraint on the part of capital. It was a tripartite arrangement of labour, capital and the state. It was supposed to be a win–win situation: public good was gained by all the people: the externalities of the neocorporatist bargain promoted growth and low inflation. Similarly, in what is effectively this sports event neocorporatism, 'private sponsors' help bring the event to 'the people'. They bring a public good to the people and at the same time sponsors like 'Coca-Cola must create a win–win situation for the governing bodies [FIFA and UEFA]. They [Coca-Cola] can't come in here and with a quick bang take over an event, paint the place red and just walk away. They need to create and work and fund an event or league or governing body that will increase, enhance the property.'[46] The property must be protected from the commercial imperatives of the brands in order to enhance its value. 'The game has not changed [in US World Cup '94] for commercial reasons: the goals and the pitch are the same. There is no chance for ad breaks' (this is the reason that sponsorship on perimeter boards is so important). The 'rules of the game' make it 'quite difficult to change it to a more commercial event'. 'We at ISL are very keen to protect that.'[47]

This perhaps characteristically European model is the long-term relationship of what informants called not clients but 'partners', between the triangle of the governing body, ISL and the sponsors. The national state is not an actor in this global and cultural (instead of national and social) neocorporatism. Protecting the 'property' that is a global public good is paramount: restraint on the commercial side is necessary. Keith Cooper, a sports journalist before his work at ISL and FIFA, says: 'In FIFA's law number two, which is the field of play, decision ten of the International Football Association Board says, "There will be no publicity on or in connection with the field of play." Now for us the rectangle, the 105 × 68 meters, are sacred. At a safe distance, put up the advertising boards. But the pitch itself, hands off, hands off. Whereas in [US] ice hockey, basketball, you see logos on the ice, on the court. No way, not on the grass. Otherwise you'll see suddenly one penalty area that is Philips, the other Gillette and the centre circle MasterCard. No way, no way. The game is worth too much.'[48]

There has been, however, a shift from a public regulation of culture and the media towards a private distribution of public goods, first through the sponsors and, from 2000, through the deals ISL makes with often private, commercial broadcasters. But this is still somewhat different from what happens in the USA, where commerce takes over in a much purer market governance. The private partners in the European set-up are more constrained. The European model is somehow public and private, corporate, with some aspects of post-national state governance, and thus not dissimilar to the EU regulation of, for example, the agro-chemical industry (Bailey et al. 1999). In the latter industry, the EU sometimes uses national bodies for test development, but in the name of the supra-national body, the EU. Often the national bodies subcontract testing and research in analysis of environment-relevant properties of products onto private groups. There is thus a mixture of the private and public, of the national and supranational here. The same is true in the cultural gover-nance of Euro '96 (also see Eder and Kousis 2000). The superior body is not a private firm but a quasi-public governing body (FIFA/UEFA), and public broadcasters share in the bidding. Relationships are informed as much by 'status' as by 'contract' between organization and sponsors; they are long term. There is a circulation of personnel between governing bodies, spon-sors, ISL and even the media. And all partners practise a certain measure of restraint to preserve what is seen as a public good.[49]

This differs from the American model. ISL competitors, the American counterpart of IMG, do not operate a rights delivery model. They don't deal with long-term multi-sponsors and sectoral exclusivity. They – and sometimes now Nike – create and put on their own events, especially in tennis and golf. They are also often agents for the sports stars. The 'gov-erning body' is IMG itself. Whereas in Europe the governing bodies, such as FIFA and UEFA, are starting to act like private bodies in some ways, in the USA the private bodies are so strong, they become almost de facto governing bodies. The same is true with Nike, the American model of buccaneering sponsorship. 'Nike has created a bad boy image through-out. They back bad boys [like Bo Jackson]. It's quite interesting now. They've suddenly realized the error of their ways and have bought Ronaldo at $200 million or whatever. Over a huge period of time. Plus the Brazilian football team.' Now Nike will 'start to compensate for their poor image among governing bodies. They know that in the long term they have got to be in with governing bodies. Ambush is great fun when you are on the up, but when you want to stay in the centre at lower cost, it's better to be in than out.'[50]

Football is currently a public good. What about other cultural proper-ties? As well as sport, notes Peet, 'entertainment and music' comprise a 'serious sized property market'. 'The strongest property company in the world is Walt Disney. They bring properties in and then in the very long term convert them into highly profitable properties.' 'Disney markets emotion, and sport is a heightened emotional environment. Disney makes more out of the toys sold off the backs of the movies [via licensing contracts] than through the movie. They invest very heavily in a movie, make a property out of it. And then invest lots of money to make sure the property is profitable in its own right.'[51]

After twenty years of serving as the main broker of such football events, ISL was declared bankrupt in a Swiss court in May 2001. They had overbid for global rights in an attempt to muscle in on new sports. Sepp Blatter, President of FIFA, was at that time subject to media reports of having had a relationship with ISL managing director Maria Weber. FIFA at first tried to save ISL, but then themselves took on marketing functions for the 2002 World Cup.

4 Art as Concept / Art as Media / Art as Life

Introduction

When we interviewed him, Sandy Nairn was Director of National Programmes for Tate Modern, Britain's national museum of modern art.[1] Nicholas Serota is Director of the Tate complex including Tate Modern, which opened in May 2000. Nairn, who met Serota as a student at Oxford in the 1970s, was then Director of Exhibitions at the Institute for Contemporary Arts (ICA), working as senior partner to Iwona Blazwick from 1982 to 1986. Blazwick was lead curator of Tate Modern's first major exhibition, 'Century City', in spring 2001, and then moved to be Director of the Whitechapel Gallery. Nairn and Blazwick have worked closely with Serota over the years: Nairn especially, in getting Tate Modern off the ground. In the early days of Channel 4, Nairn developed the acclaimed television series, *State of the Art*. Subsequently, he was a

Sandy Nairn says: 'Network television is the key. You can do things with network television in a way completely different from a newspaper. Network television provides a different kind of access. Not because everybody watches it: they don't watch it at all. But because of the idea of it and the assumptions around it allow you to do a hell of a lot else.'

prime mover in the Channel 4 coverage of the Turner Prize competition and more recently exhaustive media coverage of the launch of Tate Modern. More than anyone in London's art sector, he should know media.

Our decision to look at all seven of this book's cultural objects as media intrigued him. He asked: 'What's the definition of something becoming a medium?' 'Traditionally', he continued, 'a medium was the means and not the object; it was the means and not the content; it was the transmission and not the material. ... Obviously that changes with the modern definition ... [in] which you cannot differentiate between the means of transmission and what is being transmitted. ... Once that is true you don't have the same definition of medium or media. ... When we think of art worlds, it's true that we have not, perhaps wrongly, until recently been thinking of public art galleries as mass media.' What can Sandy Nairn have meant by this? Is he implying that art has now been mediatized? If so, how?

Rosalind Krauss considers this question in 'A Voyage on the North Sea': Art in the Age of the Post-Medium Condition. She describes the conception of medium proposed by exponents of 'high modernism', following the position of Clement Greenberg, in which the essence of a medium – what makes it specific – is its particular material properties: for painting, the 'rectangular, flat picture surface'; for sculpture, a 'volumetric object in space' (Rorimer 1999: 10). For Greenberg, 'modernist art is a self-critical art which explores the definition of its medium' (Osborne 1999: 50; see also de Duve 1999). Krauss (1999: 5) contrasts this conception with today's vision of the 'medium as aggregative, as a complex structure of interlocking and interdependent technical supports and layered conventions'. The contemporary medium is a 'layered complex relationship': a 'recursive structure', a 'structure, some of whose elements ... will produce rules that generate the structure itself'. It is a 'reflexive structure that must be able to specify itself'; to put this another way, the specificity of a medium, in this contemporary definition, lies in its constitutive heterogeneity, the fact that it always differs from itself. This notion of medium, we suggest, is characteristic of the work of the art of what were the young British artists, YBAs.[2]

Krauss suggests that the work of art is becoming an aggregation of relationships. It is becoming a 'structure', a platform; in our terms, a 'system'. This recursive structure can 'specify itself'. Such a system does not reproduce externally determined rules but instead produces the rules that will generate itself. To be self-causing in this way is to be ever-changing: its characteristic register is in excess of reproduction. Such open systems evolve and mutate by selecting information from the environment, from the reflexive description of selected information and then from its own communication. This is art as a non-linear system, a medium of flows, the flows of the global culture industry. In this chapter, then, we look at YBA, and consider how it too may be described in terms of the mediation of things.

Art as Concept

To understand young British art, we must take a step backwards and reflect on the prior emergence of what is fundamentally concept art in Minimalism in the mid- and late 1960s in the USA. Here, Robert Morris, Donald Judd, Robert Smithson and Carl Andre, amongst others, were self-consciously opposed to Greenberg's tenets. They were less concerned with form and material than with ideas. They effectively displaced Kantian assumptions of judgement with phenomenological assumptions whose focus was not judgement but experience. In this sense there were two interrelated ways out of the flatness, the materiality of the picture plane. One was into the realm of the idea. The other was into the 'vector' connecting the intentional subject and the art-object.

For Kant the art-object is a *Zweckmäßigkeit ohne Zweck*: finality without external end. Here the creator and viewer stand in a position vis-à-vis the object that rules out any interest, any attitude or intentionality. What the Minimalist does, so Krauss argues, is to 'rotate' the picture plane on its axis so that what counts is no longer the vector of its flatness but the vector connecting the intentional subject and the work of art. In this regard, she argues, structural filmmaker Michael Snow influenced the Minimalists. At issue is not so much the celluloid, or any filmic equivalent of picture-plane flatness. Instead the (art-)object becomes the cinematic 'apparatus', in which the medium or 'support' come to comprise projector, camera, celluloid, screen and audience. The implication is that cinematic apparatus will 'reveal how the viewer is intentionally connected to his/her world' (Krauss 1999: 25). Via the cinematic apparatus, there is the simultaneous emergence of the viewer and the 'field of vision', which is understood as a phenomenological field (Merleau-Ponty 1962).

In this field, the relation or vector of intentionality precedes and indeed constitutes both viewer and object. Snow's *Wavelength*, consisting of a 45-minute continuous zoom, was understood as such a phenomenological vector. Correspondingly, for Minimalist sculptor Richard Serra, art became a question not of the object but of the *vector*. Serra and his colleagues thus reread Jackson Pollock's break with easel painting. What Pollock was doing was 'rotating the work of art outside of the dimension of the pictorial object altogether'. Now the vertical plane of the object was no longer the medium: the medium became the horizontal field of vision connecting the object and the viewer. The field was an 'event', constituted in the spatio-temporally embedded moment of the intentional encounter of viewer with art-object. It was there, in that relation, that art happened. It is the event that comprises the conventions that will articulate this field – itself comprising 'differential conditions of periodic and wavelike flux – as [a] medium' (Krauss 1999: 26). The object of art here is a vector or 'mode of address'.

But how was this vector perceived? In what might amount to first-wave conceptualism, the self-enclosed picture plane is displaced by an equally disembedded field of vision. For the material space of the painting is substituted the ideational space of a horizontal vector connecting subject and object. This is the ideational space of Husserl's (1983) transcendental phenomenology (or the different yet no less transcendental realm implied in Merleau-Ponty's (1962) much more bodily version of the doctrine). The medium in this is not the material object, but the vector connecting subject and object itself. The medium comprises nothing exterior to this phenomenological relation.

This phenomenological notion of what Lucy Lippard (1997) called 'post-object art' may, as we have noted, be connected to a cinematic problematique. Video, correspondingly, is a possible model for what seems to be the 'second-wave conceptualism' of the 1990s and after. In place of Minimalism's (and structural film's) phenomenological interiority, there is instead a more wide-ranging, constitutive 'heterogeneity' and openness to the exterior. Raymond Williams (1974) and then Fredric Jameson (1990) identified these characteristics in their descriptions of television and video in terms of 'total flow'. Krauss sees Marcel Broodthaers as a precursor of what is for us this second wave.

Broodthaers looked not at structuralist, but at early, cinema in which an 'openness was woven into the mesh of the image: the flickering irresolution of illusion of movement produces not so much the field of vision but an experience of sight … a mixture of presence and absence' (Krauss 1999: 44). This practice informs an understanding of 'mediatic specificity in its self-differing, aggregative interlocking support and layered conventions'. The self-identity of the Minimalist phenomenological field of vision is displaced by the self-difference of an optico-technical system.

Sarat Maharaj, a teacher at Goldsmiths College, London, says of the 1980s: 'There was a questioning of the retinalism of the period, of the powerful conceptualism at Goldsmiths, which was also a powerful school of sheer visualism: a bit like Jackson Pollock without the intellectual torment and all that body-psycho torment which makes him a great and wonderful figure. This was a comfortable conceptualism.' There was, Maharaj says, a movement from the transcendence of pure theory to 'immersion', 'to actual involvement and immersion in the art practice'.

The 'crisis in the ontology of the artwork' that was characteristic of first-wave conceptualism was at the same time a question of the concept. Thus Sol LeWitt's 'Paragraphs on Conceptual Art' were republished in *Art and Language* in the early 1970s. For LeWitt, conceptual (as distinct from formalist) art is an 'object producing', though not an 'object based', practice. The ideas or concepts of conceptual art are a 'self-regulating series and systems of rules for the production of objects out of pre-formed materials' (Osborne 1999: 52). They are a series of propositions, systems of rules (and the parallel with the feedback loops of computers and other new media objects such as brands is worth drawing here (Manovich 2003)). They were, for Robert Morris, 'permuted, progressive symmetrical organisations [whose function was] to distribute matter' (Bird 1999).

Morris's classic essay 'Anti-Form' continued to speak of such ideational systems as 'separate from the physical by making relationships themselves another order of facts'. Morris was deeply influenced by phenomenology. In the early 1960s, when he drew on Duchamp's use of language in, for example, *Card File Index*, Morris understood art as a 'phenomenological investigation'. Towards the mid-'60s, in his most influential period of the large minimal and 'serial sculptures', a major influence was the late Wittgenstein. Here, the simple grey and white polyhedrons set up a space for the viewer: a visual space making it possible to see his sculptures as 'visual expressions' in a Wittgensteinian language game. A 'phenomenology of slight shifts is experienced by the viewer, moving in relation to the objects, so that their primary property – shape – is constantly disturbed by patterns of visual movement' (Bird 1999: 100–1).

The Minimalists – and first-wave conceptualism more widely – were also involved in a move towards object exteriority. There was an emphasis on the body, language or the site, that moved art towards relations with a more heterogeneous outside. But this exteriority itself typically became incorporated in a closed system, almost as if it were a new transcendental, understood in the form of ideas. In his later work, Morris tried to open up this self-enclosed idea-system to what seemed to be a more empirical exteriority. Influenced by Herbert Marcuse and opposing eros to form, he moved away from an exploration of the optical field to a more haptic or tactile dimension of phenomenology. In the early '70s, using video and bringing concrete blocks and pipes into exhibitions at the Whitney and the Tate for adults to climb and play with, his art became much more processual. Hence the title of his 1971 essay, 'Some Notes on the Phenomenology of Making: In Search for the Motivated', in which he gives examples of choreography, video, natural objects and performance.

In this move towards what we are calling second-wave conceptual art there is a more decisive shift away from the timelessness and spacelessness of both formalism and first-wave conceptualism towards a sort of phenomenology of socio-technical systems. Now, instead of timelessness and spacelessness there is the site-specificity of the 'here' and 'now'. In this context, Pollock's later work was no longer seen to be constituted in a timeless and spaceless vector of a field of vision, but instead as a 'gestural immersion in the process of art making'. It is an interaction of 'chance and order, body and material'. Pollock's pictorial space becomes an event, an arena for the coming-into-being or becoming of work *and* spectator in an unstable and active field. The vector thus becomes flux. Process now becomes more part of the work, one is enabled to engage more directly with the work of art, as 'forming is moved further into the presentation' (Bird 1999: 96). Hence the title of Morris's late published collection of essays, *Continuous Process Altered Daily*. Space now becomes perhaps less an optical than a performative field: as self and body are transformed into 'temporal constructs'. As spectators climb and jump on ramps, ropes, lumps of metal and cylinders, they become sites of 'performative play': the event is constituted by both the material and the spectator. These are sites for 'participatory exchange' (Bird 1999: 102); with the 'random distribution of stuff', there is a fragmentation and a scattering of intentionality itself.

Sarat Maharaj says, 'All of conceptual art comes from Duchamp's urinal'. The point is 'if you take an ordinary object and place it in the context of art, it becomes art'.

To pose the Duchampian questions of function and nominalism is to destabilize the object as painting or sculpture. It is at the same time to begin to foreground *context*. Thus Rosalind Krauss's earlier work, 'Sculpture in the Expanded Field' (1986), addressed the crisis of sculptural form, given the object's new proximity to previously excluded categories such as landscape and environment. When Duchamp brought *Fountain* into the museum, he was not just questioning the status of the art object, but that of the museum as site. He was questioning the site-generality of the museum. In his action the museum becomes one specific site among others.

Another site of exploration was the printed page.[3] Thus we have Sol LeWitt's thirty-five sentences or Lawrence Weiner's *Statements*, instructions for a sculpture. But it is not painting or sculpture, but photographs and words that typically occupy the page. Clement Greenberg, as Anne Rorimer notes, disapproved of photographs because of their indexical connection with the page. But the Minimalists and early conceptual artists used the page for the juxtaposition of ideational and indexical expressions. What Adrian Piper (1999) saw in Sol Le Witt's work was juxtapositions 'between abstract temporality and the indexical present'. Similarly, in Dan Graham's *Works for the Pages of Magazines*, the magazine itself – for example, *Harper's Bazaar* – becomes a site of display. Here we see 'the ideational space of the magazine page' counterposed to 'enterable exhibition space'. Consisting of printed material and information on a page, the work 'defines itself as the materially present page' (Rorimer 1999: 15).

Joseph Kossuth's work also set up confrontations between art systems and non-art systems. For him, artistic expression was in the idea rather than the form. Indeed, in *Art After Philosophy* Kossuth defined the 'work of art as a proposition presented in the context of art as a comment on art'. The art world now becomes the context, the artistic expression becomes the idea as comment on the context, the world. 'The art object becomes less an object of perception than an articulation of context' (Rorimer 1999: 15). Here the focus is on the propositional content that stands in for the traditional art-object. Its context is the traditional art-object and its institutions. This was the topic of Kossuth's 'Investigations', pursued from 1966 to 1968 in his *Art as an Idea* series. Notions of display and museum hegemony are disputed by his insertion of excerpts from *Roget's Thesaurus* 'Synopsis of Categories' into the advertising space of newspapers and (art) journals. There is a 'confrontation between [an] abstract linguistic system and information pertaining to sites of promotion' (Rorimer 1999:19). The page becomes 'a meaning-bearing surface', an 'exhibition site, a self-reflexive surface' (Piper 1999: 26).

Yet putting art-as-idea into the context of first-wave conceptualism is different from the artist and art *themselves* becoming promotional, as was the case with the YBAs. The content of first-wave conceptualism – propositions or series and systems of rules – is timeless and spaceless. The *content* – and not just the context – of second-wave conceptualism is often itself mediatic. There is something still transcendental about both content and context of first-wave conceptualism. There is something very anti-transcendental, something base or radically *empirical*, about second-wave conceptualism and YBA. There are a few precursors for this: for example, Victor Burgin's contribution to the New Art Exhibition at London's Hayward Gallery in 1972. Burgin's series of statements, on the face of it, resembled the work of Kossuth, Lawrence Weiner and Robert Morris. Yet the sentences were produced, less in terms of ideas and more in terms of their own materiality. Burgin saw the 'artist not as a creator of materials but rather as a co-ordinator of existing materials'. If Duchamp introduced the ready-made,

Norman Rosenthal, Exhibition Director of the Royal Academy, disputes 'academic' explanations, and insists that 'all these things come down to individuals and the fact is Damien Hirst got his act together and Charles Saatchi provided the wherewithal'.

Jay Jopling says that the YBAs were the 'conscious promotion of this generation of artists as a group', at the beginning 'by themselves' and then 'by others'. If anything unites them, he says, 'it is that almost all make art about life, make art about stuff that surrounds them, art dealing with experiential phenomena'. 'But', he says, 'they are all individual.'

Gilane Tawadros, director of the International Institute of Visual Art (INIVA), says: 'Dealers are gallery people: commercial galleries. They like to think they are slightly more than that, i.e. "cultural entrepreneurs", but they are dealers. No one gets anywhere in the public sector if they don't have a dealer. People joke about certain shows in public galleries being a "Lisson show" or a "White Cube show". You might get a show at the Hayward in which most of the artists are Jay Jopling's artists. ... That goes in the CV – that they have been chosen by a public institution. They may then be bought by the Arts Council collection, so they get a commission. He [Jopling] trades off the fact that they have got that and then they get a bigger show. Then they get a project special at the Tate. Someone from New York sees that ... .' She also adds: 'Chris Ofili, Steve McQueen, Yinka Shonibare and two or three others are the only black British artists to have dealers.'

with Burgin there is the suggestion of a set of ready-mades put in coordinated relations as materials. Burgin's sentences are in a register that is much more indexical, more materially motivated – perhaps even recursively aggregated in a substrate – than classical Minimalism. They are 'reflexive' sentences suggesting a certain non-linearity. They are to be 'performed' by the gallery-goer or reader of the page (Wood 1999: 79).[5] They are in this sense more 'events in the life of the user' than the transcendental vectors of Morris's and Serra's phenomenology. At stake is a 'distributed intelligence', including a distribution of intentionality, in which there is 'a shared-out labour of the artwork with the spectator who performed Burgin's sentences'.

Norman Rosenthal introduced Carl Freedman to Jill Ritblatt (a leading British collector of contemporary art[4]) in the late 1980s. Her nephew, Matthew Slotover, came down to London, having just completed a degree at Oxford University. He helped start Frieze, currently Britain's largest circulation art magazine. Slotover is also currently Director of the Frieze Art Fair, an annual London-based international art fair, the first of which was hosted in Regents Park in October 2003.

In the same exhibition was shown the early work of Gilbert and George, who are in many ways precursors of the YBAs. Their focus on the artist's self takes us out of both the materiality of the picture plane and the vectoral horizontality of the phenomenological plane. Their focus on the self is neither expressionist nor semiotic in the sense of Barbara Kruger or Cindy Sherman, but instead unabashedly promotional, as if in an advertisement. Gilbert and George sent out calling cards. These were somewhere between a business card and an announcement of the self as artist. At some performances their Singing Sculpture went on for as much as ten hours. Gilbert and George were not signifiers nor representations nor part of some sort of signifying structure in what was – and is still in large part – a representational culture. Rather, they are objects or things themselves: they are mediated things of the global culture industry. They are 'aware that since they were in demand there must be some value to the endeavour'. Indeed theirs was a commentary on an art world 'where valuing depends on demand and display' (Wood 1999: 79, 82). They are witnesses not just to a crisis in the ontology of the art-object, but to an institutional crisis, a crisis in value.

The first-wave concept-artists – Kossuth, LeWitt and Morris – took on the role of philosopher-critic and artist at the same time and therefore increased their power in what Pierre Bourdieu calls the field of art (Bourdieu 1993; Myles 1997; Osborne 1999). They made art and at the same time provided a legitimating function for art in a set of arguments in regard to aesthetic value (though seemingly anti-aesthetic). Gilbert and George, and later the YBAs, are not critics but *promoters* in an art field that is increasingly pervaded by the values of advertising, communication and display. Unlike the Minimalists (Morris was, we saw, influenced by Herbert Marcuse), Gilbert and George and the YBAs operate in a world in which classical critique is no longer possible. There is power and politics at stake, but they do not take place through the classical route of critique. The move to site-specificity – especially when the sites become the promotional and generic sites of the global culture industry – is a question of an immanent critique. This has nothing to do with classical critique via the negation of a transcendental. At stake is a much more Nietzschean politics of affirmation: of *amor fati*, and the inescapable grain of the empirical.

Carl Freedman – one of the organisers of 'Freeze', an exhibition curated by Damien Hirst in Surrey Docks, London, 1988 – says: 'No, there was never a kind of critique.'

Art as Media

In first-wave conceptualism there was a shift from the materials to the concept. This was a transformation of sculpture's volumetric shapes and the flatness of the picture plane into a reconstituted art-object as idea. In this move, the ontological basis of the art-object became conceptual. The ontological basis of the art-object became a phenomenological field connecting creator and viewer to object. It was a sort of *generative* field, in which linguistic and conceptual structures – in the form of propositions or a series of utterances – are the basis of events. There is the system, which is the field, a conceptually driven substrate and then the events, which may themselves be visual or propositional expressions, acting recursively on the field. With second-wave

Michael Craig Martin, teacher of many YBAs at Goldsmiths College, says: 'Pop art and Minimalism ... it's essentially painting and sculpture ... but something else comes into the picture ... this new information-based art.' 'I was at Yale in the early '60s and we were crazy about McLuhan. The change from manufacturing to information. It's come 100 per cent true. Possession of information was going to be possession of wealth.' 'By the late '60s, my generation was making things ... were making informational art.' Informational art 'is art which is essentially ideas, an idea can be transmitted, which is the basis of conceptualism, the basis of conceptual art.'

He continues: 'Conceptual art privileges the idea of the work over its form. ... The form follows from the idea.' Conceptual art is 'where something is not defined necessarily by how the work looks. If someone says the work is minimal, sculpture – then the sculpture has a look; pop art has a look ... whereas with conceptual art ... it can take many different forms, it can have content but you can't recognize one by generic form.' What counts is 'not the form or content' of the object, 'but its function'. 'When I was doing it, the content of the art was information. The content today is not the idea of information, but it certainly use[s] ... information: [art] has absorbed the idea of information and it's usable.'

'Informationalization of the art world ... starts in the late '60s essentially with conceptual art. Conceptual art was transportable without money because you could transport an idea. Artists themselves were going from one place to another and then making the work where they went. When I do wall drawings, I can go someplace with a bag of tape and a box of slides and I can create massive works.'

There's no shipping cost; there's no insurance, one of those things that normally would have impeded the movement of things.' 'This was a globalization of art which was not to do with money, but to do with ideas and the dissemination of information and ideas. Now with Damien Hirsts's generation, they went straight out of Goldsmiths into the exhibition of "Freeze". "Freeze" attracted a great deal of interest: a lot of the interest was international. So from literally day one, they have never not known what it is to be part of an international art world. They were integrated, saw themselves from the very beginning as playing on a larger field.'

conceptualism – including the YBAs – there is a recasting of the concept, which is simultaneously a recasting of the ontology of the art-object. The concept or idea is no longer a proposition or a rule or a sentence. It is instead a *communication*. The concept now becomes *informational*.

The shift from the early 'formalist' modernism of Picasso, Matisse and the young Pollock to conceptualism is a shift in the nature of aesthetic value (De Duve 1999). Aesthetic value, once inhering in the vertical plane of the picture, came, with first-wave conceptualism, to inhere in the horizontal optical-conceptual field. At stake in turn-of-the-twenty-first-century art is not so much a shift in aesthetic value and art-object ontology, but instead a *meltdown* of aesthetic value, corresponding to a certain meltdown, at least in London, of the institutions of art. It is not just a crisis in the ontology of the art-object, but an *ontological meltdown*.[6] The City, the Lottery, Development Corporations, Charles Saatchi, Goldsmiths College, business sponsors and the media make up a new complex of institutions, an enterprised-up art world (Strathern 1999).

Norman Rosenthal says of the organization of the exhibition 'Sensation' at the Royal Academy: 'Charles Saatchi came to me and there was a gap in our programme.'

The communication takes part in neither a vertical plane nor a horizontal phenomenological-conceptual one. It escapes from a Cartesian logic of the plane altogether and goes into flow, a sort of plane of immanence (Deleuze 1994). The concept for Damien Hirst is

Jay Jopling recalls that the 'second artist I took on was Damien Hirst'. 'I lived in Brixton then. That's how I met Damien. He lived in Brixton too. We met after an opening once in 1990. We worked together, organized exhibitions.'

'not a fixed idea ... but the movement of ideas, so that the more you try to contain it, the more it gets out of hand'. For Hirst this 'implies life ... dealing with life when things are out of control, where there is overlapping and over-layering of meaning given this intense activity which is like life to me, like a writhing pit of snakes' (quoted in Wilson 1994: 9). If art here is conceptual, then the values are let out into the flow: value is produced in flux (Lury 2004). Not just economic but also aesthetic value emerges in flux. In Minimalism, the value of creativity is rooted in the concept, in truth-value. In the work of the YBAs, aesthetic value undergoes melt-down. A concept-image ontology is displaced by a *matter*-image ontology (Maharaj 2001; Rodowick 1997).

Conceptual art gave priority to the concept, to knowledge, to critique. Contemporary art is not so much conceptual as *mediatic*. Conceptual art privileges knowledge. In a Husserlian sense, a phenomenological sense: it sees the concept as the phenomenological essence of the art event. The mediatized art of Hirst no longer privileges knowledge understood in this way. It instead privileges life. Conceptual art wants to *know* essences or structures. Mediatized art is *informed by* or generated from structures. Thus the ontological basis is matter, image, light, movement conceived also as 'life'. It is out of this swimming flux that objects and subjects are constituted. This is not the vector, the horizontality of the phenomeno-logical field. At stake is not a transcen-dental field, but a radically empiricist, indeed monist 'plane of immanence'. This plane is 'a surface-ness that permits oblique and unexpected penetration into a density of cultural references'. Displacing Minimalism's conceptual superstrata is a substrate that is at the same time its content. This new substrate and content are the global culture industry. At its best this sort of art participates in the ecstasy of contemporary communications. At its worst it gives us a set of idle references: a set of unproblematic cross-media utter-ances (Lury 2004). Here 'the artist's body is declarative from the outset. What it says is what it is.' As 'its own commodity the art sells itself with the clarity of advertising' (Harris 2001). Here aesthetic value gets subsumed fully under the value-form of enterprise culture (Keat and Abercrombie 1990).

Anya Gallaccio's *Intensities and Surfaces* placed a 34-ton block of ice in the boiler room of a disused Wapping Victorian Pumping Station, using salt to speed up the melting process. Gavin Turk's 1990 piece *Robert Morris Untitled 1965–1972* represented the Minimalist's four mirror cubes, only the cubes are corroded. This is an 'aesthetic born of living in a damp country', or, in Turk's words, 'a bit like Robert Morris and the Bronte sisters going for a walk'. It is 'American art arriving at this damp little island' (Archer 1996: 12). The decomposition of aesthetic value as theme is repeated in the decomposition of nature, of natural value, in some of Hirst's vitrines. It is thematized again in Gallaccio's

Jay Jopling, dealer and owner of London's White Cube galleries, says: 'The conceptual aspect is diluted because it's about things that are immediate; it is very democratic.'

Sandy Nairn says: 'The image [the YBAs] invented was of loutish and drunk and sort of partying, you know, poor white kids but find-ing money and blagging it off everybody. They were playing with working-class identity, replaying what happened in the '60s. ... And then you work it into a sort of affection. It's what Sarah Lucas has used and Tracey as well, more interesting in class terms than anything else.'

Carl Freedman says: 'I didn't have an art back-ground and I wanted to run a business rather than be in an art collective.'

sculpture for the 1988 'Freeze' exhibition (in Surrey Quays) in which she put a ton of Valencia oranges, Richard Long style, on the floor of the south London warehouse and left them to rot (Archer 1996; Mahoney 1999). The natural-value organicism of Long's work ran parallel to its embodiment of British social values, of British forms of life. Thus, in the previously mentioned 1972 Hayward exhibition, alongside Burgin and Gilbert and George, Long represented – according to curator Anne Seymour – values which were 'typically British': 'very straight use of materials, images and facts. His *Circle of Stones* alluded to an intimacy with nature, was an image repetition of an archaic practice' (quoted in Wood 1999: 84). Value *contradiction*, if not yet *decomposition*, was already implied in a comment from Art & Language's Charles Harrison.[7] For Harrison, 'Long's work was in an isolated relationship to the question of "value" based on a problematic of the placeless-ness of production with regard to the status of his documentation of art' (quoted in Wood 1999: 76).

Keith Patrick, founder editor of *Contemporary* magazines, was involved in setting up a studio complex, Cable Studios, in Cable Street, near Whitechapel. When he got there 'in about 1980, there were thousands of studios just dotted along the river. Where the old warehouses were: south and north side.' The studios had two functions. One was 'a place where people would work and second, once a year, they would hold this Open Studio Show.' But 'before 1988 they were not taken seriously. Artists would make an effort to paint out their little white cubes and they would hang their work as if it was in a gallery somewhere. You didn't feel it was a serious selling situation. From 1988, 'Freeze', Michael Landy's 'Market', 'The East Country Yard Show' and 'Modern Medicine' threw down the gauntlet to the West End Galleries, which just couldn't move as fast as the young artists. Becks started giving product: ten crate of beer to openings. These were … temporary, artist-run squat-type situations. Later Becks went a step further with limited edition labelled beer bottles.

Freedman says that what he did 'came out of a spirit of, not exactly, squatting. Into old buildings just for the fun of it. Old warehouse buildings, sometimes houses. In fact Damien used to have a squat studio with a friend of his up in Hackney. The other thing it came out of was – it was to do with, from … I don't know where things come from – I don't know, you decide, you know, wouldn't it be great to have our own gallery and to do our own shows? … We were slightly inspired by American-like sensitivities … which are far more commercial and far less embarrassed about art being promotional.'

'Freeze' was sponsored by Olympia and York Canary Wharf Ltd., a North American-based development company, which had concluded a contract for developing the Docklands with the London Docklands Development Corporation. The company also owned the building in which it was held and sponsored the catalogue. Damien Hirst's then girlfriend's father was 'high up' in Olympia and York. 'There was very little work sold at the exhibition. [The idea was] not to sell but to show. The attendance was not huge. But it had a huge impact' (Freedman).

Freedman set up Building One in Bermondsey with Hirst and Billee Sellman in 1989, partly financed by Norman Rosenthal and Charles Saatchi. It was 'a gallery. We sold stuff.' It was as if 'you've got this huge shop. … We would meet wealthy people all through networks. ... We would sit in our living-room, sending things out every day to people to get the money.'

After Building One, Freedman and Sellman began to set up Building Two. There 'was an amazing group of investors lined up', but then came the 1990–1 property crash and 'everyone pulled out'.

White Cube is a gallery established and named by Jay Jopling, 'as a slightly tongue-in-cheek parody in reference to Brian O'Doherty's essays.[8] Now, he says: 'We act very much like an agency. Few have as many staff as we do. We finance all the artists we look after. We have eighteen people working here in a very interdisciplinary way: looking after the artist from fabrication of the work right through to archiving works to organizing exhibitions; liaising with museums, selling works of art to private individuals and museums, running the accounts side. For the artists that we exclusively represent [we have] the ability to talk to the artists about ideas and be able to criticize their ideas; to be able to look after artists, creative people in a kind of caring way, to look after the financial aspects of their lives. I wanted to make a space where artists would feel they were making something very focused, very intimate, very engaged.'

White Cube is in Duke Street, just the other side of Piccadilly from Cork Street. Jopling says the idea was 'to literally make a white cube in the oldest art-dealing street in the world. Between Sotheby's and Christie's: Duke Street. St James's is where the Old Masters galleries are. And I wanted to be there because levels of artistic endeavour are internationally recognized and acclaimed, and the fact that the auction houses, which are European, are headquartered here. There's a great tradition of art dealing that goes on in this city. It goes on in this street; that's a reason I positioned my gallery in this street originally.'

Fred Manson, Chief Development Officer of Southwark Borough Council, says: 'In the early '80s, Southwark was the only Council to have its Development Plan rejected by the Secretary of State.' The plan was not one of regeneration but defence. 'It was basically saying that the workers lost the docks in the '60s and that in their place we're going to have a workers' commune on the Thames, and we are going to have two-storey houses for workers' cottages. ... And we are not going to have any of those awful businessmen north of the river coming in.' '1989 was the first time [the Council] used the term "regeneration". ... And it was just in time to make an energetic campaign for infrastructure which was the Jubilee line. Tate Modern would never have come without the Jubilee line. ... The [Southwark] Labour Party members started to realize the futility of shaking your fist at the City. Amazing that north of the river is this huge generator of wealth; south of the river someone is denying that exists, is breathtaking.'

In 1930, Britain had one of the world's largest working class (70 per cent of the workforce); by 1990, it had one of the world's smallest (less than 15 per cent). The London Docklands employed 100,000 workers in the 1930s, with some 30,000 employed directly (and many more indirectly) by the Port of London Authority (PLA). The Royal Docks were closed by this Authority in 1980, a year after the election of the Thatcher government. In 1981, Ken Livingstone became leader of the Greater London Council (GLC), and developed a (post-industrial) culture industries strategy. The GLC was abolished by the Thatcher government in 1986, and was replaced, in part, by the London Dockland Development Corporation (LDDC: one of a number of development corporations established by the Thatcher government to undercut local councils). The Isle of Dogs was declared an Enterprise Zone in 1982, giving tax allowances to developers and investors. The City Airport and the Docklands Light Railway were opened in the late 1980s. The Jubilee underground line was to come a decade later. The property crash of 1991 forced Olympia and York Canary Wharf Ltd. into administration in 1992; Canary Wharf Ltd was established in 1993 (see <www.canarywharf. com>). The LDDC was subsumed by the London Development Agency in 1999, one of ten Regional Development Agencies set up in the Blair Labour government's 1999 legislation. It is the only one answerable to a local mayor; Ken Livingstone was elected for a second term of office in 2004.

Art as Life

The YBAs are obsessed with such a decomposition of social (and political) value. For Margaret Thatcher, the disappearance of society, the withering of the social bond, was a precondition of the individualism demanded by her notion of the enterprise culture. YBAs were self-consciously Thatcher's children in the sense of 'transforming boredom into the impetus for action and provocation'. But there is another, far more telling way in which they were Thatcher's children. This is most striking in the heyday of the YBAs' group exhibitions from 1988 through to 1991. This was before the individual exhibitions in white cubes. This was site-specific work in London Docklands, Surrey Quays, Building One in Peckham, Sarah Lucas and Tracey Emin's storefront in Lewisham. Their work was site-specific in a rather different way from first-wave conceptualism. It took place in the transition-sites of disused or converted warehouses, sometimes managed by the Thatcher-initiated Development Corporations.[9] Development Corporations were institutions of urban regeneration set up alongside – and in order to circumvent – politically radical city councils. Just as the Greater London Council, abolished by Thatcher, had begun to draw up a 'culture industries' strategy, the development corporations were also adopting art as a regeneration strategy. Indeed, Tate Liverpool emerged on Liverpool Development Corporation land.

Alongside this institutional melt-down was a spatial melt-down, or a spatial emptying-out: an emptying out of power stations, warehouses and housing stock. The UK had possessed a much stronger set of institutions based on empire and social class than had other European countries, and these institutions were in a faster decline than elsewhere. Urban regeneration and degeneration figured in the work of YBAs. Thus in 1989 Michael Landy made videos of a Peckham grocer setting out his storefront fruit and vegetable display. Peckham is one of south London's poorest areas. Richard Billingham took intensive photographs of his own Birmingham council estate working-class family, beset with alcoholism, in the midst of social disorganization. Here, the focus on the self as Thatcher's child is anything but promotional. It is the self as Thatcher's child. It is the self stood in a radical exteriority to art: the self as a prism of value-decomposition in a globalizing society. Reconverted warehouses are local working-class sites in transition to becoming *generic* city sites: 'generic' sites of global exchange in proximity to the City of London, the world's largest international finance centre (Koolhaas and Mau 1995). Tracey Emin's Margate videos and installations tell the same story: Tracey as Thatcher's working-class girl in the process of generic globalization and value-decomposition. Her response is less critique than *amor fati*. Let the values decompose; let them rot. Thus the YBAs as individuals themselves have a 'status as the material possibility of the work'. In this sense they are the context and substrate of the work. Here the work (and the person) is not so much about its context: it *is* its context. The context here is understood as 'not that which lies outside of the work, but its substrate' (Archer 1996: 13).'

And this context, which is at the same time content, is surely *not* the institutions of art. When Krauss wrote about sculpture in the expanded field, she meant the environment and nature. At stake with Thatcher's children is a *really* expanded field: a field expanded outside the restricted economy of the art world to the general, global economy of cultural and financial flows. When art was concept, reflexive critique was of the institutions of art. As art becomes media, reflexivity now targets the production and circulation of culture more generally.

Carl Freedman says: 'We were politically incorrect' in contrast to 'the left-leaning art world and the old generation of artists. We were punks as teenagers. We were opportunists and weren't too soft about art as a commercial enterprise.'

Jopling opened White Cube 2 in Hoxton Square, Shoreditch, Hackney in 2000. It was 'Hackney Council's deliberate policy to allow the void left by the light industrial buildings for artists to both live and work. This has meant there is the highest proportion of artists living in a concentrated area in Europe. And the audience is there and the audience is tested.'

When Colin Tweedie arrived at Arts and Business in 1983 (then the Association for Business Sponsorship of the Arts), the amount of sponsorship given by British business to the arts was £13 million; in 1991 it stood at £141 million; in 2000, the organization had a hundred staff in fourteen UK offices. Despite this increase, Tweedie says that the country continues to lag behind others: 'Whenever I visit a Swiss, German or American office, I see contemporary art everywhere.' The money that is given tends to come more from marketing and PR budgets than from foundations, with an important additional source being corporate entertaining. 'In corporate entertaining the arts are now giving far more value than sport. ... Women don't want sport.'

Frances Morris, senior curator at Tate Modern, says of the Tate Modern, 'we have a fundraising and development office and a lot of their work is research. They work through informants to prospects. So you make a connection with someone and that connection introduces you to their friends – a bit like chain letters. The Trustees work incredibly hard at making contacts. There are weekly meetings of the development office and other departments at the Tate, literally discussing who are the next targets. You read *Hello* magazine, you read the Court Circular. You read the society pages, the business pages; you build up profiles and you move in. We have an International Council, a sort of advisory group. We hope to turn these people into donors: an incentive to become part of the Tate family, the Tate community. We have an office in New York and permanent staff there. We have an American foundation that buys art for us: American art supported by US dealers that can benefit from tax incentives. Now we have a big Internet project with the MoMA [Museum of Modern Art, New York], the global aspect really at a high level. The Tate Modern is a hybrid organization. Our Director and Trustees could say, "OK, we are going out and build[ing] a new museum without the promise of capital funds from government".'

Norman Rosenthal says he likes 'the temporary. People always think that museums are places for certainties and forever. I believe in the ephemeral, and I believe in the fragility of things.' The Royal Academy has no permanent collection. 'If people want it, they'll find it.' It receives no state sponsorship; it charges no entrance fee. Instead, it obtains a good part of its income from its 70,000 subscribers. 'Nobody could invent the Royal Academy now. It's a product of British imperial history', and at the same time a 'classic product of the kind of rules of eighteenth-century Enlightenment. The Imperial myth has kept us [the British] behind. There is now the first generation that doesn't really swallow the Imperial myth.'

Karsten Schubert, YBA dealer and gallerist in the 1990s, says the British art world has 'leapfrogged the twentieth century, going directly from the nineteenth to the twenty-first, directly from tradition to postmodernism, or from the traditional to the contemporary without ever being modern. This is the genius of the Tate Modern. ... MoMA is finding this transition from the modern to the contemporary ... very, very difficult.' This is 'because you are what you are because of your past, and if you have a past which is great and all-embracing, the next week would involve dismantling all that. The Tate's great strength is, well – there isn't anything much to dismantle.'

The architect of the Bankside Power Station, built in 1948, now converted into the Tate Modern was Gilbert Scott. He was also the architect of Liverpool Cathedral, Britain's last major cathedral. Colin Tweedie, Director of Arts and Business, says he would rate the Pompidou Centre over Tate Modern: 'I wince when the Brits say, "Look at us, we're fantastic." I say, "No, you're not; it's [the Tate] a restored power station, done actually on the cheap." The "state contribution" came through the Lottery.' Tweedie estimates the running costs of the Tate are approximately £12 million per year. The grant-in-aid is £5 million. 'After the Tate shuts in the evening … the corporate client nights make good [the missing] £7 million.'

He continues, 'British government embassies don't want any [art] … The PM's office has borrowed Stubbs and Hogarth from the National Portrait Gallery. … His [Blair's] house in Islington, David Puttnam has said to me, is all fitted carpet and Formica kitchen and no art.' On the other hand, 'there's a lot of raw edges to [the Tate Modern] … it's fantastic space and it's living.' There are 'more artists now in London than in any capital in the world. … Art in Great Britain is sexy; the Serpentine is now the sexy place to be. With the collapse of the Royal Family as a role model, royal events have lost their cache. Of course there are still certain people going to Ascot and Henley. But the rest look for the art gallery. … Sting, Madonna and Mick Jagger: you'll be seen: you want to be seen: Stella McCartney likes going to art galleries. We are not a very visual nation, but we have a superficial glamour and Charles Saatchi has made it very fashionable to be a collector.'

Site-specificity was the theme of the YBAs 1996 show in Paris, 'Life/Live: La scène artistique au Royaume-Uni en 1996'. The exhibition, curated by Laurence Bossé and Hans Ulrich Obrist, actually moved – in simulation – British art-spaces to the Musée d'Art Moderne de la Ville de Paris. In the eight art-spaces were laid out more than twenty British art magazines. Online German-language reviewer Jan Winckelmann (1996) was impressed by the 'artist run spaces' even more than the art. It is significant that 'Life/Live', like the previous year's 'Brilliant' show in Minneapolis, was as much or more about the scene (the site) as about the art. The artist-run spaces, for Winckelmann, displayed a 'kämpferische "do-it-yourself" Haltung': the artist as curator, gallerist, dealer and critic was also a 'lebendigen Professionalismus'. '[Just] Do-it' as much as do-it-yourself, as in the case, for example, of Damien Hirst's 'do-it-project, the

Sandy Nairn says, the Tate Modern started 'with not just a communications strategy, but also an advocacy strategy'. Much of the money, he says, came from abroad: 'When I talked to them, luring it from them, because you had to do the front-end work: they don't want to talk to anyone else. If I can get them to talk, what emerges is they love London. It's not just the Tate Modern they like, it's actually London they like.'

Frances Morris, Director of the Permanent Display at Tate Modern says that British art is 'kind of coming ready-made out of the artist's studio rather than mediated by the old-fashioned gallery structure'. The Tate Modern is museum in progress.' The Dutch-German review spoke of the YBAs' creation of new *Vermittlungsstrukturen*. *Vermittlung* is translatable as 'mediation'. It refers to both market intermediaries and media mediation. A prominent French online review took up the theme of mediation and argued that this was precisely why the whole YBA phenomenon was so utterly foreign to France. In France there is no tabloid media that shocks its readership through the sensationalism of art. There is no highly mediatized 'art scene at all' (Finch 2001). Not just site, but Situationism[10] was invoked in the exhibit: though where Debord was sceptical of the 'culture of the spectacle', the YBAs are already seduced and have forged a relationship with the mass media. They seem to deproblematize art and its institutions.

The 'Life/Live' catalogue describes the YBAs' engagement with social, ephemeral and everyday issues as 'abject'. It spoke of an abject or 'grunge aesthetic', also commonly seen in advertising and pop videos. Andrew Wilson draws on Julia Kristeva's *Powers of Horror* (1982) in his discussion of the 1994 Hirst-curated exhibition at the Serpentine entitled 'Some Went Mad, Some Ran Away'. For Kristeva, 'what causes abjection is what disturbs identity, system, order'. Abjection is a 'defilement', 'an object jettisoned out of that boundary'. Wilson finds the abject in Hirst's 'admiration of Bosch and Breugel for making real the most fantastic of terrors, almost delighting in the horror of an apocalyptic vision of hell, the fall and the last judgement'. In such a sense, Hirst said he conceived 'the activity between things in the show', as 'a fantastic chaos'. Yet this is 'optimistic-apocalyptic' in that 'the activity within the paintings [and

about 'the collapse of making and showing in industrial buildings' in a sort of 'open studio system'.

Karsten Schubert says, 'contemporary art has moved from being a marginal activity: it's gone mainstream. The whole notion of avant-garde was somebody who's ahead of the game. That gap has shrunk. Now there's a whole industry that just looks for the latest thing. There's a huge machine out there. But it's still couched in the language as if we have a '60s avant-garde situation. Yet in the past, the measure of something being important or of interest had to do with exactly that delay.'

Sandy Nairn comments, '[the] New York [art scene] is huge, but here [London] it's a question of whether it's more interesting'.

Michael Craig Martin says students 'arrive when they're 18 or 20. At that age you've grown up in a world of pop culture. You've come from the suburbs ... you've listened to the music your whole life, you've lived in a certain world of fashion, certain kind of design and ideas.' He says that in the 1970s, 'Most art schools founded third departments', outside of and alongside painting and sculpture. Goldsmiths 'got rid of painting and sculpture altogether and made the whole school open. ... Education [at Goldsmiths] has not been structured by either examination-type rules or even project-led. It is student-led. ... Focus is on students' ideas. If he/she wants to realize them in sculpture, he is given individual instruction in his studio by a sculptor. The same is true for digital art or video. ... Form follows ideas in this space-intensive and teaching-intensive mode of learning ... the goal is to bring as many ideas about the world, about the art, as possible.' This is the 'philosophical or theoretical dimension' to education at Goldsmiths.

Frances Morris says, 'It's not just the YBAs that create the excitement about British art: it's the higher attendances, the Venice between the objects] is celebratory ... whereas the actual meanings behind the objects are negative and depressing'. It is not the individual objects in the show in which Hirst finds sense, but in the connections and relationships between things. This sort of 'constant movement is the line to my work' and is a matter of organizing already organized elements (Hirst, cited in Wilson 1994: 7).

Pavilion, a whole network of relations and events that don't automatically spring from the intrinsic value of the artistic product. The product is also the making of stories about it: how it is branded and brought together.

The notion of the abject is as much associated with George Bataille as Kristeva. Bataille saw himself in opposition to the great classical sociologist and anthropologist, Emile Durkheim. For Durkheim, society's symbolic structures were based on exclusion, the abjection of the pathological. In contrast, Bataille celebrated the pathological as 'excess'. This in-excess of the symbolic is of course *the real*. It is the place of Bataille's flows rather than Durkheim's categories or classifications. Traditional societies exclude death: they abject the dead from their boundaries. In this context the dead give to these societies a symbolic order. The explanation of death and suffering gives birth to this symbolic order as theodicy. In modernity, this changes. With God and cosmology dead, Heidegger reworks theodicy as the individual self's being-against-death. Hirst – in his lucid moments – wants neither a Heideggerian dramatization of death nor to trivialize and compartmentalize it as do many modern institutions. He wants instead to affirm the apocalypytic-pathological, outside the symbolic, as death *and life* itself. This is the ethos of *A Thousand Years* (1990). This work is a room-sized, 800-cubic-foot glass-and-steel vitrine, a 'machine', according to Hirst, 'constructed to induce and defeat a maggoty optimism'. The 'sculpture or installation consists of hatching maggots, nutrient solutions, one skinned cow's head and an ultraviolet fly killer.' It consists of two compartments: one from which newly hatched flies emerge. An orifice connects this compartment to the other, which contains the cow's head and the insectlocutor. Here, by chance, 'some flourish', 'some fry' (Corris 1992; Lee 1995).

At issue in this work is the space of the real: at first a space of death – indeed of Freud's death-drive – but on closer inspection a space also of life. This is life not as organicist reproduction, but as molecular *production*. It is, at the same time, waste. The point, however, is not so much the life-and-death swarming – the *Lebenundtodsphilosophie* – of Bataille's excess or abjection that take place with the breakdown of the symbolic, the social bond and of cultural value. It is not the high life-and-death drama, as much as the *utter banality of the real*. Indeed, abjection itself is (b)analized as grunge. The real as charisma, as high drama, becomes routinized as communication. And the new art is amidst and amongst this. It is art, not as the sacred or as symbol, but as communication. It is art as media. Thus Hirst can say: 'I feel as if I have nothing to say. I want to communicate this.' Hirst's meaningless contradiction evokes the banality of communications (Lee 1995: 7). It is spectacle first as that which evades the meta-narratives of the symbolic, but that at the same time is sucked into the banality of everyday communication. Jean Baudrillard wrote of the 'ecstasy of communication'. At issue here is the banalization of ecstasy.

Jake Chapman, in an interview with Martin Maloney, said: 'all art works are an ideological apparatus' (Maloney 1996: 65). Note, he did not say that the institutions of art are part of the ideological apparatus of the state, nor did he say that art is somehow hegemonic. He said that art itself is an ideological apparatus. At stake is art becoming an apparatus. It is art becoming a 'thing': the thing-ification of representation. With the fracture of the symbolic, artworks function as communication. Art no longer works as hegemony. We are instead in a post-hegemonic age. Art, in an age when it is things themselves that do the mediating, has more than ever to do with power. But this power no longer has anything at all to do with hegemony. The power lies in communication itself.

5 The Thingification of Media: Animism and Animation

Introduction

In chapters 1 and 2, two key processes in the movement of objects in the global culture industry were identified: the thingification of the media and the mediation of things. This and the following two chapters will document these two processes and explore the implications of their convergence. This chapter will draw on the material we collected, tracking the biography of two of our objects: the first is the computer-animated feature film, *Toy Story*, made by Pixar Studios and marketed and distributed by Disney, US; the second is the three 'claymation' features starring Wallace and Gromit, made by Aardman Studios, UK. It will present an account of how the biographies of these two animated objects display what we call the thingification of the media. That is, although the two objects comprise films – and are thus examples of classical media – they emerge, in the course of their biographies, as things, things to be absorbed in and played with, rather than as texts to be watched.

In developing this argument, we draw on the history of twentieth-century American animation as presented by Norman Klein (1993) in terms of the possibilities of 'graphic storytelling'. This is a form of storytelling in which an 'abstract surface intrudes into the story'. It is tied to 'a memory shared by artist and audience', that is, to a historically and culturally informed sense of perception and a social imaginary of shape-shifting possibility or metamorphosis. In the case of (Euro-)American animation, Klein suggests, this memory is tied to the printed page; it is the cultural repertoire afforded by the history of the word as image. Thus, it tells its story 'in line rather than representation, as an episode rather than a novel' (1993: 15). In this history of animation, punctuation itself can feature in the action, as, for example, when Felix the cat climbs question-marks up the side of a castle, or when a word is as much a character as a figure, and figures are simplified until they resemble letters.

Klein's history of animation points both to some of the enduring characteristics of the history of line as story and to shifts in sensibility and style. He suggests that in contemporary cartoons the intrusion of an abstract surface of metamorphic possibility into the story is played out in what he calls 'the visual war of surface and object' (1993: 6). This visual war or conflict may be understood in terms of the tension surrounding how an object is recognized as such – that is, in the dynamic processes of objectification: how an object's properties or qualities emerge and are made recognizable in its appearance. In other words, the argument put forward by Klein is that animation, by its very nature, is well suited to show how an abstract surface of shape-shifting or metaphoric possibility intrudes into the object, how potentially dynamic properties or qualities are only temporarily fixed in any object's form.

This aspect of animation is also identified by the filmmaker Sergei Eisenstein in his discussion of some of the early Walt Disney cartoons. He calls it 'plasmaticness'. In describing the characteristics of Disney's images, he notes: 'Disney's beasts, fish and birds have the habit of stretching and shrinking. Of mocking at their own form' (1988: 5). Or:

In *Merbabies*, a striped fish in a cage is transformed into a tiger and roars with the voice of a lion or panther. Octopuses turn into elephants. A fish – into a donkey. A departure from one's self. From once and forever prescribed norms of nomenclature, form and behaviour. Here it's overt. In the open. And, of course, in comic form. (1988: 10)

Or:

> With surprise – necks elongate.
> With panicked running – legs stretch.
> With fright – not only the character trembles, but a wavering line runs
>   along the contour of its drawn image. (1988: 58)

For Eisenstein, in all these cases, the appeal of the animation stems from the fact that the normally indissoluble link between a set of lines and the image that arises from them is broken. However, it is dissolved or dissected in such a way that there is a simultaneous perception of them as independent of each other *and* as belonging together. Thus, '[t]he comicality of the contour of a neck elongating beyond the neck itself' is a consequence of the fact that at the same time that 'the unity of an object and the form of its representation is dissected ... their representational co-membership is persistently emphasized' (1988: 58). In short, '[t]he independently elongating contour is read as a "neck going out of itself"' (ibid.: 58): the process of forms and forms of process are both momentarily rendered present.

The capacity of animation as described here is that the link between a set of lines and the image that arises from them is simultaneously perceived as fixed *and* ephemeral. One of the characteristics of animation that makes this possible is that the object or image – whether drawn by hand or machine – is continually re-presented for action and narrative. As such, the potential of the surface to disrupt the formal constraints of the object may continually be made visible. This potential has, very often, been linked to the two-dimensionality of much animation: rather than functioning as a limit, forgoing the dimension of depth has opened up the possibility of occupying an uncertain abstract surface as the very condition of the object for animation. This is most obvious in the case of hand-drawn animation as, for example, described by Klein himself and by George (1990). However, even when the animated figures or objects are themselves three-dimensional – as in the case of models or puppets – a two-dimensional effect has frequently been reproduced through the use of a fixed camera.

Neither of the two biographies discussed in this chapter relies upon either hand-drawing or a fixed camera, however. In the case of Wallace and Gromit, the characters are three-dimensional plasticine figures, and the camera, while perhaps more frequently fixed than in live-action, is often mobile.[1] Indeed, this is one of the reasons these films are often described as cinematic, while personnel at Aardman made a point of saying that all three features were made as films, not as television broadcasts; their broadcasting was merely a consequence of the deal struck to finance their making. *Toy Story* does not make use of a camera at all. Instead, there is a 'view-finder', a computer workstation viewscreen; what it 'looks' out at is controlled by menu commands that position and steer a simulated camera 'lens' through a 'set' modelled entirely in a computer environment: 'the character models [were placed] in space, in performance areas where the apparent depth and width could change radically depending on where and how they used their "camera"' (Lasseter and Daly 1996: 62).

In what follows, it will be argued that while neither case makes use of the two-dimensionality historically characteristic of animation, a shape-shifting potential is acknowledged in the playful manipulation of colour, line, texture, depth and scale. Through their use of these elements, these two cases of animation draw the viewer's attention to the vitality of objects. In addition, both examples were intended to, and did, solicit repeated viewing, in which the process of animation itself became a source of interest and fascination for many viewers. In spite of their contrasting styles – one low- and the other high-tech – in both cases the two-dimensionality of the (viewing) screen is the representation of a surface which is not understood in contradistinction to depth, but rather in relation to an abstract space. The exploration of this space is both their method and their subject.

[There's] a coherent and rounded story and a very clear sense of sort of place and environment and Wallace and Gromit have a place in the world that is on one level comfortable and familiar but on another level is completely fantastical. I mean anyone who can build a space rocket and go to the moon you know their world is unbounded in a sense.[2]

The occupation of this surface, and of the space into which it opens out, is what makes it possible for animation to be a defining cultural form in the contemporary global culture industry.

More generally, then, this chapter will be concerned with the cultural economy of animation. However, such systems are taken to be an instance of what we call the thingification of media, and parallels will be drawn between this process as it emerges here and the movements of other objects as they are discussed elsewhere in the book. In this chapter, it will further be suggested that, despite their contrasting styles, in both *Toy Story* and the Wallace and Gromit features, the conflict between surface and object has largely been resolved in favour of an organized system of objects, a flow of things. This argument emerges from a consideration of the biographies that includes not only the films themselves but also the toys and merchandising associated with the films. In both cases, the instability or anarchy threatened by the intrusion of the abstract surface of a shape-shifting imaginary is contained in particular ways. Nevertheless, the resolution of the conflict between surface and the object in animation is not secure and emerges in unexpected ways in the experience of viewing the films themselves and in play with the toys and associated merchandising.

The discussion in this and the following two chapters of the role of our selected objects in everyday life is implicitly informed by Johan Huizinga's classic study of play, *Homo Ludens*. His understanding of representation as a '"helping-out of the action"' (1955: 15), that which incites the players to participate in the action, the event, is helpful to describe the 'doing' of culture that we seek to describe here. But, the identification of four different principles or categories of play by Roger Caillois (1961) is perhaps more nuanced. This categorization allows a consideration of the ways in which, as Meyer Barash describes it (in his introduction to his translation of Caillois' book), a detailed consideration of types of play may be used as 'a culture clue' (ibid.: ix), enabling the deduction of the patterns or basic themes of a culture. The four categories of play Caillois identifies are: agon (competition), alea (chance), mimicry (simulation) and ilinx (vertigo). Additionally, games or play from each category may be placed in a continuum from paidia, which is active, tumultuous,

exuberant and spontaneous, to ludus, representing calculation, con-
trivance and subordination to rules.³ These terms will be adopted here
and in the following chapters in order to consider some of the implications of the movements of our objects.

Animism, Automatism and Animation

In what follows, the visual conflict between surface and object that characterizes animation is explored first in relation to the comic, a subject
which preoccupied a surprising number of serious thinkers in the
early part of the twentieth century, including Henri Bergson and
Sigmund Freud. For Bergson, the comic is the observation of what he
describes as the obstinacy of matter and is a consequence of the resulting
automatism:

Settling on the surface, [the comic] will not be more than skin-deep, dealing with
persons at the point at which they come into contact and become capable of
resembling one another. It will go no further. Even if it could, it would not desire
to do so, for it would have nothing to gain in the process. To penetrate too far into
the personality, to couple the outer effect with causes that are too deep-seated,
would mean to endanger and in the end to sacrifice all that was laughable in the
effect. In order that we may be tempted to laugh at it, we must localise its cause in
some intermediate region of the soul. (1999: 151)

In these few sentences a number of significant themes are touched upon.
First, there is the contention that the comic is a surface phenomenon.
Comedy is not concerned with depth, with cause and effect, with motivation or intentionality; indeed, such a concern is seen to endanger its
very existence. Second, there is the view that the comic arises when people become capable of resembling one another. There is here a recognition of the erasure of the individual by the comic, an erasure which
stands opposed to the emphasis on individualizing characteristics, such
as the developmental continuity of personality to be found in many
forms of cultural representation, notably in narrative. In place of the
individual, comedy is concerned with resemblances, with relationships
of imitation and affinity, that is, with type or kind. And then there is the
location of the comic in what Bergson calls the intermediate region of
the soul.

Bergson proposes a deceptively simple explanation of the comic. Let us
give you an example of his thinking:

A man, running along the street, stumbles and falls; the passers-by burst out
laughing. They would not laugh at him, I imagine, could they suppose that the
whim had suddenly seized him to sit down on the ground. They laugh because his
sitting down is involuntary. (1999: 13–14)

The conclusion Bergson draws is that 'the laughable element ... consists
of a certain *mechanical inelasticity*, just where one would expect to find the
wide-awake adaptability and the living pliableness of a human being'
(ibid.: 15). The comic thus 'enables us to see a man as a jointed puppet',

but '[t]he suggestion must be a clear one, for inside the person we must distinctly perceive, as through a glass, a set-up mechanism' (ibid.: 32). In Bergson's formulation, 'The attitudes, gestures and movements of the human body are laughable in exact proportion as that body reminds us of a mere machine' (ibid.); in short, 'rigidity is the comic, and laughter is its corrective' (ibid.: 24).

Such an analysis is helpful in relation to the two biographies to be discussed here. The film *Toy Story* opens with a simple set-up mechanism, as one of the two principal characters – a rag-doll sheriff called Woody – is put through his paces by his child owner Andy, only to be thrown to one side as the boy's mother calls him away. The nature of Woody's movement, and that of his fellow toys, is first shown to be entirely involuntary, the direct consequence of their manipulation by an external force, in this case that of a child. However, this involuntariness is then shown to be an act, a show, masking a capacity for independent action. Woody, and Andy's other toys, comes to life. The believability of the life-likeness of toys is the subject of the rest of the film: an exploration of its limits provides the narrative drive, the complex possibilities of pliability and rigidity defining the personalities of the two main characters, and most of the film's comedy resulting from the manipulation of its effects.

The Wallace and Gromit trilogy[4] too features a number of set pieces in which the single-mindedness of the inventor Wallace's reliance upon machines, and his own rather mechanical rigidity, provide the basis of the comedy. These machines include the rocket in *A Grand Day Out*; the Heath Robinson device which wakes, dresses and feeds breakfast to Wallace, the train and the wrong trousers themselves in *The Wrong Trousers*; and the 'Knit-O-Matic' machine in *A Close Shave*. Many of the set pieces which introduce the machines are the episodes which are then taken up and reworked in the accompanying merchandise – so, for example, one of the Wallace and Gromit computer games requires its user to aim jam at toast as it flies through the air propelled by an unpredictable toaster.

For Bergson, there are three processes that, to some degree, underpin all forms of the comic: these are *repetition*, *inversion* and *reciprocal interference of series*. They are identified by Bergson by means of a contrast with the three characteristics that distinguish the living from the mechanical. These are, 'a continual change of aspect, the irreversibility of the order of phenomena, the perfect individuality of a perfectly self-contained series'. These characteristics are what inform Bergson's provisional or working conception of life, or of spirit, and thus of the principles of animism. *Toy Story* is a film in which this comparison is knowingly inverted. It is a comedy in which all the toys' personalities and the development of the friendship between the two main characters can only be realized when both come to terms with – and make life-like – repetition, inversion and reciprocal interference of series: when they recognize that their life-likeness – indeed, their very livelihood (to make children happy) – is that of toys, that their animism is indeed mechanical, that it is animated. The film's cleverness derives from the multiple ways in which this inversion is carried out, what Bergson calls 'topsy-turveydom'.

Most obviously, much of the plot of the film is concerned with Woody's attempts to convince the other main character, Buzz Lightyear – a toy who believes he is a Space Ranger, of the Universe Protection Unit – to recognize that he is a toy, that he cannot fly, that his gadgets are only make-believe. For much of the film, Buzz refuses so to believe; he thus embodies what Bergson pictures here:

> ... a certain inborn lack of elasticity of both senses and intelligence, which brings it to pass that we continue to see what is no longer visible, to hear what is no longer audible, to say what is no longer to the point: in short, to adapt ourselves to a past and therefore imaginary situation, when we ought to be shaping our conduct in accordance with the reality which is present. (1999: 16)[5]

In a similar inversion in Wallace and Gromit, much of the humour is provided by the dog Gromit's ability to foresee the trouble that his master's rigidity of character and his fascination with the mechanical will produce. Indeed, Gromit is generally seen to be 'more human' than Wallace; although he doesn't talk, his reading includes 'Pluto's Republic'. His creator Nick Park suggests: 'He's got more baggage. He's more aware and more emotional. He carries with him all these doubts about Wallace – you know he's been hurt in the past' (quoted in Sibley 1998: 22). As one of the fans of Wallace and Gromit whom we interviewed remarks: 'Well it's always funny when you get ... the backward meeting the forward' (Claire). In the fascination with automatism that is at work in their uses of the comic, in both examples the distinction between animation and animism is inverted.

Personality and Narrative

Bergson goes on to propose what he describes as a general law of the comic, namely that 'when a certain effect has its origin in a certain cause, the more natural we regard the cause to be, the more comic shall we find the effect' (1999: 17). This means that if the mechanical inelasticity that is the source of the comic can be located within a person him- or herself, then the comic effect will be greater. As Nick Park describes the making of *The Wrong Trousers*:

We kept discussing one particular question that was vitally important to the film: why does the Penguin want to steal a diamond? Is it, for example, because it reminds him of ice? We spent months on that question before it suddenly hit us, one day, that the reason he wants the diamond is – *because he is a thief!* (quoted in Sibley 1998: 14)

Bergson's insight also explains the comic dimensions of Buzz Lightyear, the toy that is described by one of the members of the film production team as 'a cop who got a flat tire in Podunk on his way to save the galaxy'. When challenged by Woody to demonstrate his ability to fly, Buzz does not falter. He extends wings from his shoulders, swoops down from the bed which is his launch site, bounces high into the air after landing on a ball, gets caught up with a toy aircraft hanging from the ceiling, and circles the room at a great height, finally falling back onto the bed in a perfect landing. As Woody remarks, in an example of the insensitivity that Bergson believes is necessary to the realization of the comic effect, 'That wasn't flying. That was falling with style.' But Buzz Lightyear stands firm on the bed: his chest would puff out in pride if its already excessive contours weren't already fixed, moulded in plastic. Again and again, the comic effect of the toys' personalities makes use of the same device. Their very personality is mechanical or technological, no more and no less than an effect of their physical make-up; as such, it occupies the intermediate region of the soul and provides a 'natural' cause for their actions that is not motivational. In the adventures of Wallace and Gromit, similarly, Wallace is taught the lessons of putting too much faith in modern technology by the narrative; his personality is shown to be too single-minded. He is revealed as a contraption (in 2002, Aardman released ten short films, *Cracking Contraptions*, starring Wallace and Gromit), only to be made 'human' again when Gromit's superior sensibility sets in motion a train of events that bring the adventure to an end.

Bergson's discussion of the importance of gesture to the comic is also of relevance to an understanding of the comic effects of the examples discussed here. He writes: 'instead of concentrating our attention on actions, comedy directs it rather to gestures' (1999: 129). By gestures, Bergson means the attitudes, the movements and even the language 'by which a mental state expresses itself outwardly without any aim or profit, from no other cause than a kind of inner itching' (ibid.). So, in the examples under consideration here, both Wallace and Gromit are defined through a highly nuanced series of gestures (consider, for example, the movements of Wallace's mouth, 'that gormless toothy smile'[6] (Adair 1994)),[7] while the personalities of the characters in *Toy Story* are provided by their physical make-up, their objective properties. Gesture, as defined by Bergson, is profoundly different from action on a number of counts: action is intentional, or at least conscious, while gesture is automatic; the whole person is engaged in action, while in gesture only an isolated part of a person is expressed. Lastly, and for Bergson most importantly, action occurs in proportion to the feeling that inspires it (we might say that feeling motivates action). This is what makes identification possible as we 'allow our sympathy or our aversion to glide along the line running from feeling to action and become increasingly interested'. In contrast, in gesture there is 'something explosive', something that disturbs or arouses us, and 'prevents our taking matters seriously' (1999: 130). Bergson here thus indicates both the affinity between the comic and gesture, and also suggests some of the reasons why the comic is not easily harnessed to narrative.

Insofar as it relies upon gesture, the comic is detached from the lines of motivation, feeling, intent and purpose. It is, rather, linked to the event, to 'something explosive', to the disruption of the development of narrative. And while, as will be discussed below, both examples employ a developmental narrative, this narrative is continually compromised by the demands of gesture rather than action, and is thus a narrative which is not allowed to take itself too seriously. It is repeatedly either sidestepped or brought to a halt, while 'something explosive' takes over – as, for example, in the set pieces such as the train journey in *The Wrong Trousers*. Catch phrases – such as 'Cracking toast, Gromit' or the upward movement of Gromit's eyebrows – work in a similar way; they punctuate rather than motivate the action. The emphasis is on the particularities of small gestures and details for specific comic or narrative effects rather than as expression (Wells 1998: 60). As a couple of our respondents put it: 'Gromit's the one who makes the breakfast' (Carla). 'Sort of like raises his eyes and goes – "Oh no, not again"' (Costas).

In the case of *Toy Story*, John Lasseter, the director, is renowned for the animation of inanimate objects; he works with what he calls 'the integrity of the object'. In one story relating the development of his career, one anecdote stands out:

At Pixar ... Lasseter and two others hunkered down and began making a demo film about two desk lamps. Lasseter got the idea from twisting and turning the Luxo lamp on his drawing desk. He produced dozens of wire-frame studies, exploring all the lamp's possible movements. When he showed the drawings to well-known Belgian animator Raoul Servais, Servais remarked, 'It's alive.' Then he quizzed the young animator, asking, 'What's the point?' Lasseter replied, 'Oh, it's just a character study.' Servais then imparted a lesson that Lasseter still carries with him: 'he said, "No matter how short it is, it should have a beginning, middle and end. Don't forget the story." I kept thinking, I don't have time for a story. He said, "You can tell a story in 10 seconds." So I came home from that and started working on a beginning, middle and end.' (Lasseter and Daly 1996: 34)

This short film is now distributed on the video of *Toy Story 2*, and stands as an explanation of the Pixar logo, in which the letter 'i' is replaced by a desk lamp. Here then there is some reminder of the history of animation that Klein outlines.

In the main, it is developmental narrative that dominates in many accounts of both biographies discussed here. As John Lasseter describes

Toy Story, it is 'a buddy movie: a banter-laden tale of a bitter alliance blossoming into a true friendship. It'll have a few unusual twists. First, the buddies will be toys. And second, it will be the first time an entire movie will have been created using computer animation' (Lasseter and Daly 1996: 14). Indeed, it is the narrative that was seen by the creators at least as the most important element in the making of the film: 'If the story isn't there, all the breakthrough computer graphics in the world piled onto it won't matter. You'll have made a piece of passing fashion' (Joe Ranft, story co-creator, quoted in ibid.: 53). Screenwriter Joss Whedon believes that while we laugh at Buzz, the dramatic effect is tied to the narrative development of Woody's character and it is this development which underpins the film as a whole: 'Woody is the person who needs to learn the lesson of the movie. Buzz has to learn in that he is really a toy and he's a little full of himself. But Woody is the one who needs to learn about friendship and trust and dealing with potential loss. He's the guy who needs to be redeemed' (quoted in ibid.: 42). However, the conflict between the needs of drama and the needs of the comic also structures the film and many accounts of the film's reception. Similarly, in stories of the making of the Wallace and Gromit series, the difficulties of reconciling narrative with the graphic elements of the films are acknowledged. So, for example, the scriptwriter for *The Wrong Trousers* notes:

Many aspects of the story sprang directly out of Nick's sketches – such as that drawing of a penguin in a milk bottle. A writer usually constructs a story as a series of events that lead to an inevitable climax. Working with Nick was challenging in that the climax was the first – or only – detail in place. The puzzle was how to arrive at that conclusion: there is a penguin in a milk-bottle – how did he get there? (Sibley 1998: 14)

Similarly:

'Nick talks and thinks through the pencil,' says Colin Rose, 'and the seeds of these films are all in Nick's sketchbooks. At story-meetings, he would often say: "I've got this bit of an idea and it kind of looks like this ..." and, of course his drawings are so full of life that you could see the potential in the idea. But the first thing that needed to be done was to develop some crazy rationale that could allow these various images to co-exist in a narrative space and then to refine it and refine it.' (Ibid.: 18)

The intention of *Toy Story*'s producers was that the needs of drama should predominate; that is, that the audience should identify with the toy, Woody, whose centrality to the narrative means that he is compelled to develop into more of a man. But what was apparent in the reception of the film was that it was Buzz Lightyear – the character whose development, such as it is, is to learn that he is a toy – who was the focus of interest, not only for the young children who were a significant part of the targeted market, but also amongst their parents, notably their fathers. One sign of this interest was the demand for Buzz toys in the UK for Christmas 1996, following the release of the video by Disney in the autumn. Indeed, the demand was so great that it outstripped supply, and stayed high following the release of an 'improved' model which appeared at the end of January 1996.[8] Disney stores sold more over Christmas 1997 than they had the previous year. The interest in Buzz does not seem to have been related to his role in the narrative as such, and thus perhaps is not best explained in terms of identification. As the journalist William Leith puts it:

> One of the things about Buzz is that he's utterly dim; he does not think that he is a toy, but that he is actually an astronaut. ...
>
> Serious *Toy Story* watchers [he is discussing an audience of adult men, fathers] identify with the angst and neurosis of Woody, but they love to quote Buzz. Finding himself on the bed, Buzz proclaims: 'The impact must have woken me from hyper-sleep!' People 'do' Buzz with a mock-serious face. (1996: 1, 4)

Buzz is the toy whose 'lust for life' (to use one of the song titles from *Trainspotting*) is not limited by experience: if it were, it would not be possible for him to believe, as he does, that his journey might take him 'To infinity and beyond'.

The appeal of Buzz is in part related to how his personality is not entirely tied to narrative; nor, however, as is the case with much of the animation that Klein describes, is it tied to the imaginative possibilities of the printed page. Rather, Buzz is an example of a personality that can only represent or find itself in abstract space, in a space in which there *is* a beyond to infinity. It is a space in which the relation between surface and volume, between inside and outside, between near and far, is uncertain. And each figure's trajectory of movement and every rotation are potentially open to infinite division in the computer environment they inhabit, thus creating a space of unlimited finitude for the object. Colour itself is illuminated, as translucence and opacity extend the perception of range of the spectrum, enabling the image to appear simultaneously to obey the laws of depth perspective and to display the graphic effects associated with the computer-aided manipulation of contour and contrast.

In his discussion of the many genres of animation, Paul Wells suggests that John Lasseter 'essentially three-dimensionalises the animated cartoon, using the limitations of computer animation in the representation of figures to his advantage in depicting neo-cartoon characters' (Wells 1998: 180). And the combination of graphic characterization and the comic structure of the film create a simultaneously flat and multidimensional space as is clear in the following account of the making of one particular scene:

> The layout team also had to find artful ways to 'cheat' the apparent scale of the environment – and no scene tested that skill more than Woody's attempt to get rid of Buzz atop Andy's desk. 'Buzz had to break into a full run along that desk-top,' says Johnson. Artful editing helped, but the main solution was to model a second, larger desktop 'just for the shots where you're up on top of it, so it's two different sizes depending on where you see it from.'
>
> Because computer animation creates fully dimensional settings, the layout team's 'camera' could go above, below, in and around the action as well as simply stand still. 'Our camera could do anything a real one could and then some,' says Good. That enabled layout to program in a tilt up or down, a pan, a track along-side something, or a dolly forward or back, as well as to pivot the base of the cam-era body itself on any number of axes as it made one of those major moves. (Lasseter and Daly 1996: 64–5)

The 'then some' capacity of computer viewing is what creates the uncanny perception of space as both more and less than three-dimensional in the film. This perception is exacerbated by the construction of the figures that move through (and help make as well as being made by) this space. The modeller of a moving, living character is rather like a digital-age marionette-maker, attaching hundreds of interconnected 'strings' – articulated variables or 'avars' – that pull surfaces in concert to make them look alive. Scud, the dog, for instance, has 178 avars built into him. It is these avars that are used to coordinate movement. However, this movement comes neither from without – there are in fact no strings – nor from within – it is not the result of muscle or bone, of contraction and exertion, of volume, not even of any kind of matter. It is the movement of bodies whose shape and volume is entirely a consequence of surface animation.

Types and Toys

The stabilization of the system of objects in both biographies is evident in the development of personality through gesture *and* action, notation *and* motivation, explosion *and* narrative. However, as noted in the discussion above, the intention was for action – in the sense of motivated behaviour – to dominate – and thus, in both cases, the principal characters were tied to the narrative through 'internal' development. Both Woody and Wallace come to learn about friendship and trust as a consequence of narrative developments (although Wallace seems not to carry this learning over from film to film). But, there is also another dynamic at work here, one which, initially at least, seems to cut across the movement of objects estab-lished by the dominance of a developmental narrative. This relates to the ways in which gesture, while disconnecting characters from narrative, opens the possibility of embedding them within a wider system of things, extending beyond the narrative, outside the specific medium of film: the world of toys and merchandising. This is in part possible because, as

Bergson recognizes, gesture and the comic are the province of the type, not the individual, a natural as well as a social scientific classification: 'In order that we may be tempted to laugh at [the comic personality], we must localise its cause in some intermediate region of the soul. Consequently, the effect must appear to us as an average effect, as expressing an average of mankind' (1999: 151). As exemplars of a type, the characters in the films may be reproduced without undermining their singularity. They may be disembedded from the narrative, only to reappear in different media – on cards, key-rings, fridge magnets, toothbrushes, bath plugs, accessories, clocks, T-shirts, bags, mugs and as 'real' toys – thus becoming available to be re-embedded in other spaces, other times, in play.[9] Bergson notes that whereas in drama characters and situations are tied together, in a comedy any situation might equally well be chosen to introduce a character. In other words, while the characters are tied to the films through the internal development made possible by a linear narrative, their comic aspects work to disengage them from their narrative role, constituting them as exemplary of a type, 'a possibly common sort of uncommonness, so to say' (1999: 152), true to themselves whatever situation they find themselves in. As two of our interviewees put it:

Claire: It [the merchandise] might refer to a, to a particular story but it's not, it wasn't that ... it's like, it's like the calendar, it's keeping the characters [from Wallace and Gromit] in character in a different situation.

Ashley: I was going – I must admit I did, the, the calendar for this year I do think that's a, looks a clever –

Claire: And it's, it's original. Creative.

Ashley: Yea I've no doubt they're linking it to, to classic films and, and the –

VM: Oh yea.

Ashley: Um and the way –

Claire: Preston [another dog character] is King Kong –

Ashley: Yea.

Claire: And it's stuff like that and you know and they put the porridge gun trying to get him and that.

Ashley: Yea I think it's, it's that sort of, I mean that really is sort of you know branching out into, to, to different cultural references but –

Claire: There's a bit from *Cleopatra* and stuff yea.

Ashley: Yea and it's which characters they choose to, to play whatever and I think they've got a scene from *The Great Escape*. The one, you know at the end of it where Steve McQueen's trying to jump over the, the barbed wire fence and it's obviously, it's Wallace and Gromit in the motorcycle but it –

Claire: With the sidecar.

Ashley: Yea but the, the –

Claire: 'I don't think it's going to get over.'

Ashley: And they've got you know, and, and Gromit's doing this kind of thing cause he um ... and I think that sort of given that there hasn't been a film that sort of extends their sort of life beyond you know they're, they're still there and you can almost imagine them being involved in these other great films.

As described in chapter 2, the process of transferring the figures from one medium to another is captured in the notion of transposition, a process articulated in the following discussion of the relative merits of different characters (Gromit the dog and Feathers, a penguin villain) for merchandising. Specific intensive features relating to Gromit are carefully identified, while Feathers is seen to have a more limited capacity for transposition:

Ashley: ... but you know as I say I think probably Gromit with, with sort of Feathers is another sort of interesting option, but I think it's er, Gromit seems to live more in the film, they've obviously been extended out and you, you can, you can almost in the products that come out they're all, have that sort of, they tend to capture a particular expression about him.

VM: Um.

Ashley: Um —

Claire: Well it's like the bubble bath, isn't it, where you know he's sort of looking at this sponge that Wallace is holding above him and thinking 'oh my God what is he going to do with that?'

Ashley: Um. Whereas I think with, with Feathers it just starts with one thing, with you know a thing with a rubber glove, a glove on his head whereas I think the artefacts do tend to capture something about Gromit. You know the, the, it's not, it's frozen in time, it's either some physical expression or it's something about him which makes a lot of the things that you, you can buy about him immediately recognizable over and above him being a little plastic object.

Claire: I think it's the silence —

VM: Um.

Claire: The silent sufferance isn't it. That you know everybody can relate to that.

Ashley: Um. Um.

Claire: Which makes him just so attractive.

The effectiveness of the processes of transposition in the two examples being discussed here relates to the way in which, as Wells notes, animation can 'operate beyond the confines of the dominant modes of representation to characterise a condition or principle in itself, without recourse to exaggeration or comparison' (1998: 122). The animated type – the representation of a principle or abstract concept in itself – is what makes such characters especially suitable for merchandising. This principle emerges when and as the application of a set of rules – the pulling of draw-strings – makes something come alive. Significantly, it is the merchandising tie-ins that make animation the most lucrative part of the film industry. Both biographies show that this possibility was exploited extensively.[10]

The BBC, which owns the worldwide merchandising rights for Wallace and Gromit, subcontracted to around fifty-five licensees in the UK, who in turn produced about three hundred different products for the films. Internationally, the BBC either makes use of its own offices or contracts the services of a licensing and merchandising agency, such as Fording Union Media in the USA. Such agencies have a key role in the development of the system of objects outlined above. As Cathy McCarthy from Fording Union Media in the USA puts it, 'We don't create products; I should say we create opportunities for companies to create products.'[11]

Alternatively, the objective of such agencies is described as the 'representation of intellectual properties' in categories such as 'toys', 'apparel', 'gifts', 'stationery' and 'collectibles'. Such representation involves negotiating with product manufacturers across a range of material media, developing a public relations strategy (press releases, costume appearances and one-off events for the properties and, sometimes, their creators), liaising with retailers (sorting out details of display information, signage, theming), setting up promotions (such as deals with Typhoo and Kellogg's) and auditing the progress of properties. The agencies may, or may not, also have the rights to representation in the more conventional media of publishing (books, film, television, video). Such media are seen to have special importance since they are what give the properties their initial 'exposure'. The lack of any sustained exposure in such media was one of the problems facing Fording Union Media in their representation of the property of Wallace and Gromit in the USA – they were reliant on the broadcasting of only three half-hour films, and did not even control the terms of that. As Cathy McCarthy rather gently puts it:

Aardman is very involved. And as the property owner they should be. And they are. The BBC is much like what we are doing, they are their agent. ... But they are very involved in the programme. And that's good. It's good and bad. I mean for us it's nice when you can kind of do what you think you need to do and not have any involvement. But of course, it's also a good thing because they are the creators and they know best for the property. So that's fine. That's good.[12]

It is the first medium of exposure that typically comes to define the core attributes of the property: 'Like, if it's TV it's usually pretty close to the TV show storyline. If it's a movie, it's probably stills from the movie.' However, a book is often seen as the richest medium from which to develop the representation of a property:

If it's a book it's – it's just whatever creative process that people go through for a book, it's usually closest to the property itself. You'll get ... you can't tell a story through a T-shirt usually, or through a coffee mug or through cufflinks, so that's why those products are great and they say something about the property but they don't say a lot about the property. But a book can. A book can tell a story.[13]

In the case of Wallace and Gromit, for example, McCarthy reports, 'part of the story between Wallace and Gromit ... you can try to do that through images but you won't get the same emotion'. Certainly, the merchandising frequently depicted the two principal characters together: what was typifiable here was a relationship, the relationship between 'one man and his dog'. (In one interview, Nick Park goes so far as to suggest that they are one character, two halves of the same person, while the two characters were sometimes referred to as 'he' by those involved in licensing the property.[14]) As one of our interviewees puts it: 'Yea I think that if, if there's a pair it's Wallace and Gromit, it's not well Wallace and Wendolene [a female human character] you know, um, however unnatural that might be' (Ashley). But Zita Carvalhosa, Director of the São Paulo Festival of Short Films (Festival Internacional de Curtas Metragens), says that while Aardman 'create[s] characters, [what they do] above all [is] styles. It seems to be the characters that win empathy from the public, but in fact it's the way it's made.' And

McCarthy acknowledges that what was also important in the development of the properties was the detail, the ornament, all that was extraneous to the narrative:

I mean the music in the videos is as important as the wallpaper in the videos, as important as what Wallace is saying to Gromit and the fact that Gromit's not answering but he's answering with his eyes. There's so many different things that go on in every single video that the whole thing's unique.[15]

And certainly this was confirmed in our interview with Wallace and Gromit fans: 'I like the noise of Gromit's feet when he patters about' (Jack). And:

I don't know, yes probably the characters and obviously the voices are quite funny as well and the fact that Gromit can't talk but he's really clever and you can tell just from all his facial expressions and things and all the things he does and I think just everything about it. Cos obviously Wallace when he's inventing things and when things go wrong he gets ... he gets all bothered about them but Gromit's just 'Oh, whatever'. (Helen)

In addition, however, the commercial possibilities of transposing characters from one medium to another in these two biographies is a consequence not simply of their immediate context – such as the comic elements of the narrative – but also their wider, mediated context: what is known in the business as 'the platform'. Thus, for example, while the merchandising for Wallace and Gromit in the UK began when only two half-hour films had been broadcast, their repeated screening by the BBC at peak viewing times – for example on Christmas Day at five o'clock in the afternoon – helped give them recognition across all age ranges by situating them in a familial environment. The International Licensing Manager for Wallace and Gromit at the BBC comments:

[P]romotions are very important to use but we would only pick a product and a company that really reflects Wallace and Gromit, that would be part of Wallace and Gromit's life. So, for example, cereal and [Kellogg's] cornflakes which is a premium brand, a family brand, fits very nicely with Wallace and Gromit ... and cheese, Wensleydale cheese of course. Crackers, we're working on.[16]

In this respect, there is a contrast between *Toy Story* and Wallace and Gromit. In the former, there is less respect for the 'lives' of the characters themselves, and a much greater push towards merchandising – with the demands of merchandising playing a much greater role earlier in the production process.[17] In the latter, as indicated above, care is taken to find a fit between merchandising and the 'lives' of the characters. '[T]he real joy is when you find a way of making something totally unique to that character. So, so it works you know for that character and you couldn't imagine it for anything else.'[18]

This care was appreciated by those who took an interest in Wallace and Gromit merchandise, as is evident in this response to the question as to which of the many items owned by the couple being interviewed were favourites:

Ashley: I think the cheese stuff definitely. Um, I think the egg cups and the salt and pepper were I think they're the sort of things that Wallace himself would have done, they seem to make sense. I mean they're just –
Claire: He's always eating in the films.
Ashley: Yea.
Claire: Sort of breakfast or meals or whatever so it kind of ties in with that.

Such items were contrasted with those perceived to be nothing to do with the lives of the characters concerned:

Ashley: ... there are certain things that you think I am being sold something just because it's you know somebody said right well if we stick whatever on the side of it somebody will buy it and those are the sort of things that I think 'No, I won't buy that' sort of, unless they're, they're particularly well, either well made or interesting but ...

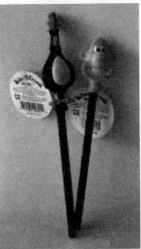

Nevertheless, while many of those involved in the licensing of Wallace and Gromit (in the UK at least) were keen to make an explicit contrast between their own approach and that of Disney, in both cases manufacturers of products were required to work from style guides provided by the property owner. As Cathy McCarthy said:

The style guide was made by Aardman working with the BBC. You give the licensees all this information so that when they are making the products they have it right in front of them. They know what fonts to use for the logos, they know what fonts to use for any copy. I assume Aardman crafted this [pointing to an example on one page]. I don't know at what point they did it. WG normal. So that's Wallace and Gromit's own font. And then they put together suggested patterns and styles, packaging also.

In addition, the promotion of Nick Park[19] also played a part in the exploitation of the property of Wallace and Gromit, especially in the publicity given to Oscars he has won. On one occasion, part of this promotion involved the story of the loss of models of Wallace and Gromit on the night of the Oscar ceremony: put in the back of a taxi in New York, they were sent on another great adventure while Nick Park collected an Oscar. Outside the UK, the Oscars may have been the first time the maker of Wallace and Gromit acquired any media visibility at all. Cathy McCarthy comments: 'I don't know that he's that big a character yet. Nick – not the characters. But I can only imagine that's how people were introduced to him – through the Oscars. Or maybe a trip to the UK where they saw the product or the property. And now it's through the videos.'

Toy Story, in contrast, was able to benefit from the more tightly integrated global distribution operations linked to Disney, including the Disney broadcasting channels, Disney Worlds and Disney retail stores. In 1995 alone, profits from tickets, merchandise and videos from *Toy Story* were over $500 million. With this and other Disney releases, the promotion and merchandise may often precede the films themselves as well as continuing for some time after. Yet the operation of this global package is by no means always smooth; so, for example, in Brazil, *Toy Story* did not have substantial merchandising sales: the scale of its success was not anticipated and plans for importing merchandise were delayed and slow.

Make-Believe

The resolution in favour of a commercial system of objects with personalities that can be disengaged from narrative does not mean, however, that the abstract surface of imaginative shape-shifting is not present as an element in the two biographies. Thus, for example, the surface which emerges in viewing *Toy Story* is linked to a tactile, embodied memory; indeed, it seems that the intrusion of the surface was explicitly manipulated by the cartoon's makers to make 'seeable' some of the non-visual aspects of perception:

The tactileness of this world, even though it has never existed – the sense that you can reach out and hold what you see on the screen – is very significant to the appeal of the film. If you tried to make it look like real life, you would fail, because it will never look like real life, but it can be touchable life. (Thomas Schumacher,

Senior Vice-President, Walt Disney Feature Animation, quoted in Lasseter and Daly 1996: 28)

The abstract surface of shape-shifting is also accessed through the use of a variety of non-visual sources that helped constitute the 'look' of the character; so, for example, 'casting Tim Allen to voice Buzz helped the character to gel'. Similarly, casting the Yorkshire actor Peter Sallis as Wallace is said to have helped Nick Park realize the nature of the character.

Describing the way in which the toy-objects were given personalities, John Lasseter says: 'The task of bringing *Toy Story* to life began with thinking through each toy's physical and conceptual essence. How is it made? What was it built to do? What are its physical flaws and limitations?' (Lasseter and Daly 1996: 16). The key to defining each of the toys' personalities was to try always to derive their traits from the realities of their physical construction, respecting what Lasseter calls the 'physical integrity of the object': 'Mr. Potato Head ... is a natural malcontent. ... "You'd have a chip on your shoulder too if your face kept falling off all day"' (ibid.). When describing the methods used to animate the famous green army soldiers scene, he notes: 'Practically every American male had little green army men as a kid. ... The one standing with the mine sweeper, the one on his knee with the bazooka, all of that. We had to be true to that burned-in memory' (ibid.: 24). To this end, 'Pete Docter nailed a pair of old running shoes to a big board, and his dedicated corps of artists took turns hobbling around the hallways, studying each other's awkward steps. ... "That gave us some ideas about where your energy goes when you can't move your feet, and how your hips would move relative to a base, if, um, you had one"' (ibid.: 24–9).

Yet none of the animators 'could actually replicate the hippety hop locomotion they finally engineered for their characters'; and Docter notes, 'That's why you animate something. You can give it moves you'd never see in the real world.' In other cases too, it is apparent that knowing how the characters work as objects was seen to be important in creating a sense of 'touchable life': 'All these holes for screws and rivets, so there's no question in your mind exactly how he's [Buzz] put together. ... From existing action figures, the designers appropriated arms with "karate-chop action." Since flying is high on every five-year-old boy's obsession list, Buzz sports pop-out wings with landing lights' (ibid.: 29).

Similarly, in the case of Wallace and Gromit, their appeal is understood in terms of 'the fact that you could feel that you could pick them up. ... I don't actually think it's the narrative because the stories themselves aren't that brilliant.'[20] As one of our interviewees says: 'I think Wallace and Gromit, some Wallace and Gromit things, I think there was, because of the sort of plasticine form it does lend itself to ... a certain form of reproduction which you know is quite cute' (Mary).

As figures of folklore, the merchandise items enter into the rituals of everyday life. As companions to the mundane routines of daily life – as

alarm clocks, as mugs, as key-rings, as back-packs – the resulting merchandise offers the reminder of a child-like ability to be beside oneself, to
be transported beyond oneself. They provide at least the suggestion that
the routines of waking up, of gulping down breakfast and leaving home
to attend school or go to work need not only be mechanical, are not com-
pulsory; that there is a pleasure to be found in accomplishing such
actions, a pleasure 'which lies outside and above the necessities and seriousness of everyday life' (Huizinga 1955: 26). And in such merchandise
the graphic elements – of shape, colour and scale – were often manipulated so as to suggest the coming-out-of-itself-ness that Eisenstein
delights in. Consider, for example, the way in which Shaun the Sheep,
another character in Wallace and Gromit, has been transposed into a
knapsack, with his body more wool than hold-all, and his arms and legs
uncannily mobile, given life by, but not apparently connected to, the
movement of the human body which he adorns.

As this example suggests, elements of the animated features may,
then, become figures in and of make-believe in everyday life. Obviously,
the toy models associated with *Toy Story* were frequently adopted and
adapted in play of all kinds, as were puzzles and games of various sorts,
including computer games. And here, neither the size of the toy-market
nor the dominance of licensing in the industry should be underesti-
mated. Three-quarters of all toys purchased in the USA are licensed, and
while this proportion is currently only a third in the UK, it is growing
rapidly (Fleming 1996). To take just one example of such games: the animated CD-ROM storybook for *Toy Story* did not simply feature the storyline of the movie, but provided 'clickables' on screen, allowing the users
to extend the story. In one scene, the user can click on Woody and he
does a disco dance. Also included are five games linked to scenes in the
film, including one using the cursor as the 'claw' to try to pick up
Martian dolls, reproducing an episode in the film. In many of the free-
standing games, two aspects of play identified by Johan Huizinga – a contest for something and a representation of something – are combined. In
the Wallace and Gromit computer games, with the move from viewing a
character whose life-course is perverted by technology to taking up a subject position as a user of technology oneself, the enjoyment of a comic
effect is mixed with the desire to master the technology. Indeed, it may
be that in this and other examples of games, the element of contest or
competition acquires a greater significance than the element of representation ('helping-out the action').

At the same time, however, the characters from both *Toy Story* and
Wallace and Gromit also feature in merchandise other than toys or
games. And while much of this merchandising is not described as toys,
this does not mean that it is not taken up in play. It seems clear not only
that the manufacturers of such toys attempted to manage the transposition across media by highlighting catch phrases, but also that the use of

such catch phrases is actually what enables audience members to enter into a space and time apart from reality, to enter into play. In many respects, then, animation may be seen to contribute to a culture of play, of returning the adolescent or the adult to a state of childhood, in which characters 'pop up' to enliven the everyday world. 'The characters [Wallace and Gromit] have almost become part of the British psyche. It's amazing. They really seem to pop up everywhere ... in cartoons, in the newspaper, references in chat shows.'[21]

Toy Story was clearly made for repeated viewing in a family context, and in that sense was aimed at both children and adults, but Wallace and Gromit are especially interesting in this respect. In the analysis of viewing statistics for the films, the International Licensing Manager at the BBC noted that they were the 'flattest set of figures' he had ever seen; that is, they appealed equally across the age range, amongst men and women, boys and girls. Nevertheless, the majority of the early merchandising was explicitly targeted at adults, especially the category of gifts. However, the merchandising was dealt with by the Children's Publishing Division within BBC Worldwide (a wholly owned subsidiary of the BBC charged with looking after its commercial activity). This was not because the target audience for the Wallace and Gromit broadcasts was children alone, but because it is the Children's Publishing Division that appears to have (first) developed the ability to exploit a property across many media. As Ian Grutchfield, the International Licensing Manager, puts it:

The key factors I would say in building that business [Children's Publishing] are the relationship with the broadcaster, so for us as we're children's, it's primarily children's television, but it's also with other types of output that have the same appeal across different media. So Wallace and Gromit did not come through children's television, it came through BBC Bristol, the Animation Unit, Colin Rose, and similarly output may come from ... it could come from BBC Scotland ... . Even a project such as 'Animal Hospital' which comes out of the Features Department, because it has obvious appeal across many media and is appealing to a children's market as well, the skills we have should relate to that property. In terms of TV programmes in general, very few types of output have appeal which go across many forms of published activity, aside from children's the only other form of output which really stretches across book, video, magazine is wildlife programming.[22]

In the USA, Cathy McCarthy was determined that the Wallace and Gromit merchandising should be focused on the adult market, 'even though kids like it for the programming and I think that they are definitely a secondary audience and something we will consider going to in the future'. There are a number of commercial factors at work in the staggering of merchandise production: 'It's very hard to bring a property that's a children's property up to adults, to make adults and teenagers buy products, but it's easier to bring it down over the years.'[23] Adults are more able to pay higher prices, and it is common for gift, cult or collectible merchandise to be made available before mass-market goods.

The Standards of Play

Given that it is the graphic elements, the comic and the use of gesture which are of most relevance in explaining the special appeal of both cases, the notion of identification seems somewhat inappropriate for understanding audience investment in them. From our interviews with audience members or fans, it seems that mimicry is central to the play encouraged by the thingification of the media; as one of our intervie-wees puts it: 'Yes, with my sister, even though we are twenty years old, both of us, um we still try, whenever we have new stuff, we still ... play and have voices you know and as stupid as it may sound we do' (Marley). However, while imitation is indeed central to the comic not only for Bergson but also for Freud, it is a process that they both view somewhat ambivalently. This may in part be because, as Caillois suggests, in rela-tion to play in which mimicry dominates, 'the sentiment of *as if* replaces and performs the same function as do rules' (1961: 8),[24] that is, the rela-tion between representation and the real is deliberately confused. This reliance on 'as if' may explain both the embarrassment evident in the extract above and the contemporary anxieties expressed concerning the supposedly harmful effects of watching cartoons and computer games.

Caillois describes mimicry as that kind of play in which the subject 'forgets, disguises, or temporarily sheds his [or her] personality in order to feign another' (ibid.: 19); in short, this is a type of play in which the subject 'plays a part'. Caillois uses the English word mimicry here 'so that the fundamental, elementary, and quasi-organic nature of the impulse that stimulates it can be stressed' (ibid.: 20). Significantly, he suggests that 'acts of mimicry tend to cross the border between child-hood and adulthood' (ibid.: 21). Bergson too points out that 'there can be no break in continuity between the child's delight in games and that of the grown-up person', and that 'comedy is a game, a game that imi-tates life' (1999: 65). However, he is unwilling to specify a more definite relationship between the child, imitation and the comic. Freud, howev-er, is more certain: imitation, he says, is childish; more specifically, it is without regard for rules or standards. Indeed, Freud develops a thesis concerning the relationship between the child, imitation and the comic:

If we were permitted to generalize, it would seem very tempting to transfer the desired specific character of the comic into the awakening of the infantile, and to conceive the comic as a regaining of 'lost infantile laughter.' One could then say, 'I laugh every time over a difference of expenditure between the other and myself, when I discover in the other the child.' Or expressed more precisely, the whole comparison leading to the comic would read as follows:

'He does it this way – I do it differently -
He does it just as I did when I was a child.'

This laughter would thus result every time from the comparison between the ego of the grown-up and the ego of the child. The uncertainty itself of the comic difference, causing now the lesser and now the greater expenditure to appear comical to me, would correspond to the infantile condition; the comic therein is actually always on the side of the infantile. (1938: 794–5)

Yet, according to Freud, the child cannot him or herself appreciate the comic. He writes: 'the child lacks all feeling for the comic'. Freud explains this lack in sensibility in terms of the child's reliance on imitation which he contrasts to the adult's use of comparison, a process that relies on the acceptance and availability of standards, the basis of judgement. He writes: 'Let us again take comic motion as an example. The comparison which furnishes the difference reads as follows when put in conscious formulae: "So he does it," and: "So I would do it," or "So I have done it." But the child lacks the standard contained in the second sentence, it understands simply through imitation; it just does it' (ibid.: 794).

So it seems for Freud that the satisfactory appreciation of the comic requires a particular development of imitation; in the process of comparison that leads to such an appreciation, imitation is carried out in relation to standards. In a similar vein, Bergson also identifies the importance of standards or social norms in the recognition of the comic in laughter; he believes that there is an intention to correct behaviour in laughter. Indeed, he suggests that there is a wish to humiliate. He then goes on to claim that typically, 'it is the faults of others that make us laugh by reason of their *unsociability* rather than of their *immorality*' (1999: 125). And it is such 'standards' of sociability – as well as commercial practices and technical conditions of distribution – that are vital to the movement of the objects discussed here.

For both Bergson and Freud, however, there seems to be some uncertainty about how the individual can both recognize a comic situation and uphold the standards or norms that are necessary to appreciate – to laugh at – the comic. In both accounts, on the one hand, it is only on becoming a socialized adult with a distinct identity that the self is able to appreciate the comic in others. Yet, on the other, the propensity to recognize the comic or be comic is an aspect of the self which undermines the [adult] individual. So, while, as noted above, Bergson believes that 'comedy is a game, a game that imitates life' (ibid.: 65), he also argues that 'In a vice, even in a virtue, the comic is that element by which the person unwittingly betrays himself – the involuntary gesture or the unconscious remark' (ibid.: 131). For Bergson, it is through the comic that the individual is most likely to betray him- or herself, to come closest to that which he opposes to life, to spirit – that is, to matter and the mechanical. Perhaps this is also why Caillois describes mimicry as relating to the quasi-organic. Moreover, such betrayal is not uncommon; thus Bergson argues that in some respects all character is comic, if one understands, as he does, character to be the *ready-made* element in personality, the mechanical or automatic element. He writes: 'It is ... that which causes us to imitate ourselves. And it is also, for that very reason, that which enables others to imitate us' (ibid.: 134). Indeed he goes so far as to suggest that, 'we begin, then, to become imitable only when we cease to be ourselves' (ibid.). It is to this paradox that Buzz Lightyear speaks.

Indeed it is because of the possibilities for the comic to undermine an individual sense of self that it must necessarily be answered by laughter. So while Bergson argues that comedy is a surface phenomenon, that it cannot involve a relation of depth, that it cannot occur if we are affected or touched by another's personality, that it begins with 'what might be called *a growing callousness to social life*', he continues that '[i]t is the part of laughter to reprove his absentmindedness and wake him out of his dream' (ibid.: 121). It is perhaps this last sentiment which explains Bergson's decision to foreground 'laughter' in the title of his essay. Certainly, the conclusion of his line of thinking is that laughter, rather, unconsciously and without regard for morals, pursues the utilitarian aim of improvement. Yet, he also remarks, the comic cannot so easily be reproved by laughter: 'And yet there is something esthetic about it, since the comic comes into being just when society and the individual, *freed from the worry of self-preservation*, begin to regard themselves as works of art' (1999: 24; our emphasis).

For the toys in *Toy Story*, the worry of self-preservation is the overriding narrational compulsion: to be secure in the affections of their owner, to play, or rather to be played with, is their goal. 'Every man-made object is manufactured for a reason, and their reason for being is to make children happy', says Lasseter. 'Anything that interferes with that is unsettling to them.' (Lasseter and Daly 1996: 19). In this respect too, then, the narrative is such as to contain the possibilities of imitation, thus stabilizing not only a system of objects but also their relation to the development of individual subjects, sociability and behaviour. This stabilization is central to what we mean by the thingification of media and helps organize the flows of which it is comprised. Nevertheless, as accounts of the film's reception presented here and elsewhere suggest, certain phrases – 'To infinity and beyond', 'The claw, the claw' and 'That's falling with style' – were frequently taken out of narrative context. They were disengaged from reason, both functional and narrational, and used as catch phrases to isolate and condense feelings of being out-of-control, of recognizing the impossibility of self-preservation and claiming a kind of freedom in this recognition, of occupying what Bergson calls the intermediate region of the soul.

6 The Mediation of Things: *In Medias Res*

Introduction

In a stunning few sentences in his essay 'Transparencies on Film', Adorno draws on Kracauer's study of cinema and anticipates that of Deleuze. He suggests that the most plausible theory of film technique – by which he means the most plausible internal organization of film, its inner logic – focuses on 'the movement of objects', giving Antonioni's *La Notte* as an example of a film that illustrates the power of this technique. But, so he goes on to say, the scope and power of this cinematic technique is limited by the representational tendency of the photographic process of film. This representational tendency is what explains the 'retarding aspect of film in the historical process of art'. It 'places a higher intrinsic significance on the object, as foreign to subjectivity, than aesthetically autonomous techniques'. Thus Adorno says, 'Even when film dissolves and modifies its objects as much as it can, the disintegration is never complete. Consequently, it does not permit absolute construction: its elements, however abstract, always retain something representational; they are never purely aesthetic values' (1991: 157). Yet, as Deleuze will go on to argue, there is more to this technique than Adorno allows. While (photographic) film may, in some respects, be continuous with its object, in other ways – such as the framing of time – it is discontinuous (even if usually standardized). This discontinuity allows for a multiplicity of possible ways of constructing the movement of the object of a film; for Deleuze, cinema is not merely representational, it is – and can reveal itself as – matter-image, whether this is as movement–image or time-image (1986, 1989).

Our previous discussions of the films *Trainspotting*, *Toy Story* and Wallace and Gromit have suggested that, in these instances at least, cinema is becoming less and less defined by representation: that it is more and more to do with the manipulation and exploitation of matter-image, more and more a process of the thingification of media. However, the decreasing significance of the representational tendency is not here accompanied by an increase in the development of aesthetically autonomous technique, in Adorno's terms. Instead, it may be understood in terms of the intensification of the processes of mediation described earlier in terms of translation and transposition, and by what Adorno, scathingly, describes as the intentional integration of the consumer 'from above'.[1] In the case of *Trainspotting*, for example, we have suggested the life of the film is as much a matter of the movement of the poster, the music and the T-shirts as it is of the celluloid print itself.[2] This is in part a consequence of the fact that technique (in Adorno's terms, internal to the object) and technology (the distribution of an already completed, discrete, closed object) cannot be disentangled. This is a point made most famously by another of Adorno's contemporaries, Walter Benjamin in his essay, 'The work of art in the age of mechanical reproduction' (in Benjamin 1992). As Adorno summarizes this argument, 'the cinema has no original which is then reproduced on a mass scale: the mass product is the thing itself' (1991: 155).

But what might Adorno mean by 'mass product'? Raymond Williams (1975) notes that uses of 'mass' continually reflect two basic early meanings – 'something amorphous and indistinguishable' and 'a dense aggregate'. As Robert Cooper suggests, it is 'a term that resists easy interpretation'; he continues:

Its early, religious interpretation saw it as prodigious, life-giving matter that could be shaped into the multifarious creative expressions of human culture. Later, in classical science, it was physical substance that could be handled, weighed and measured. Later still, through the relentless interrogations of modern science, mass seemed to evade precise characterisation; its mutable nature exposed it to infinite interpretation; it could only be expressed as a specific product of a specific experimental set-up. (2001: 16)

It is in this latter sense that it is understood and adopted here in our attempt to understand the global culture industry. As Cooper argues, drawing on Benjamin, mass may be viewed not in the traditional sense of physical substance and volume, but as 'a mutable and inexhaustible source from which worlds are continually being made through the repeated double movement of collection and dispersion' (ibid.). 'The society of mass production is essentially to do with the production of mass in the special sense of producing and reproducing the mutability and "bewildering abundance" intrinsic to mass' (ibid.: 23). Mass products – the crowd, the public, the mass market and the mass media – are transient 'in the multiple sense of being evanescent, incomplete and moving on' (ibid.: 17–18); mass products may thus be understood as the movement of complex and variable relations.[3] For Benjamin in particular, modern technologies such as cinema entangle mass as a source of ever-changing possibilities: 'With its 'shots' of the world and its edited 'cuts', film displayed its products as versions of mass convertibility in which mass audiences took part' (ibid.: 38).

In our study of the biographies of global cultural products, the movement of the object of the combined technique and technology of cinema – the mass product described by Adorno – does not pre-exist its mediation. The object of cinema, the mass product or thing, is itself constructed – coordinated, organized and integrated – in mediation, in mass movement. And in this movement is transformation. The suggestion here is that the role of reproduction or distribution has become more and more important in the double movement of mass as collection and dispersion (Cooper 2001), differentiation and integration (Deleuze 1994). The operation of the culture industry can no longer adequately be described as, 'from the beginning, one of distribution and mechanical reproduction, and therefore [as something that] always remains external to its object' (Adorno 1991). Reproduction is no longer mechanical and is no longer – if it ever was – external to the object, but is, rather, internal; technology and technique are intertwined. As Kracauer put it, rather more memorably: 'A glittering, revue-like creature has sprawled out of the movies: the total artwork [*Gesamtkunstwerk*] of effects' (1995: 324). The tendency, towards what we have described as the thingification of media, thus marks a further stage in the industrialization of culture, a stage that is simultaneously a vitalization.[4]

This chapter though – which maps the biographies of the consumer brands Swatch and Nike – is concerned with how (manufacturing) industry itself is coming to be more and more like the global culture industry. This tendency too, we suggest, is in part a consequence of the increasing significance of not simply mechanical, but more especially electronic, (re)production (Benjamin 1992). Indeed, our point is that reproduction – in the economy more generally as well as within media – is no longer mechanical, a matter of standardization and identity, but rather, is vital, a matter of mediation, of differentiation and difference; no longer 'after', it is 'within', 'in and of' production. In this regard, what is at issue is a culture of circulation (Lee and LiPuma 2002). Our study suggests that brand commodities such as those associated with Swatch and Nike are

not produced as fixed, discrete products, and then mechanically reproduced or distributed, but rather that brands are 'mass products' in the
sense outlined above. That is, we found the brands of Swatch and Nike to
be objects of a process of mass production that is non-linear, a dynamic
set of relations of power or force, with each moment or stage of production occurring in relation to every other, not a two-step process with a
production phase followed by a distribution or exchange phase (Lash
2002; Lee and LiPuma 2002; Lury 2004). While it may sometimes seem
that the functions of marketing and distribution are simply added on to
production, or that production and distribution are a series of transactions happening in sequence along a time-line, one after the other, cul-
minating in consumption, this model is not adequate to describe the
biographies of the objects we studied here. Rather, our study suggests
that brands such as Swatch and Nike progress or emerge in a series of
loops, of the collection and dispersion of mass, and an ongoing process
of (product) differentiation and (brand) integration.

While this distributed, discontinuous, open-ended mode of endurance
posed problems for our methodology, our approach was not to suggest
either that the brands Swatch and Nike do not have mass or that they are
without duration (Lury 1999). Rather, we sought to pay attention to the
processes of integration, organization and coordination (Kwinter 1998)
in which the abstract singularity of these brands emerged. Such
processes do not map straightforwardly onto either the social history[5] of
the brand or onto the complicated sequence of transactions in which a
specific (branded) product is produced and consumed. In this (and the
next) chapter then, there is no attempt made to provide a historical narrative of the development of these brands or to consider their biographies in terms of a simple sequence or chain of transactions. Rather, the
aim is to explore some of the complex and variable relations in which
the 'eventive' (Malik 2005) characteristics of the abstract machines Nike
and Swatch emerge.

Swatch

What is Swatch? technology, high precision, creativity, humour, imagination,
quality. A world full of life, fantasy, fun. People of all cultures joined together by
the same passion. Exciting surprises, suspense and craziness. Fabulous events –
astonishing and unforgettable. (Hayek, Swatch CEO, quoted in Taylor 1993)

The venerable Swiss watch-making company ASUAG was founded in
1931, while SSIH was established a year earlier through the amalgamation of the companies Omega and Tissot. Both groups included watch-
making companies that were between 150 and 200 years old. These two
companies were themselves merged in 1983, as one of a series of initia-
tives to lift the national watch-making industry out of a period of intense
financial crisis, precipitated, in part, by competition from the production of cheap, digital watches in East Asia. The losses of the ASUAG group

alone ran to a billion Swiss francs in 1980; unemployment across the industry was considerable, peaking in 1981; and the banks were brought in to take control in June 1982. One of the joint projects of the newly merged company was the research and development of the object that has become known as Swatch, a project funded initially by a loan (at a preferential rate) from the Department of Public Finance of the Swiss canton of Solothurn.

So successful has the object for which this loan was sought become that its name is now that of the largest watch-making company in the world, The Swatch Group Ltd. Comprising numerous global brands, The Swatch Group Ltd. not only makes watches (it represents 22–25 per cent of the watch production sales in the world), but also supplies movements to most of the rest of the watch-making industry in Switzerland and to a more limited extent beyond. In 1998 the Group produced more than 118 million watches, movements and stepping motors, representing 327 billion Swiss francs (CHF) in yearly sales. In 2000, gross sales went up to CHF4.26 billion (+17.6 per cent) and a net income of CHF651 million (representing an almost +50 per cent increase over the preceding year). The company currently has some fifty production centres, mainly situated in Switzerland, but also located in France, Germany, Italy, the Virgin Islands, Thailand, Malaysia and China. It owns its own network of distribution organizations, and in 2000 began to develop its own retail structures. In 2001, it launched an e-commerce platform in the USA. As well as dominating the watch-making industry, the company also delivers high-tech components to other industrial sectors such as computers, telecommunications, medical applications, automotive industry and electronics. In 2001, The Swatch Group Ltd. and the International Olympic Committee agreed a long-term partnership (the first in the IOC's history) in which The Swatch Group will provide timing, scoring and venue results services for the Olympic Games (the Olympic Games and Olympic Winter Games) until 2010. In a press release (21 January 2001), Nicolas Hayek, the company's CEO, commented: 'The Olympic Games fit perfectly with Swatch's strategy.'

But what is the Swatch strategy? At first, an important dimension was the intention to develop a project to reverse the growth in national unemployment and reinvigorate Swiss national pride in the watch-making industry. For this reason, any products produced as a consequence of this strategy needed to be made by Swiss labour. And the location of many aspects of production in Switzerland is integral to Swatch: the very name Swatch is a contraction of 'Swiss' and 'watch', while the Swatch logo usually incorporates the Swiss flag. Nevertheless, the operationalization of Swatch also came to involve an association with mobility and a cosmopolitan lifestyle; that is, its own movement is facilitated by the way in which it opens up access to selected channels of movement for consumers. As Swatch publicity puts it, 'Why stay an outsider any longer? It doesn't suit your style! So change your status here and now on the membership hotline of Swatch the Club International or call your national club (if already established).'

While the movements of Swatch occur in relation to a clearly defined country of origin, the distribution of products occurs through retail outlets in airports (Heathrow, Manchester, Amsterdam, De Gaulle, Copenhagen, Montreal, O'Hare, Newark and Havana International among others), train stations, shops in holiday resorts, franchise outlets in department stores and arcades and malls in tourist sites in major cities, principally in Italy and France and to a lesser extent in the rest of Europe,[6] North America, Australasia and elsewhere (in Brompton Arcade, Covent Garden and Oxford Street in London, Galeries Lafayette in Paris, Falkoner Alle in Copenhagen, Shinjuku-Ku in Tokyo, among others). Swatch aspires to present itself as a global passport, presenting a face (as in a passport) that enables movement through certain select channels. To take one example which makes this explicit: the Adamaster Swatch Access is described in promotional materials as a watch, an electronic admission ticket, a key to the interactive activities at the Swatch Pavilion (at Expo '98 in Lisbon), and a donation to a World Wide Fund for Nature

(WWF) Project. In these ways then, Swatch draws on and extends the pre-existing use of the watch to link together modalities of time-telling and coordinating movement (Manovich 2003).

In order to be competitive, however, Swatch watches also had to be cheap. In one of the initial formulations underpinning the development of the brand, it was described as an 'economical' watch that was also desirable: a cheap watch that everyone would want to own. The production of such a watch was not antithetical to the Swiss watch-making industry as such, as the historical example of the 'Proletariat' suggests. This was a watch designed by a famous Swiss watch-maker Abraham Louis Breguet in the late nineteenth century, manufactured to give the working classes an individual means of access to the correct time.[7] For the Swatch to be economical in the late twentieth century, however, its assembly had to be automated. And from very early on in the development of Swatch, it was decided that there was to be an integral back-plate, enabling assembly from above. This is itself typically moulded in a strong, synthetic material (plastic), using a high-precision, micro-injection technique which was original to the Swatch.[8] There was also to be a substantial reduction in the number of parts (from the ninety-one or more characteristic of an electronic quartz movement to fifty-one), a reduction made possible in part by means of the use of simple, multi-function components. As one of the key players in the research and development team notes: 'When you change all the sparking plugs of a 2CV, you only change two sparking plugs ... Your valves go? There are only two of them anyway ... using this as a basis, I was convinced that the fewer the parts, the lower the risks of breakdowns or problems during assembly' (Jacques Müller, quoted in Carrera 1991: 38).

In the production process as it came to be organized, multi-part modules are pre-assembled and pre-tested, so that only two or three 'components' need to be put into the watch during the final phase of construction. One of the last details of the original design to be agreed was the hinge connecting the strap to the casing, the patent for which defined its purpose as 'the resolution of mechanical resistance to an aesthetically pleasing system' (Carrera 1991: 62). This hinge is a feature that still enables a Swatch watch to be distinguished from imitators.

Crucially however, the economical watch of the late twentieth century was intended not so much as an affordable time-telling device for the thrifty worker but as an expendable accessory for the fashion-conscious consumer.

It was a decision from the start to promote the Swatch as an accessory, following a study made in 1980 by one of the big marketing consultants which had confirmed the up-and-coming popularity of the fashion accessory. To make the product so that it would fulfil this requirement was an important point; it was something to be worn, to match clothing, mood, occupation, and easily changeable, like a scarf or a tie. Needless to say all of these ideas had been discussed, written down and drummed into everyone working on the 'non-watch' project, long before they had started to design anything concrete. (Ibid.: 55)

In its functioning as a non-watch, then, Swatch may be seen as a contraction of tradition and innovation, an intervention

It was not until the early 1930s that the Swiss watch-making industry started to export more wristwatches than pocket watches, but in the period that followed, the wristwatch was established as 'the outstanding clock genre of our century' (Kahlert et al. 1986: 12; see also Freake 1995). Worn on the wrist, the watch is more constantly available for private inspection; at hand for frequent reference, it allows for precise and individualized time management. As an object of individualization and miniaturization, the wristwatch has always been an intimate machine (Freake 1995); or, as Baudrillard puts it, it is 'an intimate and highly cathected mechanical talisman which becomes the object of everyday complicity, fascination (especially for children), and jealousy' (1996: 94).

The arrangement of the 'hands' and 'face' of watches and other timepieces reflects the circle of the sky and the position of the sun, and thus situates the observer in relation to the cosmos. It makes an attenuated reference to a 'natural' sense of time (the 'daily round' of time) that watches and other time-telling devices have in actuality made less and less relevant to modern life. And the continuing relation between wristwatches and larger cycles of time is evident in their frequent use as gifts on occasions that mark the stages of life (birthdays, anniversaries, engagements, marriages and retirements). Yet, such gift-giving is increasingly subsumed by the Swatch strategy within an economy of waste (see chapter 7), in which exchange is detached from the life-cycle of subjects, and is increasingly unpredictable and unlimited. In this economy, the Swatch face acts as a switch to channel movements: it 'define[s] zones of frequency or probability, delimit[s] a field that neutralizes in advance any expressions or connections unamenable to the appropriate significations' (Deleuze and Guattari 1999: 168).

At 10 to 2 – the position in which the hands of a watch are conventionally displayed – the hands of a Swatch watch do not simply give a smile-like expression to the watch's face, but also display the watch's brand name. The logo intensifies the complicity of the wristwatch in relation to the long-standing in the spatio-temporality of the production market of making, buying, selling and owning of devices which tell the time. This restructuring of the spatio-temporality of the market (which may itself be seen as a collection and dispersal of the masses) brought an advantage for the Swiss watch-making industry at the level both of competitiveness – a watch to compete in terms of price with East Asian watches – and consumption – a watch to be worn as an accessory. Indeed, it is this intervention in the market – the reconstitution of the watch-making industry in relation to the rapidly emerging priorities of the discipline of marketing – which marks out the biography of Swatch.

The centrality of the performance of multiple identities – the production of a brand experience – was emphasized from the very beginning: a member of the core team, Franz Sprecher, a marketing expert brought in from outside the watch-making industry, prescribed a principle of unity-in-variation: 'they should be restrained but at the same time have an attractive appearance, with sufficient variety to please all tastes. Transforming the "crazy" idea into a mass-produced item' (quoted in Carrera 1991: 58) This principle was introduced almost immediately, first with the availability of a range of colours of the watch-face and then through the introduction of variation in the size of numbers on the face. But while the introduction of the principle of fashion into the watch-making industry was deliberate and systematic right from the start – the selection of colours adopted for the first range of Swatch was made after visiting the Paris ready-to-wear

preoccupation with watching and being watched, of surveillance and visibility. As Baudrillard puts it: 'The clock is to time as the mirror is to space. Just as the relationship to the reflected image institutes a permanence and a kind of introjection of space, so the clock stands paradoxically for the permanence and introjection of time' (1996: 24). But in the case of Swatch, it is as if both time and space (the space of oneself as an image) are introjected, and while the image may change as one model is replaced by another, the introjection itself is still intended to be permanent. Indeed, a number of our interviewees attested to the reluctance with which they replaced one watch for another (even if they had deliberately purchased the new one as a replacement themselves), and indicated that the old model was usually kept for a period, perhaps in a drawer, or by the side of the bed, as if its ability to watch over the owner, to make some claim on the owner, continued long after its use.

The watchfulness of the watch may be understood in relation to Huizinga's discussion of the evil eye, in which 'The terrors of childhood, open-hearted gaiety, mystic fantasy, and sacred awe are all inextricably entangled' (1955: 13). However, in the case of Swatch these qualities are aestheticized. Watching and being watched is presented as a game. This emerges most clearly in a consideration of the relation between the playfulness of Swatch and secrecy. As Huizinga notes, there is a 'feeling of being "apart together" in play [in] an exceptional situation, of sharing something important, of mutually withdrawing from the rest of the world and rejecting the usual norms'. Indeed, he argues that this feeling produces a sense of a play community, and that '[t]he club pertains to play as the hat to the head'. And our interviews suggest that the organization of Swatch owners as a club by the company supports not only an aura of exclusivity but also a sense of superiority by the watch wearer in relation to others in so far as he or she is communicating through the form of a secret. One attempted interview with a Swatch collector failed to take place because he believed the interviewer (one of the researchers on the project) was a member of a secret surveillance service, possibly linked to the government or to Swatch itself.

clothing fair – it has been hugely intensified over the course of the last twenty or so years. Today, Swatch, like the fashion industry, typically organizes the introduction of new models via 'seasons'. Additionally, some new models are launched independently: for example, Swatch.beat is a theme whose interpretations are differentiated by function and so-called 'animation type'. Other ranges are distinguished by the attribution of their design to named artists; some of these are produced in 'limited editions'; others are made available in special packaging. In the Spring-Summer Collection 2001, a watch was featured that is part of a shoulder bag, and another that is part of a bikini (as the tag line puts it, 'bikini included'). In these and other ways, the status of the Swatch as accessory (among other accessories) is made explicit.

The use of plastic in the manufacture of Swatch watches did not only allow for greater automation. It was essential not only to the innovative production process that was employed but also to the development of the distinctive design features that marked Swatch out as an accessory. The use of plastic meant that the face and strap of the watch could be easily coloured, decorated and altered in size, thus aiding the rapid turnover of models. In short, the use of plastic afforded a potential for the performance of a variety of (forms of) appearances, contributing to the production of a brand experience, or what CEO Nicolas Hayek calls an 'emotional product': 'We are not just offering people a style. We are offering them a message. ... Emotional products are about message – a strong, exciting, distinct, authentic message that tells people who you are and why you do what you do' (quoted in Taylor 1993). In the terms of design theorist Ezio Manzini, plastic is a 'new material' which is able to present more than one 'sincere' image of itself (1989; see also Barthes 1973). Its performance capacity enabled Swatch both to make use of a wider variety of 'forms' than was conventional in the originating product category (a watch) and to be constituted across product categories. In short, not only did the Swatch products involve the use of new materials, but also the commercial innovation of the brand itself – new product development and brand extension, for example – was dependent on the capacity of these materials to perform identities.[9]

But these design features, a consequence of the implementation of the decision to make an economical (non-)watch that would be desirable to everyone, meant that the final product could not be opened following its manufacture for repair. In other words, identity performance requirements mean that the Swatch watch is unrepairable and thus has a limited life expectation (to put this another way, each individual product's life is subordinated to the need to keep the brand alive). This was in conflict with the conventional technical standards sustained by the Swiss watch-making tradition that had nourished the concepts of longevity and service after sale. The technical challenge therefore was to ensure that the characteristic of 'non-dismantleability' became synonymous with the non-necessity to repair. This condition was met to a large extent by high standards of accuracy, precision and durability.[10] However, from the accessory-making point of view, the inability to repair individual products (watches) simply fed into the promotion of a brand, a mass product or abstract machine, whose individual, concrete parts were intended to be replaced regularly by another (albeit independently of wear and tear, or of faults requiring repair). Alongside their presentation as fashion items or accessories, the brand Swatch is thus additionally presented as the source of an (open-ended) series of products for collection. Some models are introduced in terms of limited editions, others are presented in special display packages, others still in small sets united by themes (the packaging of which itself was ideally not to be opened). At the same time, the annually renewable membership of the Swatch Club includes ownership of a limited edition Swatch, a newsletter and opportunities to participate in 'a world of Swatch collecting'. As the organization of a series of accessories,

Swatch could and does have a very different biography from that of a company making watches.

In this respect, consider also the involvement of The Swatch Group Ltd. in the design and production not simply of watches, but of telephones and other personal electronic devices, and also of a car.[11] The so-called Smart car is manufactured by MCC – Micro Compact Car, a subsidiary of Daimler-Chrysler – and was engineered by Mercedes-Benz. The basic model has a 599cc, three-cylinder Suprex turbo-charged engine that is situated at the rear; transmission is via a semi-automatic gearbox with six gears and no clutch. The car is only 2.5 metres long, and 1.51 metres wide. Fuel consumption is low, and the car itself is nearly 100 per cent recyclable. In publicity for the car, in line with the Swatch interpretation of the watch as accessory, the consumer is invited to 'Design your own Smart' – 'with many optional extras you can create a car that is as individual as you are'. Options include: leather upholstery, radio/cassette/CD player, interchangeable coloured body panels, alloy wheels, air conditioning, baby seat, drinks tray and racks for bicycles and skis. At an early stage in its development the *Swatch World Journal*, reporting on a preview presentation of the car during the Olympic Games

The Swatch identity is informed by a playfulness in the ways in which the designed properties of space come to represent relations of time: 'How long is a Swatch minute?'. Typically, the forms and values of substance and durability are overturned. So, for example, the material properties of the classic plastic Swatch lines communicate lightness, rather than heaviness. This lightness is an aesthetic presentation of the overturning of the temporal values associated with watches made to last a lifetime or mark the rites of passages associated with the life-cycle (coming of age, marriage, retirement). There is, for example, a range of watches called 'Lightness' ('Lightness', according to Swatch is 'fun, brightly colored, playful, obvious, and direct') and another called 'Skin' (to indicate how thin it is); above all, as a Swatch motto states, 'Time is what you make it.' Different Swatches communicate different ways of 'making' time. Consider the metallic line of Swatches, titled Irony. In the promotional literature for this line, introduced by the phrase 'The other face of Swatch', the individual watches in each of the sub-divisions – Big, Medium, LadyLady, Scuba and Chrono – are accompanied by a cartoon-like photographic illustration of the metallic face of everyday things. These are: Face #1: Whistling town gas cover; Face #2: Astonished rice bowl; Face #3: Laughing boat pulley; Face #4: Wondering showerhead; and Face #5: Patient padlock. And this design intensivity is not confined to products. Swatch is typically distributed through a set of dedicated franchise retail outlets, alongside franchise spaces in department stores and other leisure spaces. These spaces are designed to be very light and self-consciously modern, with conspicuous use of plastics in the window- and display-cases, making use of bright, artificial colours.

in Atlanta, reported the following comments from visitors: 'Does it tick?' 'Is it the car that shrinks when you wanna park it?' 'Does it use the same batteries as the Swatch watches?' 'It looks like an overgrown roller-skate!' However, while The Swatch Group was involved in the concept, development, production, marketing, distribution and launch of the Smart car, in 1998 Daimler-Benz AG took over its already reduced 19 per cent shareholding of Micro Compact Car. The company that produces Smart car is now a 100 per cent subsidiary of Daimler-Benz AG.

In Europe, the Swatch strategy has been commercially successful, but its global expansion policy outside Europe, in the potentially large markets of Japan, India, China and Brazil, is being rather unevenly implemented and received. In July 1998 we interviewed a representative of the advertising agency in Rio de Janeiro that had the Swatch Brazil account. The agency was actually just about to lose the account to Young & Rubicam, which was increasingly handling Swatch accounts worldwide. Not surprisingly, the representative, Gasparini, thought this 'was a mistake'. Young & Rubicam 'want to regularize throughout the world. But we know the media here, and the competitors'. Swatch had performed 'rather poorly' in Brazil, but Gasparini saw it as 'Switzerland's fault'. The advertising budget had declined from US$400,000 to US$250,000 in the previous year, and their competitors such as 'Casio, Magnum and Du Monde had annual budgets of US$15 million.' Moreover, 'Switzerland was slow at getting watches in the shops'. Casio's new models, he said, were ready to be sold some forty-eight hours after release, while Swatch models took thirty to forty days, coming circuitously via Manaus. Swatch was too centralized in Europe, Gasparini argued: the 'General Manager for Brazil lives in Italy!'. The Bureau of Media that bought Brazilian television time and resold it to Swatch was Europe-based. The problem is, 'Switzerland didn't understand that, in Brazil, people – unlike in Europe and the USA – didn't know what is a Swatch'. Even the personnel at radio stations where Gasparini 'did promos' – giving away Swatches with footballs or Team Brazil T-shirts – 'even the radio stations don't know Swatch'. 'When they (the radio DJs) saw it, it was "Wow but this is amazing – look at this watch". So we gave away 150 watches, but we needed to coordinate this with the World Cup (France '98). And the new watches arrived late!' Swatch group's Omega costs US$300, and we wait thirty days for a new model. A Swatch costs US$80 and you wait thirty to forty days. With Casio and Timex it's forty-eight hours.'

Nike

Nike can come in plural numbers, for she has no personal character that demands confinement in a single body. (Warner 1987: 129)

The origins of the Nike firm are in a company called Blue Ribbon Sports, which Phil Knight, a former runner at the University of Oregon and now

Nike CEO, and Bill Bowerman, Knight's former track coach, created in 1962. The company initially did no more than distribute running shoes in the USA for a Japanese company (Onitsuka Tiger track shoes[12]), but then shifted to designing its own shoes and outsourcing their production to East Asia (although it did have factories in Exeter, New Hampshire and Saco, Maine, until the early 1980s). At this stage in its history, the company's competitiveness was characterized by a series of performance-oriented product innovations – most famously, the 'waffle' method of aerating the rubber sole of shoes – and an early mastery of the spatial dynamics of out-sourcing.

The early and continuing manufacture of Nike products in shifting locations in the Pacific Rim is linked to the availability of cheap and plentiful labour and a developed network of raw materials and parts suppliers in this region. The exploitation of cheap labour is not unique to Nike, but they have been among the most commercially adept, and the least shamefaced, in their reliance upon a very powerless labour force. This large volume production by semi- and unskilled labour is, however, but one element in a complex web of design, manufacturing and distribution extending across numerous countries:

The Air Max Penny, for example, is a truly global product. As the *Far Eastern Economic Review* described it, the shoe is designed in Oregon and Tennessee (where Nike's 'Air' technology is perfected), with input from technicians in South Korea and Indonesia with some fifty-two different components from five countries (the United States, Taiwan, South Korea, Indonesia, and Japan). During the assembly process, a single shoe is touched by some 120 pairs of hands. (Vanderbilt 1998: 84)

In the late 1980s, manufacturing of Nike trainers began to be moved from Korea to Indonesia; it then moved to China, as Korean wages increased. As late as 1990, Korea produced nearly 57 per cent of the athletic shoes imported to the United States, but by 1994 it assembled only 14 per cent. Nonetheless, it continued to supply a large proportion of the materials used to produce the shoe throughout the 1990s. Increasingly during this period, press accounts of violations of labour law (such as minimum working age and minimum wage requirements) and poor working conditions, including what Donald Katz (1994) has called 'management by terror', has drawn attention to the conditions in which many Nike branded products are actually manufactured.[13] For much of the 1990s, the company Nike refused to pay much public attention to such claims, insisting that any responsibility in such matters lay with the subcontractors. Thus, while Nike issued a Code of Conduct in 1992, their response to complaints was often slow, and did little to transform the situation in which worker abuse is widespread.

The biography of the Nike brand is, however, not only dependent on spatial outsourcing, but also, as is the case with Swatch, a matter of the temporal reframing of the market (Callon et al. 2002; Lury 2004), and then a reconfiguring of production processes more generally in relation to the 'shots' or 'cuts' of the mass made by marketing. In this regard, the decision to rename the company as Nike, the Greek goddess of victory,[14] in 1978 – with sales and profits doubling every year – was especially apposite. According to internal company mythology, this was also the moment that graphic design student, Caroline Davidson, was paid US$35 for the now famous Swoosh logo, supposedly representing the wings of Nike. As described by Marina Warner:

The [mythological] figure of Nike, flying in to land on the victor's ship or hovering overhead with the garland of victory, cancels time's inauspicious vigil on her subjects' lives; she materializes as form in art the point at which the destiny of a single person converges auspiciously with time. Like time she is travelling at speed, but unlike time, she is not moving regardless of us. She has become conscious of our passage into the future. The arrest of Nike in mid-flight, her halt over the head of the victor folds together the moment of unutterable good fortune when we come to the attention of destiny instead of hurtling on willy-nilly while undifferentiated time streams by. When she comes to a standstill in mid-flight over us she tells us that time now augurs well. And for a moment time's dread fades. (1987: 134–5)

The temporal restructuring that characterizes the biography of Nike has emerged in stages, many of which overlap, producing a dynamic mass (market) that continues to present both problems and opportunities of convertibility.

In its early years, the market for sports shoes was relatively stable. The basis of the introduction of a model was sometimes related to technical innovation within the production process (often no more than an ad hoc process of trial and error), and this is how Nike initially sought to frame its market. However, while Nike's growth was fuelled in the 1980s by the rise of jogging as a national pastime in the USA, what Rothenberg calls a sports-as-culture trend (quoted in Vanderbilt 1998: 130), in the mid-1980s the company lost its footing. It was overtaken in market share by Reebok, which had tapped into the growing (female) aerobics market, deploying a new understanding of the trainer as accessory or fashion good. Nike was forced to accept this reframing, in which the basis of innovation was not technology-driven, but marketing-driven. However, they were unwilling to acknowledge the shift in target market in their self-presentation; indeed, they continue to insist that their shoes are for athletes and not for leisure use. Nevertheless, in retrospect Phil Knight commented:

We made an aerobics shoe that was functionally superior to Reebok's, but we missed the styling. Reebok's shoe was sleek and attractive, while ours was sturdy and chunky. We also decided against using garment leather, as Reebok had done, because it wasn't durable. By the time we developed a leather that was both strong and soft, Reebok had established a brand, won a huge chunk of sales, and gained the momentum to go right by us. (Quoted in Willigan 1992: 92)

]The set-back was a defining moment in company history, as Knight goes on to suggest in his description of the ensuing transformation in the company's understanding of itself:

For years, we thought of ourselves as a production-oriented company, meaning we put all our emphasis on designing and manufacturing the product. But now we understand that the most important thing we do is market the product. *We've come around to saying that Nike is a marketing company, and the product is our most important marketing tool.* What I mean is that marketing knits the whole organization together. The design elements and functional characteristics of the product itself are just part of the overall marketing process.

We used to think that everything started in the lab. Now we realize that everything spins off the consumer. And while technology is still important, the consumer has to lead innovation. We have to innovate for a specific reason, and that reason comes from the market. Otherwise we'll end up making museum pieces. (Quoted in ibid.; our italics)

The change in orientation was successful: in 1991, Nike held 29 per cent of the global market for trainers and sales topped US$3billion.[15]

Phil Knight describes the resulting growth of Nike as a result of:

breaking things into digestible chunks and creating separate brands or sub-brands to represent them. If you have something that's working, you can try to expand it, but first you have to ask, does this expansion dilute the big effort? Have I taken the thing too far? When you come to the conclusion that you have ... then you have to create another category.

...

We've created lots of new categories under the Nike brand, everything from cross-training and water sports to outdoors and walking. But what's interesting is that we've sliced up some of the categories themselves.

... As we thought about it, we realized that there are different styles of playing basketball. ... We had to slice up basketball itself.[16] (Quoted in Willigan 1992: 94)

However, Nike's continuing growth also involved a (grudging) recognition of the relevance of fashion to product development.[17] Knight notes: 'We have people who tell us what colours are going to be in for 1993, for instance, and we incorporate them' (ibid.). Most important, however, was the new importance that was attached to market research:

Even though 60 per cent of our product is bought by people who don't use it for the actual sport, everything we did was aimed at the top. We said, if we get the people at the top, we'll get the others because they'll know the shoe can perform.

But that was an oversimplification.

... [W]e do a lot of work at grass-roots level. We go to amateur sports events and spend time at gyms and tennis courts talking to people.

Beyond that, we do some fairly typical kinds of market research, but lots of it – spending time in stores and watching what happens across the counter, getting reports from dealers, doing focus groups, tracking responses to our ads. We just sort of factor all that information into the computer between the ears and come up with conclusions. (Ibid.)

At one level, the transformation of Nike into a marketing company simply involved more promotion and more advertising (already in 1980, Nike had started what was to be a long-standing – and unusually close – relationship with advertising agency Wieden and Kennedy, also based in Portland, Oregon). Nike spent $5 million between 1984 and 1986 advertising the coloured leather shoe, the Air Jordan. In 1987, they launched a

10-model 'Air' line. The television advertising campaign that year was said to cost $20 million, a figure to which the annual costs of not only print advertising, but also ever-increasing numbers of team sponsorship deals, individual contracts with global superstars and arrangements with summer basketball camps to use Nike products (known colloquially as a result as 'shoe camps'), should be added if some idea of the global sum allotted to advertising is to be reached. It also involved – somewhat belatedly – a new attention to the women's market, including the setting up of special teams in the advertising agency Wieden and Kennedy (Katz 1994). But perhaps most significantly, in the years 1995–8 Nike doubled its design staff and tripled its research and development budget, and its three hundred designers sustained a relentless flow of new product technologies and designs. In interview, Gordon Thompson III, Vice-President of research, design and development said: 'On average the design time of a shoe is about 6 months – that's design development to the sales meeting. Average design time, itself, is about three months. Then, it takes a year to commercialize the product' (quoted in Vanderbilt 1998: 56). In short, marketing was not simply an add-on to a pre-existing process of production; it led to a redefinition – and fundamental reorganization – of the production process and the company itself.

The overarching aim of the coordinated functions of design, marketing and advertising was to build an emotional relation with the consumer that would provide the basis for repeated purchase. Nike marketing and advertising is explicitly intended 'to create a lasting emotional tie with consumers', and to this end Nike 'uses athletes repeatedly throughout their careers and present[s] them as whole people. So consumers feel

A further insight into the making of mass products is provided by the perspective outlined by Norman Klein (1993) in the discussion of animation discussed in chapter 2. As was elaborated there, Klein points to the ways in which an abstract surface of metamorphic possibility continually intrudes into the object or figure in animation. He describes this in terms of 'a war of surface and object', a conflict surrounding how an object's properties or qualities emerge and are made recognizable in its surface appearance. Rather than functioning as a limit, foregoing the dimension of depth has opened up the possibility of occupying an abstract surface as the very condition of the object in animation in movement. Moreover, the war between

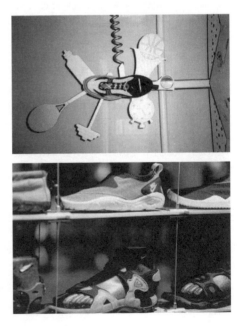

that they know them' (Knight, quoted in Willigan 1992: 92). To this end Nike has made extensive use of the marketing technique of personification, in which the properties of a product or series of products are associated with the characteristics of a person. This technique operates at many levels, including not only the sponsorship of individual sports figures and the use of these individuals in advertising campaigns ('Bo knows', 'I am Tiger Woods'), but also in the design of products, including the AirMax series of shoes, and other named shoes:

The Air Jordan: it's all about obsession.

'Guys who are now full grown say, "Yeah I really wanted Number Four, but my mom didn't have the money, and when I couldn't get it, I cried all night!"', says Tinker Hatfield, designer of the Air Jordan series since the AJ3. 'We can reissue them like Disney does *Bambi* and *Snow White*, and they can communicate with young people who didn't see them before. The retro shoes let people buy a piece of Jordan.'

The Air Jordan's success is largely about this: commodification of a person and a personality. Michael Jordan is, in the words of Nike, 'an icon for excellence'. He, like his shoes, is beyond sport. For anyone with or without hoop dreams, he came to embody a heroic amalgamation of skill, style and ... niceness. (Cook and Kabat 1999: 90)

But the personality implicated in the Nike logo is not always that of a real individual. Think here of the Swoosh, the tick that supposedly represents the wings of the goddess Nike. This graphic sign has no (or very little) subjective individuality, but is an abstract personification, first of desire, the desire for success, and then of its realization, success itself (Warner 1987: 129). In this and other cases, what we can call the 'faciality' (Deleuze and Guattari 1999) of brands – or the physiognomy of logos – is of major importance in the brand's relation to consumers, since

surface and object is now increasingly able to draw on the imaginative possibilities afforded by the abstract face of the (computer) screen and what Klein calls consumer cubism: 'The door of a refrigerator (or any appliance) became the ultimate grid for consumer gratification, opening like a little diorama into the new highway or the new airport. By cartoon logic, the consumer object arrived (or was packaged) to the happy consumer at right angles' (1993: 210).

Klein argues that cartoon memory entered into real space in the grid of the new suburbs and shopping centres in 1950s USA, and has recently been extended in themed environments across the globe. A wonderful example of this is provided in a cartoon entitled *Design for Leaving*, in which Daffy Duck, as salesman, chases Elmer up and down his house trying to sell him robotic gadgets designed to make the world come to you. These include a

it underpins the affective relations between brands and consumers. Think here of the mantra 'I am Tiger Woods. I am Tiger Woods. I am Tiger Woods' super-imposed over the images of young sports-players and fans. Such relations of implication, attachment and entangle-ment are nurtured in the marketing practices that build brand relationships and brand loyalty and typically include some degree of trust, respect and good-will, but may also include playfulness, cynicism and sometimes dislike.

A further aspect of the transformation of Nike into a marketing company is the management and coordination of a series of events in which they seek to ensure that time is on their side, that they are on the winning side. In describ-ing the Goddess Nike, Warner writes:

Nike belongs to the salubrious, sunlit, upper air, and her wings mark her out as other-worldly, at one with the sky above and a spirit of concord and harmony. ... But, most impor-tantly, she represents a power for whom speed is of the essence, yet who hallows and glori-fies the spot of her temporary halt. This makes Nike resemble an aspect of time itself, or more precisely a way we see her relation to time. She represents the propitious event that interrupts the ordinary flow and singles out the lucky winner. (Warner 1987: 133)

The attempt by the Nike company to resemble this aspect of time itself (to present a time-image in Deleuze's sense) involves the close control of the sponsor-ship of individual athletes and teams. So, for example, the basketball player Scott Pippen 'hired' Nike to attend to every detail of his professional life. In the terms of this contract, Nike guarantees the player a certain annual salary composed of a Nike endorsement plus other endorsements. Nike lawyers also help negotiate the player's salary from his or her team. This example is not

hydraulic device for bringing the sec-ond floor down stairs to you instead of you taking the steps (see Koolhaas 2001 for a discussion of the impor-tance of the elevator to the rise of shopping). The point being made here is that the exploration of this new sur-face space further contributes to the making of the contemporary mass product, not only in animation or computer games but also in architec-ture, design and everyday thinking with things.

The logic that Klein describes is evi-dent in the architecture and layout of Niketowns (and also perhaps in the layout and design of some urban spaces). In the LA Niketown, for exam-ple, spaces are both clearly defined or discrete *and* connected. The space is divided by light and sound as well as partitions. The lines between inside and outside, here and over there, are multiple, not always overlapping. The partitions themselves are usually not

exceptional; Nike has established a sports agency unit to take greater control of the endorsement opportunities that come the sports star's way.

At times, the Nike drive for consistency is such that it may override other sponsor's messages carried by a sports star or team. So, for example, in the Barcelona Olympics, Reebok had paid for the uniforms of the US basketball 'dream team', but when the medals were handed out, the athletes who (were paid to have) endorsed Nike as individuals covered the Reebok patches on their jackets with American flags. (Nike officials say the company had no role in this.) Similarly, Nike is notorious for 'ambushing' sporting occasions (as when their advertising featured prominently in the English cities in which Euro '96 played despite the fact that they were not an official sponsor. Crucially, Nike's ambition to ensure that time is on their side involves the management of the environments in which the brand appears in such a way that, as Warner puts it, the 'ordinary' flow of time is interrupted. Of course, this does not always work out in the way intended. Nevertheless, they seek to organize events almost as if they took place in a large-scale social laboratory; the word 'experimental' was attached to Nike's Sports Marketing and Entertainment divisions in 1996. In such event-based marketing, 'a global surplus of effect, a kind of booster-effect' (Massumi 2000: 191) transforms the situation into one of '(un)control'.

Let us consider one example: In 1997, Nike signed a ten-year $170 million (£104 million) sponsorship deal with the Brazilian Football Confederation (CBF), which committed the national team to playing fifty Nike sponsored interna-

solid, but have gaps, don't reach the ceiling, are suspended. There is a 'shoe tube' connecting all the different sections, bringing stock up from the basement, moving it around. Again and again, the Nike logo is embedded in sports balls – we walk on the outlines of logos, stools are covered in their stitching, every circle or elipse is a ball of some kind, and the response invited is to reach out, to touch, to catch the ball. Differences of scale and perspective are used both to disorient and direct the visitor. Standing at the front end of the first floor, looking out, you can view the inner wall of the outside porch, which is covered by a large photograph alongside which is written 'Just Do It'. From the ceiling of the basketball section is suspended a large metal ring – it is a basketball hoop that opens onto the retail space beneath. The floor of this space is marked as if it were a flattened ball. So as consumers we are caught in movement, the movement of the brand as mass object.

As a system 'based on co-ordinated pauses' (Klein 1993: 211), Niketown produces 'pleasure designed off a short, grid-like menu'. In these and other spaces, as Klein notes, consumers 'act out stories in cartoons' (ibid.: 253). In linguistics, the phatic is the name given to the signals which maintain discourse or dialogue, and have little or no intrinsic meaning, such as, 'How are you?' In graphic media such as comics, phatic communication refers to panels, the presence of framing devices such as lines, balloons, rules and escapements, and the deployment of motifs such as speed lines or arrows (Eisner 1985). Phatic devices capture and direct the attention of observers; they indicate possible relations between separate frames;

tional games over ten years against opposition teams of Nike's choice (including club as well as national sides). The requirements of the contract are that the team must include at least eight first team regulars. Furthermore, the contract states that the CBF cannot play a friendly against a team in Europe, the United States, Japan or South Korea if Nike has arranged or intends to arrange a match with that team in the same year. Furthermore, the requirement for at least eight first team regulars to play in such matches is potentially problematic since many play for European teams and their clubs are only obliged to release them for five international friendly games each year. The company is able to sell the worldwide TV rights to the games it organizes, thus abrogating a commercial opportunity which had previously been the responsibility of sporting bodies (see chapter 3).[18] In addition, considerable income is accrued by selling replica shirts.[19]

they maintain movement, change location, shift focus and direct the action. Such devices, both linguistic and graphic, proliferate in the American retail environment; in particular, the statement, 'How are you today?' disturbed me as I wandered around the store. What worried me was the 'today'. It was as if the speaker (the retail assistant) knew how I had been the day before, and was interested in knowing whether I was any better on that particular day. It was as if she was actually talking to me. I was disturbed (I tried not to be, to take it in my stride), because I was taking seriously the nowness of the statement, its attempt to bring me – including some recognition of my past, some supposition that I was not just someone who had walked into the store and was just about to walk out – into the Nike frame. But this nowness was only so the assistant could move me along to the next frame: 'Can I help you?' or 'What can I get you?

The 1998 World Cup saw ten national squads bearing the Nike insignia: the Netherlands, Italy, South Korea, the Czech Republic, Poland, Russia, the USA, Portugal, Nigeria and Brazil. The latter were the championship favourites. However, when the Brazilian national team returned home, after losing the final (to France), they were met at the airport by disappointed fans holding the national flag modified so that in place of the slogan 'Order and Progress' was the word 'Nike'. In January 2001, the Brazilian footballer Ronaldo was questioned by parliamentary investigators on the role that Nike had played in the performance of the national team (as part of an investigation into the

organization of the game in Brazil). He was asked by congressmen why Brazil lost the 1998 World Cup final 0–3 to France. 'We lost,' he said, 'because we didn't win.' Questions focused on whether Ronaldo (a star player who also has a personal sponsorship deal with Nike), who had a convulsion (and had taken a tranquillizer) before the final,

One of the figures (Haraway 1997) that instantiates the mass product Nike is Michael Jordan, perhaps the most famous Nike-sponsored athlete. Jordan appeared not only in numerous advertising campaigns, sporting promotions and events, but also in a logo, the Jumpman, that adorns a very successful line of shoes and apparel (Lury had been forced to play by Nike against medical advice. It was also suggested that without pressure from Nike, the player would not have had a convulsion at all. The commission called 125 witnesses, including other players, the team doctors and former FIFA president João Havelange. But the testimonies did not incriminate Nike; as Ronaldo put it: 'There is no clause [in his contract with Nike] saying what I had to do during the World Cup. My relationship with Nike is very good. They never demanded me to do anything. The only thing they wanted was for me to score some goals wearing their boots' (quoted in Bellos 2001a). Instead, criticism was ultimately directed towards the CBF.[20] The final report presented evidence to prosecute thirty-three people for corruption, including CBF president Ricardo Teixeira (the former son-in-law of João Havelange) on thirteen counts of fraud. The communist congressman Aldo Rebelo, who had called for the commission, commented: 'Disney didn't sell Mickey Mouse, but the CBF sold the national team to Nike. It should have sold the spectacle, not the product' (quoted in Bellos 2001c). But spectacle and product cannot be separated in the workings of the brand Nike, as the interviewees we spoke to during the summer of the World Cup recognized.

We spoke, for example, to Angelo Franzão Neto, a senior executive at McCann-Erickson, the advertising agency for Nike in Rio de Janeiro. McCann-Erickson opened a branch in Brazil in 1935, at about the same time as another of the largest agencies at the time, J. Walter Thompson: they were the first outside agencies on the Brazilian market. Brazil is currently the 'fourth market for McCann-Erickson, after the

1999).[21] In this figure, Jordan, the basketball player, is represented by a silhouette of a jumping figure, caught at the moment in a jump when you are both going up and coming down, rising and falling, flying and dying. He is caught in an instant which is no more than a shiver of time, a moment of chronic ecstasy. In addressing the significance of the Jumpman, consider what the filmmaker Spike Lee (who is a not uninterested contributor to the value of the Nike brand[22]) has to say about Michael Jordan:

> Michael Jordan changed ball. Jordan was multi-dimensional, up in space, in the air, explosive, and saw all the horizontal creative passing angles, with added shot-blocking and psychological warfare edge. ... Jordan is now the top of the line. I doubt we'll see anything like him again. ...
>
> I can't say I saw Babe Ruth, Jack Johnson, Ty Cobb, Joe Louis, Jim Thorpe, Josh Gibson, Sugar Ray Robinson, Ben Hogan, Cool Papa Bell, the Herculean guys, but now we are in the presence of one of the greatest athletes ever and we're able to see this gentleman perform.
>
> I consider Jordan an artist. Not all athletes are. Not all make it to that level. Jordan is like John Coltrane, Louis Armstrong, Ella Fitzgerald, James Baldwin, Toni Morrison, Paul Robeson, Jean-Michael Basquiat. When we speak of Afro-American artists, I think we now have to include Michael Jordan. Muhammed Ali would be up there too. (1997: 20)

Clearly Michael Jordan is a lot of things to Nike.[23] He is up in space, in the air, the top of the line, a gentleman, an artist. He is all these things because he changed ball. He changed how people throw a ball around in space, and in doing so he changed space. This is how he is an artist, a gentleman. But it is also how he (and Nike) changed time.

The use of a silhouette in the

US, Britain and Japan'. The agency has three hundred employees in Brazil, fifty in the Rio office. Franzão had worked for a Brazilian-owned advertising agency before joining McCann-Erickson in 1980. McCann-Erickson has had the Nike account in Brazil, Argentina and Columbia since 1994–5. At first, though, the account was mediated by Footline in Argentina: Nike dealt with Footline and Footline with McCann-Brazil. But since 1997 Nike began working directly with McCann-Brazil. All the creative aspects of Nike advertising are worked out in the USA at Weiden and Kennedy, but the implementation of strategy in non-US markets is largely handled by McCann. Their role is in media and strategic planning. Other McCann-Erickson accounts in South America include Coca-Cola, Gillette, Oréal, Mastercard, Motorola and General Motors. In each case, Franzão says, the brand wants to put across a uniform offering, but in each case McCann-Erickson has to 'nationalize' the content.

Nike, he says, is different from Coca-Cola, which is a more 'traditional product'. Coca-Cola does its own manufacturing, close to the consumer market because of the weight of the product and its vulnerability to heat. Hence, there are Coca-Cola-owned manufacturing facilities in all major Brazilian cities. Coca-Cola was the Brazilian football national team shirt sponsor from 1991, and at one point sponsored some thirty Brazilian club sides. By 1997 this had been reduced to none (Salim interview). From the mid '90s, Coca-Cola's sponsorship switched to beach soccer, Carnival and racing cars. Coca-Cola advertisements are oriented, thinks Franzão, to 'younger kids' than those targeted by Nike. 'Nike campaigns', he also notes, are aimed at 'class ABs, Mastercard also at ABs, General Motors at

Jumpman – in conjunction with the sponsorship of Jordan himself – catches him, stops the artist, arrests the gentleman moving in space, and in transferring that trace of movement onto shoes and clothes, opens up an entry point to the depth of time for the Nike corporation.[24] This is the time of no-time-at-all; as Michael Jordan himself puts it:

The first time you hit a jump shot with no time on the clock, you can always go back to that moment. You have the confidence because you've done it before. ... I was in that situation and I came through. Now when I get in that situation, I don't weigh the negatives and the positives and hope the positives win. I just go back to my past successes, step forward and respond. (Quoted in Vancil 1995: 36)

Or as one of our interviewees put it:

A: Yea, and I really enjoy these shoes. I really enjoy how they make you feel, how you and you walk and you walk through air. It's so, so light. ... Well I always when I think of Nike –

VM: Yea.

A: I always picture a black man ready to, I don't know why, maybe it's the advertisements and I just picture like that um a black man standing ready to run –

VM: Oh yea.

A: Yea, yea. So wearing the Nike outfit, the Nike shoes and ready you know to start running and win the trophy or something.

VM: You don't have anybody [in particular in mind?] –

A: Just anyone yea.

VM: Yea.

A: Just the best of the best or something.

VM: Yea.

A: Yea I always picture something like that.

However, there are few athletes who have the ability to embody this

AB and Cs, and Coca-Cola at everybody'. In contrast to Coca-Cola, Nike focuses on the sponsorship of individuals and individual teams like Selecao Brazil.

apostasy, and Nike, ever more urgently since Jordan's retirement(s), have adopted a variety of strategies to intervene in the spatio-temporality of the market.

Nike is also different, however, says Franzão, in being a more 'demanding client'.[25] 'They ask us to pay attention to television scheduling, all the time, every hour of the day.' This is not easy for the agency, as typical practice is to buy media time a long time in advance of specific campaigns. 'You have to check the whole day TV schedule. You don't want to be on in the middle of a soap 'cause Nike is not soaps but football.' So 'we need constantly to negotiate with Globo. But they need us too. And you have to create a direct line to Globo.' For example, 'if Brazil goes to the final, we have to create special action for Nike'. But this cannot always be done. Nike's contract with Seleção included the requirement for the team to play five or six friendlies per year, but 'when Globo transmitted the Mexico game, they had their own sponsors and cut the Nike logo'. In 1998, eight Selecão Brasil players had individual contracts, including Rivaldo and Ronaldo, but not Djunga. 'When Nike has a party, they ask for the whole Brazilian team to participate. Djunga says no: he needs to train.' On the other hand, 'Nike protect Ronaldinho in terms of image'.[26] 'You have to consider not just one media for Nike because these people, young people are very dynamic and don't have traditional media behaviour.'[27] 'You have to follow the people ... if Brazil win tomorrow and Sunday, I hope we will use billboards and use alternative media.' Furthermore, 'The Nike commercial is different ... it suggests an action, suggests an environment and suggests different behaviour of the TV viewer.' In relation to the audience for football, the advertisement needs to be 'the right day, the date, the right moment: *for soccer in this market is in the moment*'. The mass (product) is in the shot.

We also interviewed Ronald Radomysler, Managing Director of Drastona, a manufacturer of leisure apparel based in the suburbs of São Paulo. Drastona is a manufacturer for Nike, and a licensee for Adidas. In 1993, the company had 3,000 employees; in 1998, at the time of interviewing, it had 700. Radomysler says: 'Next to Mexico, the second country that visits Disneyworld is Brazil. Mexico is just a two-hour flight [from Disneyworld]. For us it is much more expensive. It is unbelievable – because we are not a rich country – to have so many people travelling. But [we] are crazy for the US.'[28] In the past, he says, 'everything was oriented to, came from France. Even President Fernando Henrique Cardoso was a Professor of Sociology at the Sorbonne.' But the French connection 'was a cultural elite' and now 'everything is geared to the US'. He continues: 'What these brands do is try really to impose a cultural standard that is valid or that is accepted everywhere. The ads they run in English sometimes: sometimes without subtitles!' Another interviewee, Juan Carlos

Salim,[29] the Marketing Director of the Confederação Brasileira de Futebol, confirms this.[30] Like Franzão, he says, '[Nike] wants everything. Pictures of the players sleeping, taking baths, everything.' Nike 'makes their own movies. A Nike cameraman comes to every match played by the national team.' Nike has 'some control over the advertisers showing when Brazil [national football team] is on TV'. It is as if Nike is a co-producer of the national football team and of the media itself.

As a Nike supplier, Drastona makes clothing to order: 'They come in with an order of so many thousand units – like the Brazilian home jersey – and I deliver them. I don't know what they do with them.' For Adidas, however, Drastona is the 'exclusive licensee for the Brazilian market', and its role is correspondingly greater; 'we manufacture, sell and distribute'. We are 'basically manufacturers, a firm of manufacturers. But with Adidas we have a contract. With Adidas we have a big part of marketing, product selection, range building, pricing and distribution.' 'We are involved in how the product range is built, in terms of pricing, if it's sports-specific or a leisure-oriented product.' Drastona has been a non-exclusive supplier for Adidas since 1976, when Radomysler's father ran the firm. Then, says Radomysler, 'they placed the orders, and we delivered the goods and they [did] everything else.' But 'when Adidas had problems at the beginning of the '90s, they could not do all the work on the ground any more in Brazil.' 'We were the best and largest supplier so we made a contract with them for exclusivity in 1993.' Since then, 'we are exclusive licensee for the whole textile range in Brazil.'[31] This relationship – licensor–licensee – is itself complicated and tense. At the time of interviewing, Adidas had a fully owned subsidiary in Brazil, 'whose president reports directly to Germany. We deal with the subsidiary.' The subsidiary does 'not want licensees. They are not renewing contracts. They want to shop around and sell by themselves.' As a licensee, 'I pay a royalty fee to them and I take the risk. I buy and sell. When they buy and sell, they have the risk 'cause if they buy too much *they* end up with too much inventory.'

At the time of interviewing, Nike had also recently established a fully owned subsidiary in Brazil (previously they had had a licensing agreement with a Brazilian firm). This company took on more functions than Drastona has done for Adidas. Now Nike 'will start doing business for themselves'. Nike had a licensee here:

because they don't know the market and they didn't have the manpower to control the market. [They] didn't have the investment to put an office here. The licensee worked and is doing pretty good business. But now they [Nike] want to take control so they are buying back the license. They want to run the business themselves because Wall Street wants brands to control the business. Wall Street wants to know that the Brazilian market is served by Nike, not a licensee. Wall Street wants Nike in control directly of all the markets. It's the Wall Street mentality. Wall Street wants an organization with globalization that can work in Brazil, Argentina, India and Pakistan. (Radomysler interview)

On the one hand, Radomysler acknowledges the commercial sense of this strategy: 'And they're in a way right. Because there is more in common between a teenager from Brazil and from Japan than there is between a Brazilian teenager and his father. So all over, they do the same design, the same product.' But on the other, he counterposes a Brazilian logic, a different temporality: 'All these companies have a global source structure. They buy in China and Indonesia and Malaysia. To do this they must place orders six months ahead of time. In Brazil six months is like an eternity. So they need local suppliers.' They should use 'local businesses to run the business for them, because we are able to understand the markets better'.

Salim also identified the pivotal role of Teixeira, the son-in-law of João Havelange, a previous president of the CBF who had gone on to be president of FIFA. Prior to Teixeira's appointment in 1989, the single national team sponsor was Topper, but Teixeira negotiated sponsorship through the Brazilian sports sponsorship company, Traffic. Traffic itself bought rights to the Selecão's image. 'We sell to Traffic and Traffic has the right to negotiate the symbols ... our logo.' 'The television rights to games and to friendly games we sell to Brazil TV.' Traffic had negotiated with Pepsi, which was team sponsor from 1991 to 1993; subsequently it was Coca-Cola. Pepsi and Coca-Cola's level of sponsorship was about $4 million per year. Nike's is of a different order: $20 million. But, at least so Radomysler says, it is widely thought that Nike's deal with the CBF 'was not for Brazil'. Nike and Reebok are geared basically to the American market. To be global you need to have a relation to 'the world's most popular sport'. But according to Radomysler, 'Nike does not know a thing about soccer 'cause its tradition is basketball. So they think "if you don't have a heritage, you buy one". Hence the Brazilian team: $200 million over ten years. This is similar to what the deal with Tiger Woods or Michael Jordan is over ten years.' 'They could have had it for less. This is different from the deal Adidas does with the German or Spanish or French federations. It includes five friendlies in the Far East and the US.' And 'Nike will spend another $100 million on ads for the Brazilian team. The message is "Nike understands soccer". They have [Brazil], everybody's second favourite team.' Nike is 'pouring money into club football: getting the best clubs everywhere.' Of Nike's individual contract with Ronaldo, Radomysler says: 'Now they're retailing the Ronaldo boot for $200. They won't sell many of these but they will upgrade their whole soccer profile. What they wanted is to sell a very *expensive* Nike soccer boot so people will know that the brand can be a standard of excellence in soccer.' Still, however, Radomysler continues, Adidas is not only the leader: 'It is the standard. If you're going to buy a running shoe, a Nike shoe is $100; then if you are Adidas you'll have to sell the same shoe for $90 or $80. If you are a soccer brand, people go to see the price of an Adidas boot. If the Adidas boot is retailing for $60, your similar boot, even a Nike, has to be cheaper.'

Radomysler also points out that the majority of the population of Brazil, like the majority in many other countries, is outside the brand economy. 'Of 160 million people, maybe 20–25 million, like a country half the size of England, are [in the brand economy].' Of the 'workforce of about 30 million, only 10 million pay taxes.' They buy soccer boots. 'People go Sunday, have a team, play with each other. They must have a uniform, but they cannot afford a Nike or an Adidas jersey. So they buy one that retails for ten *real*, or seven or eight. Soccer shorts you can pay 3–4 bucks. You buy cheaper boots. Brazil's biggest seller of tennis shoes is not a branded company, but a sporting goods manufacturer. It's Olympicus because of price. It sells several times what Nike sells.' But working-class consumption has increased with stabilization of the *real*, and its pegging to the dollar. In the recent past, Brazil had experienced '30 per cent inflation per month. [The working classes] had no bank account to pay in their wages, so they needed to spend it to buy food. Every day the money they earned, if it was in their pocket, it was losing value. Now, with stabilization, they can save money. And buy TVs, fridges. There are instalment plans everywhere.' Here, as in many other countries then, there is a complex, changing stratification of consumption, with only a small but increasing proportion entangled in mass products, part of the global brand economy.

Mass Products and the Mediation of Things

In mapping the biographies of the brands Swatch and Nike, the writings of Adorno (1991), Benjamin (1992) and Kracauer (1995) on 'the mass product' are of enormous relevance. For all these writers, '[t]he society of mass production is to do with the production of mass in the special sense of producing and reproducing the mutability and "bewildering abundance" intrinsic to mass' (Cooper 2001: 23). In their writings, a heterogeneous public is made visible to itself in mass products such as the media (in particular cinema) and the market (in relation to the emergence of a modern consumer culture). Mass products draw in the public at the level of the senses, and lead to the restructuring of the very conditions of experience, subjectivity and the body. In mapping the biographies of Swatch and Nike, we came to the view that they are examples of the brand as mass product in the sense described by these writers, but we also came to focus on developments in both the ways in which production and reproduction are collapsed (in which technique and technology become irretrievably entangled), and the consumer is incorporated into a culture of circulation.

If we return to Adorno and his understanding of the technique of film as to do with the movement of things, it may be helpful here to consider the logos of the brands Swatch and Nike as techniques which operate in the same way; that is, they are images which also open on to – indeed help organize – a particular movement of things. Let us elaborate this claim a little further. In his discussion of what he calls a movement image, Deleuze emphasizes that this kind of sign is not analogical in the sense of resemblance: 'it does not resemble an object that it would represent'. Rather, the movement-image 'is the object; the thing itself caught in movement as continuous function. The movement-image is the modulation of the object itself' (Deleuze 1989: 27). From this perspective, just as a cinema shot is the mobile section of the duration of an object, so may the logo of a

brand be seen. As a section of duration, the intensive ordinates of movement that are the logos described above may be turned on the one hand towards their object (the abstract objects, the brands Swatch and Nike), and on the other towards an expanding whole of relations that changes in time (the media, a flow of products, promotions and events, and also the movements of consumers). Such logos are not signs of interpretation, but of intensity, of association and of linkage; they coordinate the movements of the mass objects of the global culture industry, the mediation of things.

7 Flow: The Practices and Properties of Circulation

Introduction

In the previous two chapters, the dual processes of the thingification of media and the mediation of things were outlined. In this chapter, the convergence of these processes will be considered, and the way in which they contribute to the organization of the global culture industry as flux and flow will be further addressed. The chapter draws on materials collected from the study of the biographies of *Toy Story* and Wallace and Gromit again, and also those of the brands Nike and Swatch, and will attempt to elaborate further what might be meant by 'flow', or a culture of circulation. In doing so, it will draw on, add to and develop the theoretical sources briefly introduced at the end of the previous chapter. These include anthropological understandings of exchange (Mauss 1976; Bourdieu 1977; Appadurai 1996), sociological interpretations of the contemporary economy (Castells 1996; Callon 1998; Barry and Slater 2002; Lee and LiPuma 2002; Thrift 2004), and the accounts of mediation that are part of what might be called media theory (McLuhan 1997; Williams 1974; Deleuze 1986, 1989; Lash 2002; Bolter and Grusin 1999). The aim in this chapter is to address what is sometimes called 'reception', sometimes 'the audience' and sometimes the 'consumer market', but all these terms are somewhat problematic for the perspective adopted here. They imply that this moment is in some way a final stage in the biography of our objects, as if an object was actually used up in its use. We prefer a term such as 'entanglement' (Thomas 1991), since it does not presume the end of the objects whose biography we have mapped, but their continuing existence and transformation in use. We would also stress that there is no simple beginning or end point in a culture of circulation, but rather a dynamic of forces.

Little Presents

To begin to explore the entanglement of objects and subjects in the flux and flow of the global culture industry, consider two examples of the acquisition of free gifts or licensed (merchandise) goods. First:

Alex: I, when I go, when I go to McDonald's I always try to get the kid's meal whenever it has an artefact or whatever it is of a film ... this particular one, from [the Disney film] *Hercules* my father came to England and then he went to, he left from London airport and he bought them for me.

VM: Um.

Alex: I don't know why. I mean I don't why he bought the Hercules stuff for me. Maybe because he knows, he knows that I like them or something and he just, he um mailed it back from Greece and, in a big box you know with Hercules stuff in there.

And second:

VM: But yea so when did you first get interested in collecting the Wallace and Gromit merchandise?

Ashley: Um my version of it is that Claire bought me the clock, the alarm clock for a birthday present. I think that was the first time that I was sort of aware of how much –

VM: Christ!

Ashley: How much material that, that there was and I suppose that that was an excuse –

Claire: You'd been saying you liked it and you'd been saying you wanted one and we'd watched the movies and, and liked them hadn't we. Thought it was all very cute and silly.

Ashley: Yea I think that was it, and I don't know whether it was coincidental but then at the, the sort of time that there were all these, these sort of free you know give-away promotions on, on packets and, and we're the sort of, we're the marketing person's dream. I think we go around supermarkets going ooh isn't that nice, whatever it is you know, two hundred weight of Domestos [domestic disinfectant] and if it's got, got something that we're interested in let's have it.

In both these interview extracts, merchandise goods are acquired as gifts. In the first, a plastic figure of a mythical character, acquired as a 'free gift', is given by a father to a daughter after parting, and in the second, a young woman gives a customized alarm clock, bought as a commodity, to her boyfriend as a birthday present. This prompts the couple to begin to build a collection of Wallace and Gromit goods, including some acquired as 'free gifts', some purchased as commodities for themselves and others given to them as gifts by members of their families and friends. These examples suggest that merchandise goods may be located in relation to long-standing rituals of gift-giving (Mauss 1976; Carrier 1998; Miller 2000; Berking 1999). These and other goods are exchanged as tokens of a relationship, giving substance to relations of kinship, of affinity and difference, and contribute to ways of living, to home, family and community, to understandings of space and time in terms of presence and absence, staying and going.

In this respect, merchandise goods function as part of a gift economy, and seem to have the characteristics of what Pierre Bourdieu calls 'little presents' (1977), which he describes as halfway between 'gratuitous gifts' and 'the most rigorously forced gifts'. So, for example, another of our interviewees described such gifts as 'the small thing'. Such presents are, as Bourdieu notes, typically 'of modest value and hence easy to give and easy to match'.

Lucy: Yeah I think, I think my brother bought me this when he went on his school trip. My friend got me that one when she went to Florida and I got that when I went myself to France.

VM: Yeah.

Lucy: So if I look at them I think of when I was there.

VM: Oh yea.

Lucy: That, that one I bought when I was, I saw my boyfriend. It reminds me of when I went to EuroDisney in Paris.

VM: Yea.

Lucy: I don't think of it just as, I don't think of it as Eeyore, I think of it as the thing I bought when I went away there. I think it means more than –

VM: Em.

Lucy: Just what it is.

In Bourdieu's analysis, such gifts function within the logic of 'surprises' or 'kind thoughts' rather than according to the mechanisms of ritual, and are sharply opposed to what he calls the extraordinary gift.

In many cases, of course, the giving of merchandise goods is linked to the consolidation of a relationship between those who give and those who get. And sometimes the relationship made substantial in the gift is further developed in the ways in which the object is inserted into the practices of the production of home, family and community. So, for example:

Claire: We like, we like the Angel Delight [an instant dessert] big face things [moulds].

Ashley: Yea I, I –

Claire: And it's quite, that's quite silly surprising people when you plonk this Angel Delight and it's like Wallace and Gromit in front of them, it's like –

Ashley: I think Angel Delight frozen is disgusting you know. It just tastes like sort of frozen water with a fake flavour or something which they really do sort of [but] done as exhibits rather than practical things. ...

Claire: That's right.

Ashley: You know I think at the end of a dinner party bring these things in – well, 'my god what's that?'.

Or, more vaguely, but still powerfully:

Alex: So I don't know, I, I suppose I, I suppose I enjoy having them. They
remind me of childhood experiences and fun and I don't know
what.

There is even some sense in which
the collection of such goods may
be organized in relation to their
ability to sustain a notion of generation underpinned by the inheritance of personal property:

Ashley: Well yea but whereas the, these are sort of interpretations of the drawings
but er I think they look pretty, they're nice for, for all that and again they're
something that I think won't be as commonplace as other things. I suppose
that's sort of me and my *Antiques Road Show* mode of thinking [a UK television
programme in which 'ordinary' people have their antique personal possessions
assessed and valued by experts] um you know when I've got my –
Claire: That's your mother and her 'trash and treasure' thing.
Ashley: When my, my relatives of the future go – there's my mad such and such a relative collected these but they're worth oh ummm nothing but, but, but they're
very interesting.

At the same time, such gifts may contribute to a sense of regional or
national belonging:

Ashley: And I think that, that Nick Park has sort of anchored some of it in this part of
the world and characters like Preston, Wensleydale [towns in the north of
England], and Wensleydale cheese I think that was, um that must be I suppose
a sort of northern encultural endearism.

In these ways, such little presents contribute to a sense of the personal
ownership of things that is linked to the social relationships of patrimony and secured by the relative fixity of domestic capital, what
Baudrillard describes as 'an economy of the proper place'.[1]

For some of our interviewees, however, merchandise goods were generally not something that they would purchase for themselves. It is not
that such things were not appreciated when they were received as gifts,
but rather that, as one interviewee puts it, 'I don't think it's something
that you go out and buy for yourself'. She elaborates:

Lucy: I think it's stuff you buy as, buy as presents and it's in things like Clinton Cards
and Paper Tree [gift shops].
VM: Yea.
Lucy: And sort of in gift shops where you associate with buying presents for special
occasions that's where you find most of the things.
VM: Yea, yea.
Lucy: I actually, I think you wouldn't buy it for yourself, you'd buy it for someone
else.

There are a number of ways to understand this last statement. In the assertion that merchandise goods are not to be purchased for oneself is the implication that the value of the object is recognized to be precisely its circulation within a gift economy (see Miller 2000 for a discussion of 'treats'). It is as if merchandised goods make it possible explicitly to acknowledge that what is being marked is the act of giving itself. For some people in some countries, of course, such acts of giving (and getting) are frequent. Indeed, in the experience of many of our interviewees in the UK, the exchange of such little presents is so frequent – and sometimes so arbitrary – as to be almost without logic at all. Rather like the exclamation marks introduced into everyday life by the gifts described by Bourdieu, presents that punctuate the events of day-to-day life, these gifts are simply little tokens or packets of goodwill, and the constancy of their circulation is such that they are often taken for granted. It is almost as if they cannot be avoided. So, for example, in the course of one interview it emerged that the interviewee's collection of Wallace and Gromit merchandise was an almost incidental accumulation:

Liz: It seems strange that I haven't really seen all the [Wallace and Gromit] films but I've got a lot of the stuff.
VM: Yea yea. well I mean that's, that's, that's one of the things I guess um.
Liz: Yea.
VM: So are, like are you a huge fan of the film or is it –
Liz: No I wouldn't say I'm a huge fan of the film.
VM: No.
Liz: But I like the things that go with it. ... I think it's the cuteness of the characters and you see them like the Shaun the Sheep Bag.
VM: Yea.
Liz: And I think, I don't know perhaps an image thing because it's seen to be sort of trendy liking Wallace and Gromit so you see a lot people carrying the Shaun the Sheep bags around.
VM: Yea.
Liz: I think normally if you were carrying a rucksack with a sheep on your back people might look at you a bit strange but you say oh it's Shaun the Sheep from Wallace and Gromit.
VM: But it sounds like maybe the Wallace and Gromit stuff is more or less a coincidence. The, the fact that your brother is probably more into it.
Liz: Yea.
VM: And er –
Liz: I think it was him. Yea, just a coincidence.
VM: Um.
Liz: Yes and it just kind of rubs off.

In this respect, such little presents are not only so ubiquitous as to be almost obscene (Baudrillard 1994), they are also obsequious (Bourdieu 1977). As Bourdieu notes, the term 'obsequium' was used by Spinoza to denote the 'constant will' produced by the conditioning through which 'the State fashions us for its own use and which enables it to survive' (ibid.: 95). Bourdieu adopts the term to designate the public testimonies of recognition that are set up in every group between individuals and the group. Here the term may be seen to apply to the 'constant will' called into being by the taken-for-granted, almost unavoidable availability of free gifts or little presents in (over-)developed consumer societies. Knorr Cetina (2000) describes something similar in her discussion of the ways in which the open-ended object contributes to the emergence of a vagrant, serial, chain-like structure to wanting.

The Pressure of Time

While there is clearly an element of (subjective) will in the culture of circulation described here, and this is partly what animates this system of objects, it is in many respects a will without purpose, that is, there is in part also a kind of (objective) automation. (This is perhaps partly what provokes Rosalind Krauss (1999) to include a discussion of automatism in her discussion of the medium.) This automation is a consequence of the terms of availability, the logic of circulation, of such little presents – that is, of the logic of flows. Their movement is such as to modify, sometimes even to neutralize, the action of time (and the time of action). So, for example, many of the practices of giving and getting we documented do no more than ensure the continuity of interpersonal relations, maintaining the channels of communication, in short, sustaining the flow.

Helen: Because people know that I like it then I get it and obviously if I know them and know they like it I'd do the same, depending who it was.

But more than this, we suggest, an intensive temporality of flow, in which the interval between giving and getting is marked by the logo (see chapter 6), is sometimes superimposed on the recurrences and periodicities of gift-giving, the substantive relations of kin and household and the inheritance of a shared past.

Let us elaborate this claim. Consider a more detailed account of how some of our interviewees came to acquire particular items:

Ashley: So that was when we, we sort of started collecting and I think once, once we got bits and pieces ... I mean I, I mean I've never been one of those that go in shops and say 'ooh that's nice'. I think we've, most of the things that we've got have, we've acquired have been um given, you know sort of trade promotional give-aways but –

VM: Um.

Ashley: Um but our friends and family have, have recognized the fact that we're interested and a lot of the things have been given as gifts.

VM: Oh yea.

Ashley: And it's a sort of you know –

Claire: It's a nice easy thing, isn't it?

Ashley: Yea and that's something that, that will go down well and I think probably half of the, the, the commercial things that are on sale have been given to us as gifts which –

VM: Yeah.

Ashley: Is great.

Historically, authenticity has been one of the most important values realized in the movement of goods. Indeed, Appadurai (1986) argues that the mass production of goods has seen a shift in the regime of value associated with many kinds of exchange. This is a shift from a regime structured in terms of *exclusivity*, where the value of goods was indirectly regulated by the costs of acquisition, to one that is structured by *authenticity*. In this latter regime, value is typically established in relation to an origin – that is, to an individual, an event, organization or place that is established as pre-existing the object or work. The good is then a trace or an index of that individual, event, organization or place. The argument being put forward here is that this regime is being supplemented, if not surpassed, by a regime of value structured in terms of iconicity, or intensive qualities (rather than indexicality). This is a regime in which value is established not in relation to either price (as a mark of exclusivity) or origin (as a mark of authenticity), but in relation to information (that is, as a mark of distinctiveness).

In some of the interviews discussed here, the basis of the value of authenticity (uniqueness or specialness) of goods is recognized but is perceived to be uncertain and held to be easily manipulated and thus undermined. This seems to be because of an awareness of the routine intervention of market mechanisms in the production of an artificial scarcity of goods. This recognition leads to a certain weariness or scepticism as to the specialness – or value – of authenticity:

Ashley: I mean one I got as a gift and one I picked up from the Internet. When they, when Nick Park got the CBE, OBE or whatever he got.

VM: Yea, yea.

Ashley: They produced a fridge magnet of Wallace and Gromit in a top hat and tails going off to the palace which I thought that was you know different and those are the only two we've got. But you know I don't sort of rush into Boots [a UK national retail chain] and go ooh I haven't got that one. ...

Ashley: I mean I don't know whether it was true but it was Aardman sort of said, 'well this is a you know a special thing we've done' which I suppose that word 'special' everybody goes 'ooh I must have that 'cause it's special'. What does it mean 'cause it's special'?

Claire: Limited edition to ten million.

Here, while there is a recognition of the conventional markers of authenticity – the commemorative association of an item with a particular event, an acknowledged indexical link to the author (Nick Park) or producer (Aardman) – such signs are not given any great value: 'what does it mean 'cause it's special?' Significantly, however, another source of value is put forward, and this is to do with the particular temporality of the availability of the 'free gift', as the continuation of this interview indicates:

Ashley: ... Um I suppose some of the give-away collectibles have a certain scarcity 'cause they're on the shelves for a certain amount of time and then they completely disappear.

Claire: We got, got them all over the country as well, didn't we?

Ashley: Yea.

Claire: It was you know various sorts of trips to see people and it was quite an adventure collecting them wasn't it.

Ashley: I think, I think that was, yea I don't know what went with that promotion 'cause it didn't seem to be in all the stores at the same time. I was, sort of when I was um down south and I got them and I, assuming that they would be in every Sainsbury's and Tesco's and it wasn't the case. There, there were some were quite scarce. ... either they were scarce or um the stores weren't stocking them, so um when we did see them we sort of look right we've got, we're, we're, we've got a Wallace, we've got a Gromit, can you see a Preston [another character, but also the name of a town in the north of England] or whatever, um and I think there, there was a certain scarcity value about that and I suppose that in a way that there isn't about some of the ... things that are on sale cause they're you know they don't seem to have that. You know they're all, there's no sort of time pressure on them. If they run out one week they'll be back again.

In this elaboration, the interviewee presents the value of the free gift or promotion – in contrast to the commodity – in terms of its restricted availability ('then they completely disappear' as opposed to 'if they run out one week they'll be back again'). And while this value is described in terms of scarcity, this is not a scarcity that is marked by price, but is rather to do with an irregular periodicity, the manipulation of temporal pressure or a temporal logic of circulation.

On the one hand, free gifts – and merchandise goods given as gifts – are something for nothing, extras, freebies. For some people, they are something that no one really wants enough to buy for themselves, not 'goods' at all, and individuals must exercise restraint if such little presents are not to multiply without limit. They are not so much free gifts as give-aways, as even devoted fans acknowledge:

Ashley: Um and in fact no, not as far as fridge magnet collection goes I think you know we've got –

Claire: Quite restrained really.

Ashley: We've got two and some ones that come with cards.

At the same time as being unpredictably available, such free gifts or promotional goods are almost unavoidable. Anything and everyone may be included in the movements described here. Or to put all this another way, in their movements, such goods create and reinforce binding yet symbolically attenuated social relationships, a flow in which it is as if individuals are 'compulsorily included' (Barry 2001: 112). It is in this sense that one might describe them as junk. 'Junk is the "ideal product" because the "junk merchant does not sell his product to the consumer, he sells the consumer to his product"' (Hayles 1999: 272).

On the other hand, sometimes these gifts acquire value, not in relation to price, or an origin, but in relation to the conditions of their availability, that is, in relation to the flows of mediation. In these cases, what gives something value is not its persistent or permanent availability (albeit for a price, as is the case with the commodity), but, rather, its restricted availability, or more precisely, its availability at a particular time in a particular place for a particular person ('everyone doesn't want something ...'). So, for example, while a free gift may be given away as a matter of course with other purchases – a packet of breakfast cereal, a box of tea-bags, or a McDonald's meal – it is a matter of chance which one of a range of linked gifts will actually be acquired by a particular individual, or even whether the stock available in a particular retail outlet will be linked to such marketing. This indeterminacy adds a certain kind of 'adventure' to the processes of getting and giving: as the interviewee above says, the promotion wasn't in all the stores at the same time: particular items were hard to find.

Flows of Disjuncture and Difference

But what is the particular temporal logic at issue here? In the case discussed above, the terms of availability of the promotional gift are identified in contrast with the temporal constancy of the commodity, the more or less predictable 'limited edition of ten million'. In this comparison, the commodity 'has no time pressure'. In other words, as it is presented here, the consumer commodity market is such as to ensure the persistent, predictable – almost permanent – availability of consumer goods (for a price). In contradistinction, the free gifts described here have a time pressure. This time pressure is an indication that the value of the thing is determined by the role it plays in an open-ended system (or series) in which it is a small part. Of course, most branded products, including those of Nike and Swatch, are not available as free gifts. Branded products have a price (and 'free' gifts themselves are of course usually attached to commodities with a price); that is, they must be purchased by someone (if not the final recipient) as (sometimes expensive) commodities.[2] But, so we suggest, this is not what gives either free gifts or branded products their specific value in the flows of the global culture industry (which, we want to stress, is not to say that price does not matter). What gives both free gifts and branded products value, what makes them special, are the temporal and spatial conditions of their accessibility for someone, their occurrence in a culture of circulation. Consider an example here:

K: These have been a favourite and they're a really popular shoe as well because everyone doesn't want something that's too in your face, that's too over the top. Nobody wants to stand out too much, but at the same time you want to be wearing something that's with the fashion, that's simple, but makes a statement. So that's why I think the simpler trainers, even Adidas, even these look quite fancy. It's just a simple white shoe, but the sole and stripes make it stand out. These were in about, I think it was last year they came out but they're not as popular now. Well I think they are with certain groups, but students I know they tend to go for the more retro kind of shoe.

While many brands aspire to be ubiquitous, their manifestations – and this may be as products, promotions or events – are often unpredictable and discontinuous for any particular person. Such discontinuities open up space for possible interventions.

If we take the first of our two biographies of brands, Swatch is both artful and systematic about its manipulation of conditions of availability, drawing on mechanisms of production and distribution long established in the culture industry. As such, in its intent, at least, it falls within the continuum described by Moulin between those goods that 'combine the manipulation of signs of authentic rarity with [those that involve the] manipulation of rarity'. The aim of such strategies is, 'on the one hand, to establish a certain type of rarity as artistic and, on the other, to create artificially the rarity of what has been established as artistic' (Moulin, quoted in Miege 1989: 43). Most important among these methods historically has been the author function (Foucault 1976; Lury 1993), an operation by which the value of a work or object is produced as originality or authenticity in relation to a subject, or author. So, for example, a set of watches designed by commissioned artists is described in the following terms in *The Swatch World Journal*:

Six artists with very different aims and styles have applied their favorite themes to a Swatch product. And here's the result: for the third Swatch The Artists Collection, three multicolor watches and three in black and white. Each model will be produced in a series of only 50,000 and will be sold in a special pack. There will also be a limited number of collectors' presentation cases containing all six models.

Compare the career strategies of two of the sales staff in the LA Niketown we met in 1997. The assistant we met in the basketball section is called Jarvis, and he is effusive in his praise for Nike, both as an employee and as a consumer. His admiration, one might almost say devotion, to Nike is expressed most cogently when he claims that Nike is 'seventeen years' ahead of its rival Reebok. Such loyalty is clearly understandable in terms of an employee's acceptance of the corporate philosophy of Nike as a way to get on, to get ahead. Indeed, he tells us that he wants to get on, to move to London to work in the Niketown there (he says this before the store at Oxford Circus has opened). When we visit again – on a Sunday – we encounter a lot of business studies and marketing students working there on a part-time basis to support their studying. Most say that work experience at Nike is a good career move. But it is also personal, at least for Jarvis. He says that when he was a child he always wanted Nike trainers; that he had quarrels with his parents, when they wanted to buy him cheaper shoes. He now has about twenty pairs of Nike shoes; even before he worked in the store he had owned five or six pairs. Another assistant we speak to, on the other hand, is almost ahead of himself, he is so fast. Papa is entrepreneurial and charming, telling us that normally assistants have to do two months training, but that he only needed to do five days. What is important in his selling philosophy is talking to people. When we raise the plans for a London store, he makes it clear that it is not simply the stock in Europe that is out of date for him, but Europe altogether. Instead – originally from Senegal – he is teaching himself Japanese; and he shows us how to write his name in Japanese.

Further restrictions to availability are formalized in the Swatch Club, whose 'benefits' include 'VIP invitation to events', 'Limited edition Club Special', 'Extra chance for Swatch Specials' and 'Swatch merchandise'. The letter welcoming new members in 1998 promises: 'Now you're part of the exciting world of Swatch, you will receive all the latest information you need to keep you one step ahead – from special events to special editions – as a member you'll be in the know from day one! Happy Swatching!'

Other brands also restrict the availability of products, although perhaps in a less orderly fashion.[3] Alongside the compulsive innovation of a yearly cycle in which there may be as many as four seasons, Adidas recently reissued a 1984 shoe in very limited numbers (600 pairs in the UK). In 1996, Reebok trickled out 5,000 pairs of 'The Question', a $100 name shoe, before releasing an initial shipment of 250,000. Later that year, Converse distributed limited numbers (300,000) of a shoe: 'The brand needs life injected into it. ... We want edge and image. Market share will come with that' (Jim Solomon, head of marketing, quoted in Vanderbilt 1998: 73). Nike routinely distribute only limited numbers of Air Jordans to keep customers waiting and wanting. Additionally, Nike is said (but refuses to acknowledge officially) to 'probe' the market, by letting it be known, by word of mouth, that a very small number of a certain kind of shoe (perhaps no more than three or four pairs) will be available at a certain retail outlet. In early 2001 Nike sought to tantalize its most avid consumers; it was promising, but not yet delivering, a shoe designed in collaboration with Junya Watanabe of Comme des Garçons. It had only been sighted 'in Japan and on the web (<www.mars.dti.ne.jp/~motonike /index.html#new>)' (Hill 2000: 9). 'In 2004, police threatened to shut down a specialist trainer store called Nort 235 on New York's Lower East Side, as it seemed that trouble was brewing. Word had got out that Nort 235 was to be the first store to stock Nike's Lucky 7 Dunk Hi Pro SB, which had a limited run of 777 pairs' (Davis 2005: 22). Recently, Adidas redesigned a version of the Superstar shoe to commemorate the thirty-fifth anniversary of its launch, with thirty-five limited-edition styles being manufactured and distributed to specialist shops, with the caveat that they would go on sale simultaneously on 1 January 2005. The retail price was £150; within the week, one pair had been sold on eBay for £600 (ibid.: 21).

In this open system of goods, points of access to brands such as Nike and Swatch include not simply the point of purchase of particular products, or even associated advertising and promotion, but also 'special' events, such as openings, competitions, launches, visits and performances. Take, for example, the Swatch-sponsored visit of Nike-sponsored athlete Michael Johnson to the Swatch store in Cologne in December 1996 to promote a watch named after him. The visit was written up in *Swatch News* and supplemented by an interview with the athlete, providing a further point of access.

Nike, in particular, is well known for such events. Opportunities to participate in the brand include advertising on television, in the streets or in magazines, sports events themselves and their broadcasting, product placement in films (from *She's Gotta Have It* to *Forrest Gump*) and interviews with celebrities in magazines and on television. Additionally, however, Nike is also visible in reports of unplanned events, as when it was reported that the members of the southern California's Heaven's Gate cult were all found dead in matching black Nikes in the summer of 1997. Less dramatically, but still strikingly, the Nike logo, the Swoosh, is to be seen, lovingly hand-painted, on the back of many vehicles in Cuba, despite, or perhaps because of, the US embargo on the export of goods there. In contrast, Swatch is a legitimate presence in Cuba, but is more or less confined to the international corner of Havana airport. (See chapter 6 for a brief discussion of the presence of both brands in Brazil.)

Crookedtongues.com is a sneaker information site set up by Russell Williamson in 1999; it receives 10,000 hits a week. Williamson has since gone on to set up a creative agency called Unorthodox Styles, whose clients include Nike and the Home Office. (Davis 2005: 22)

In the early 1990s, British entrepreneurs started to import discontinued lines from the US. 'We used to go to close-out merchants in Miami, Louisiana, Staten Island, tons of places', says Richard Wharton, who is now managing director of Offspring, the London-based specialist sneaker chain. 'We'd buy up Nike Wimbledon, Adidas Trimm-Trab, whatever was around at the time. I was buying Puma Clydes for $4 and selling them for £45.' Now reissued styles are often Nike and Adidas's biggest money-spinners. 'It took them a long time to realise, though', says Wharton. 'It was like turning a boat around in the Suez Canal'. (Ibid.: 24)

Whatever the intent, the outcome of the strategies of both Swatch and Nike is not the artificial limitation of products in relation to artistic notions of uniqueness, authenticity or special-ness. Rather, it is the multiplication of points of access to an open-ended system of products, events and experiences distributed in discontinuous time and space. This system, we suggest, is based on pattern and randomness (that is, of organized but open-ended relations between products, advertising, events and so on), rather than presence and absence (that is, either some specific product – or person – being in a particular time or place or not) (Hayles 1999; Lury 2004). It is what organizes the movement of the products of the global (culture) industry – mediated things and thingified media – as flows of disjuncture and difference (Appadurai 1996). Fundamental to this kind of system is the recognition that 'an infusion of noise into a system can cause it to reorganize at a higher level of complexity':

Within such a system, pattern and randomness are bound together in a complex dialectic that makes them not so much opposites as complements or supplements to one another. Each helps to define the other; each contributes to the flow of information through the system. (Hayles 1999: 260)

Sometimes randomness is introduced deliberately (as appears to be the case for Nike), but what is significant is that in any case it is inevitable as the introduction of a strategy at one level is radically transformed in unpredictable ways at others. Indeed, brands such as Nike and Swatch rely – to some extent at least – upon this transformation as they monitor and respond to the unintended effects of their products in use. Elements of an (un)controlled event will be used – via a process of intuition, interpretation or scientific analysis – into a new direction of product planning and development as the brand mutates as it evolves. Hayles writes:

Pattern can be recognized through redundancy or repetition of elements. If there is only repetition, however, no new information is imparted; the intermixture of randomness rescues pattern from sterility. If there is only randomness, the result is gibberish rather than communication. Information is produced by a complex dance between predictability and unpredictability, repetition and variation. ... Mutation is crucial because it names the bifurcation point at which the interplay between pattern and randomness causes the system to evolve in a new direction. (1999: 265)

What we observed is an open system of goods, a system in which the value or meaning of any particular item – free gift or expensive branded product – is understood in terms of 'a difference that makes a difference'. This is, of course, Gregory Bateson's 'deceptively simple' definition of information (Malik 2005; Bateson 2000 [1972]). It is introduced here as a way of understanding the value produced in the movements of the flows of the global culture industry. As Suhail Malik (2005) so succinctly shows, while information has been widely understood as inimical to meaning or value (Lyotard 1984), it is not necessarily so. Malik argues that the information conveyed in a system as regards its transmission depends on the system as a whole *at the time in which the transmission is taking place*. This is a radically relational determination of information.

This invites questions: a difference in what (What are you paying attention to?), about what (What matters?), for whom (Who is asking, who is affected?). Asking these questions leads us to focus on the knower, a knower who always has a particular history, social location and point of view. (Oyama 2000: 147, quoted in Malik 2005: 33)

In relation to the open systems described here, the information provided by price retains its meaning (it is important because it contributes to availability and the stratification of consumption), but it is not the difference that makes a difference. Similarly, the meaning or value of authenticity fails to register, because it is intrinsic to the system (it is an index of something that pre-exists, such as an author or a place of origin), and does not require any alteration in the established structure, organization or memory of the system. Instead, what we are calling distinctiveness is produced in – and produces – a system that is temporalized; the difference that makes a difference is an event. As such, it is recognized as having a distinctive value.[4] An event is what produces a time pressure, or, as Malik puts it, a 'before' and an 'after', either for the system itself – as (a brand) experience – or for an observer, that is, the consumer, as communication, as an emotional message, as 'adventure'. In this sense, distinctiveness is not opposed to meaning, but is rather 'a vector of meaning's transmutations' (Malik 2005). It is what makes something – free gift or branded product – 'more than just what it is'; it is one way to realize value as difference.

The Properties of Circulation

But while the temporal logic of flows has been described here as openended, this does not mean that it is open to all: while users may acquire goods as personal possessions (as toys, as collector's items, as cult objects, as functional things), the brand is not their property. The flows entangle users in snares. In this regard, consider the current legal definition of trademark: 'any sign capable of being represented graphically which is capable of distinguishing the goods or services of one undertaking from those of other undertakings' (TMA 1994, s 1(1)). In adopting a role in the development of a sign such that it may function as a trademark, the law implicates itself in what we have called the mediation of things.[5] And, as the following discussion outlines, this role involves deciding whether and how a sign recognized as a trademark is capable of distinguishing goods or services, that is, precisely, of acting as a mark of distinctiveness.

A number of recent shifts in trademark law are relevant here, of which three will be considered (see Lury 2004 for further discussion of trademark law in relation to brands). The first concerns the kind of signs recognized in law as capable of being trademarks. In the USA, the Lanham Act of 1946 has for a long time provided protection for a diverse range of symbols, including, among other things, sounds, smells, numeric radio frequencies and alpha-numeric telephone numbers. But in the UK it was not until the 1994 Act that smells, sounds, colours, gestures or movements, as well as catch-phrases, names and three-dimensional shapes, could be registered as intellectual property. This first shift expands the kind of signs that may be the subject of trademark law in the UK, enhancing the possibility that qualitative intensities that characterize icons may be recognized in law as signs.

In a second change to the action of trademark law, there has been an expansion in the range of goods and services that a sign recognized as a trademark may take as its object. Until recently, the originator of a mark was unlikely to be able to control the use of a mark in relation to products in different trade classifications of goods (either by retaining exclusive use or by licensing its use). This was because it was held there was unlikely to be confusion as to the origin of trade if a similar sign was used to mark, for example, T-shirts and a film or a television series. However, following the so-called Ninja Turtles case (*Mirage Studios* v. *Counter-Feat Clothing* (1991)), the application of a mark across classes of goods can now be prevented by the originator of the sign, under the law of passing off, if that originator has a business selling the right to use the sign. This bolsters the value of a sign recognized as a mark in relation to the possibilities of licensing or merchandising. The plaintiffs in this case licensed the reproduction of fictitious cartoon characters, the 'Teenage Mutant Ninja Turtles', but did not manufacture any goods themselves. The defendant made drawings of turtle characters using the concept but not copying the plaintiff's drawings, and licensed them for use on clothing. The plaintiff sued for copyright infringement and passing off. The court held that there was a case to answer in passing off on the grounds that the public would be aware of the licensing industry and would assume a connection between the plaintiff and the defendant. This second shift secures legitimacy in law for a more or less unlimited transference of the sign, a legitimacy that supports the growth of licensing and the associated practices of merchandising.[6] As earlier chapters indicate, such practices are more and more central to the global culture industry.

A third change is the movement away from a 'confusion' definition of infringement (as to the origin of the product) towards a broader 'dilution' definition, which precludes all unauthorized uses that would lessen (or take advantage of) the mark's distinctiveness. It used to be the case that trademark infringement would only be found where the use of a protected mark by someone (X) other than its owner (Y) was likely to cause consumers to be confused as to the origin of the product to which the mark was attached. The issue was whether consumers would think that X's product actually came from Y; that is, it was an issue related to authenticity. Now it is increasingly being suggested – with varying degrees of success – that if X's use of Y's signs on its product causes consumers to be reminded of Y on seeing X's product, even while knowing that X and Y are distinct traders, infringement has occurred. In other words, what is emerging is legal protection for the use of a sign that does not have to rely on a privileged relation to an origin (as is the case with the object of copyright), but is developed through the creation of associations. The development of such signs is becoming established as the exclusive prerogative of the trademark owner: associations created by other producers can be legally prevented. In this way, the value of distinctiveness in an open system can be made subject to legal monopoly.

In sum, recent shifts in trademark law increase the range of intensities of the signs recognized in law, extend the terms of exclusive ownership and control to signs created through association, and support the unlimited transference of signs in such a way as to support and protect practices of licensing, merchandising and franchising. As a consequence, trademark law is growing in relevance to the global culture industry, and contributes to the emergence of a regime of value organized in terms of distinctiveness. Intellectual property law thus increasingly makes possible an exclusive monopoly of not simply a static sign, but of a sign that is an entry into, an opening onto, a flow of things; trademark is as – if not more – important than copyright to the accumulation of capital in the global culture industry.

The Logic and Practice of Flows

In documenting the terms of the circulation of our selected objects here, then, we are suggesting that ordinary, everyday or generic uses of goods are continually being undercut – or overridden – by the culture of circulation we describe above. On the one hand, this dynamic is such that the mediation of things can be seen as the production of a kind of planned waste, or junk, while their communication is continually on the verge of degenerating into noise. But this communication may also be perceived as creating distinctiveness, a difference that makes a difference. On the other hand then, our analysis suggests that although what might be called the informationalization of culture (Lash 2002) does not preclude meaningful or subjective relations, it does transform them. Our argument is that global flows are one of the factors making the production of locality – as a structure of feeling, a property of social life and an ideology of situated community – increasingly difficult, but not impossible. We do not believe that flows of cultural goods simply move through specific places untransformed or untransforming (see Appadurai 1996: 188–99). Instead, global flows are both constituted in and constitutive of 'local' occasions and events such as self-identity, family and community, but at the same time, a new logic is superimposed. The general effect is that a vertical form of the transmission of substances, organized in terms of product durability, inheritance and a fixity of domestic capital is overlaid by the flux of a horizontal movement of things, a global fluidity in which the relations between ideas and stuff, substance and sociality, space and time are constantly being redrawn. Global flows thus add to, as well as take away from, the intensive and implosive practices in which locality is produced.

This exploration of the logic of flows may be further elaborated through a consideration of the temporality of practice. There are two interrelated issues here. The first is the extent to which the modification of the role of the interval or delay between objects or products in global flows contributes to the displacement of an aesthetics of duration by one of ephemerality (Appadurai 1996). Our argument has been that the mediation of things does not simply contribute to a displacement of durability by ephemerality, of the durable by the deliberately obsolescent. Instead, we suggest that the constitution of the value of objects, such as the brand in terms of distinctiveness, is a means by which the temporality of consumption is endlessly multiplied and divided, resulting in an 'unlimited finitude' of occasions of giving and getting, the interpenetration of patterns and randomness. Thus, in contrast to Bourdieu's view that little presents 'draw the continuous out of the discontinuous, as mathematicians do, through infinite multiplication of the infinitely small' (1977), we argue that it is the fractal geometry of an open system of events that emerges in the movements of the global culture industry.

The second issue we want to address here is the extent to which the processes of exchange and circulation described in this chapter modify the functioning of the interval between giving and getting that Bourdieu argues is constitutive of agency itself. For Bourdieu, the interval between giving and getting, the gift and the counter-gift, is fundamental to 'the deliberate oversight, the collectively maintained and approved self-decep-tion without which symbolic exchange, a fake circulation of fake coin, could not operate' (ibid.). For Bourdieu, gift-giving is a scheme which 'works itself only in and through time'; and it is the interval – the delay and difference in practice – which makes possible strategy, the manipula-tion of the tempo of the action. Indeed, this temporal modulation is the essence of practice for Bourdieu. Thus he argues that the passage from highest probability to absolute certainty that a gift will be reciprocated is 'a qualitative leap which is not proportionate to the numerical gap' (ibid.: 9). It is the reduction of this qualitative leap to a quantitative calculation which is at the root of Simmel's discussion of the cultural consequences of money (1990). But what we describe here is a transformation in what Bourdieu calls the partial operations of 'a probablist logic'.

Such a logic is hard to describe. Agnes Heller, theorist of everyday life, elaborates perhaps one of the most comprehensive accounts of an every-day notion of probability (see also de Certeau 1998). She describes the objective basis of action in everyday life as being based on a probability provided by 'habit and repetition' (1984: 168). This notion of probability can 'extend from action based on nothing more than impulse, to action based on moral reflection or on calculation', to action based on 'belief' (ibid.: 170). But this heterogeneously orchestrated everyday probability is increasingly, in the descriptions presented above, supplemented (although perhaps not supplanted) by an additional logic of pattern and randomness, the distinctions of waste, of junk. On the one hand, this non-linear logic creates value in the production and recognition of dis-tinctiveness, the difference that makes a difference, and thus goes some way to overcoming what Heller describes as 'the rough treatment of the singular case' in everyday life. On the other hand, in the ubiquity and arbitrariness of its movements, it often results in the orchestration of the merely 'possible'. Heller herself observes: '[a]ction undertaken for no bet-ter reason than it is *possible* is not a reliable guide in the business of every-day living: it lands us in too many catastrophes of everyday life' (ibid.: 168). However, it seems that the (over-)production of the merely possible is as good a guide as any to the business conduct of the global culture industry (and may help explain why it is that nine out of every ten new products are said to fail). It is what underpins the neutralization of agency and banalization of contemporary culture.

What has further been suggested here is that the delay that Bourdieu identifies as so vital to practice has been the site of systematic intervention such that the global culture industry contributes to the functioning not of a collective symbolic exchange, but of a ubiquitous, dispersed non-purposive will. However, it is also argued that this will, while without purpose, is not without intent (it may still be meaningful). In this regard, it is helpful to consider Gadamer's description of play in terms of non-purposive rationality (see also our earlier discussions of play in chapter 5). Gadamer maintains that the movement that characterizes play is not tied down to any goal (it is, in his words, 'self-movement'), but this does not mean that it is not intended: 'the end pursued is certainly a non-purposive activity, but this activity is intended. It is what the play intends' (1993: 23). On the one hand, insofar as we play, we participate in excess, a superabundance, and in this excess we may outplay the capacity for purposive rationality. Or to put this another way, insofar as we lose ourselves in play, we may find 'something more'. On the other hand, while the player may be able to project his or her presence beyond the limits of his or her body in play (he or she occupies a multiply mediated space and time), this engagement is increasingly subject to 'arbitrary, imperative, and purposely tedious conventions' (Caillois 1961: 13).

Nevertheless, we may further speculate that the play at issue here is compelling for many of its players because it provides a meta-communicative frame. Thus Bateson (2000) points out that play acts as a frame which both organizes relations internal to an activity and instructs the player not to extend these (particular) premises of self-organization to the ground or environment which surrounds it. Yet, the paradox of play is that this delimiting may itself be redefined in the playing out of play. As he puts it, in play, map and territory may be both equated and discriminated. It may be that the peculiar holding power of the open system of objects – the global culture industry – described here is its ability to draw the subject into a constantly transmuting flow, an intensely dynamic (and dynamically intense) relationship between map and territory. In the provocation to play, the objects of the global culture industry tantalize our capacity to deal with wholes and parts, continuity and discontinuity, synchrony and succession (Gell 1998). They extend and disrupt the space and time in which we move. They are the media of flow, a culture of circulation in which we are entangled, sometimes snared.

8 Culture Industry in Brazil: Image, Market, Display

Introduction

In Brazil, only a few European movies are shown on terrestrial television, although a greater number are shown by HBO Brazil, a cable television channel.[1] The company was established in the early 1990s. It pays HBO in New York for the use of the brand name (HBO), and has 'the licence to operate HBO in Brazil'. HBO New York, Sony, Warner and Buena Vista are all part owners of the station, and HBO Brazil has an agreement by which it can show their films.[2] But HBO is majority owned by TVA – or, as it is commonly known, Abril, a magazine and cable TV dynasty owned by Robert Civita, which together with the company Globo until 2004 shared the cable market in Brazil. Apart from HBO, TVA's pay channels include Cinemax (also an HBO channel), the Euro Channel, the Sony and Warner channels, ESPN, VNN and CNN-Espagnol.

We interviewed Angela Jesus at the HBO Brazil headquarters in Rio. HBO Brazil is a large operation, with 150 staff. Jesus is number two to Rubens Edward Filho, the channel's Director of Programming and Production. Filho, a long-time movie critic, has worked in cinema for some thirty years. He shares responsibility for deciding what HBO Brazil will buy rights to broadcast with a Miami based HBO-Brazil executive called Robert Rios, who runs the Acquisitions Department. Filho attends film festivals – Cannes, Sundance, Venice, and Berlin – while Rios attends the markets for independent films, the most important of which are Milan's MIFED (Mercato Internazionale del Film e del Documentario) and AMFA (American Film Market) in Los Angeles. HBO Brazil negotiated exclusive pay-TV rights to both *Trainspotting* and the Wallace and Gromit films in Brazil. They showed each of these some eight to ten times. The pay-TV rights for *Trainspotting* were bought from André Sturm at Pandora, who had bought rights to theatre distribution and distribution to pay and free-to-air TV. Angela Jesus says of Sturm: 'Not all of his films but a lot of his films come to HBO. We have a kind of agreement. It's a "free" agreement but it works. We can buy his movies and he always has good films. He has "the window". We had [*Trainspotting*] on cable. Now it can be on free TV.' Some Miramax-distributed films are shown on HBO:[3] sometimes via Brazilian distributor Lumière, sometimes as a consequence of direct contacts with Miramax. HBO Brazil showed *The English Patient* ('did well') and *Jackie Brown* ('only did OK'). *Trainspotting* 'did a bit like Jackie Brown'. Angela Jesus says that Filho saw Wallace and Gromit 'at a festival probably. He knows everything about animation.' He 'knew the product'. HBO has 'always done some product from the BBC. They [the BBC] would say: "Well, look at this, it's very interesting. I'll send you a tape." We have this kind of relationship with the BBC.' 'André gets the rights and then he phones you and says, "Do you want it?"' With *Trainspotting*, 'Ruben had already seen the film: "Got to have it on HBO".' HBO and Rios buy packages from distributors.[4]

Toy Story was not on sale for showing on HBO, as it was the property of the Disney Channel (although Touchstone and Hollywood Pictures productions, owned by Disney, are shown on HBO). Disney Channel Brazil was launched in April 2001, as a Portuguese-speaking channel, with some local content. This was nine months after the launch of Spanish-speaking Latin American Disney. Previously, television viewing of Disney cartoon films was possible on DirectTV, a pay-per-view cable channel that has a contract with Disney. Studio Disney has only five or six employees in Brazil. Buena Vista International does all international distribution for Disney. In Argentina, Buenos Aires-based Buena Vista Home Entertainment does video distribution. In Brazil, Buena Vista has sold rights to exclusive video distribution to Abril Video, and distributes only to theatres directly. For both theatre and video, the distribution company allies with an advertising company. In *Toy Story*'s case, the marketing and advertising campaign was developed by the Brazilian agency, Giovanni Comunicações. The nationwide release was of eighty prints.

Jacqueline Lee of Abril Video works with the marketing manager of Buena Vista Home Entertainment in Buenos Aires, Argentina (that is, not with Buena Vista International in Brazil) to discuss market strategies and target audiences. Disney animations, she notes, have a much higher video:theatre ratio than films from other majors. They are the unchallenged leader of the sell-through video market; indeed most of their video revenues come from sell-through. Video products are divided into classics, cartoons and direct-to-video, with each category having a certain per cent of royalty. *Toy Story* was uniquely sell-through; in 1998 there was no rental. 'The video did better than theatrical, though theatrical box office was really good.' The Abril Group has had a long relationship with Disney (although it is also a licensee for Fox, HBO and others). Indeed Abril's first magazine, brought out in the 1940s, was *Donald Duck*. Disney was 'aware of Abril's professionalism and achievements in other areas'. For *Toy Story* and other Disney merchandising there is an exclusive licensing[5] office in Brazil. This is Walt Disney Co. Brazil. Ana Silvia Stabel is Marketing Director of this small office. *Toy Story*, she says, did not have substantial merchandising sales of products in Brazil. This was because, as elsewhere, the scale of the success of the film was a surprise to Disney, so plans for importing the toys were late. 'The success of *Toy Story* surprised Disney: they were not sure an audience would like a computer-animated movie.' But 'Brazilian critics commented on the quality of the story's script. ... Adults were captivated by the computer animation: children by the story.'

Three Stages in the History of the Brazilian Culture Industry

In Latin America, and in emerging economies worldwide, the culture industry is vastly different from Anglo-Saxon and even Continental European media regimes. It is much more closely tied to the state and to politics. Historically, there has been what might be characterized, very schematically, as a three-stage model, outlined here with a special focus on Brazil, the national-territorial focus of this chapter. In an initial stage, the Latin American culture industry – especially radio and fledgling television – was tied on the one hand to the state and on the other to the large American broadcasting companies, notably NBC and CBS. In Brazil in 1931, for example, a government decree gave the state the right to regulate broadcasting services in the national interest and set up licensing procedures, defining the rights and obligations of licence holders. The most powerful network to emerge was Diários e Emissoras Associados (Associated Dailies and Broadcasters), with five stations, twelve newspapers and a magazine. The Diários network was to persist as Brazil's largest media firm until the end of the 1960s. The second early large network was Radio Bandeirantes, set up by the group of Raul Machado de Carvalho in 1940.

The second stage in the Latin American culture industry runs more or less parallel to Fordism in Europe and North America, that is, to mass production and mass consumption. Given this context, the idea of a national economy – and the building of national identity – is of far greater importance in Latin America.[6] In 1962, a Telecommunications Code – adapted from a framework deriving from a series of industrial codes beginning in 1953 – was proposed. The Code gave licensing guarantees to particular broadcasters. It centralized telecom services under federal government (Fox 1997: 57), and it specified that there could be no contractual agreements between Brazil's private media and foreign capital. This provision was formally rescinded only in June 2002, although it had commonly been violated before. It was during this second stage that every state telephone company – in the twenty-seven Brazilian states – became part of the federal holding company – Telebras. Further, a state telecommunications fund was set up, with revenues coming from a 30 per cent tax on all communications services. Meanwhile, in the private sector the TV Tupi network also began to develop. By the early 1960s it comprised thirty-one newspapers including *O Jornal do Rio de Janeiro*, eighteen television channels, thirty-six radio stations, a news agency, an advertising agency and a lifestyle weekly, *O Cruzeiro*, Latin America's most popular magazine until 1967. Diários' chief executive was then Jao Salom, who was also head of the broadcasters' trade association. In Argentina, television was nationalized by Juan Domingo Perón in 1973, while a substantial part of Mexican television was nationalized in the 1970s.

Popular unrest and street demonstrations led to the military assumption of power in Brazil in 1964. The military gave a licence to the private sector company Globo for Channel 4 in 1965 and TV Globo was born.[7] Globo was the third large group to enter into Brazilian national television. Roberto Marinho – Globo CEO – had entered into a five-year US$5 million contractual relation with Time-Life in 1962. The company's production and transmission technology was thus of a far higher quality than their competitors, as was the programming professionalism. However, the award of this licence was still popularly seen as unconstitutional. The broadcasters' trade association and parliament itself protested. The military, however, turned a blind eye. By now the Brazilian economic 'miracle' was in full swing, with growth of 6 or 7 per cent per year. Between 1964 and 1984 the national product increased fourfold, although in the same period of time the proportion of national income earned by the lower 50 per cent of earners decreased by some one-third. The Minister of Finance from 1967 to 1974, Delfin Neto, adopted a policy of supporting champions in particular sectors thereby promoting economic concentration, while the military embarked upon a programme of national integration. This included the vast expansion of a telecom infrastructure through Embratel.

The close relation with Globo gave the government control of both national integration and expansion in broadcasting. Globo broadcast an image of stability and national integration, paid for by credits from state banks, fiscal exemptions, co-productions with state organizations and state advertising. In 1968 the government invested in microwave relay stations and also, incrementally, began to put money into satellite reception and transmission (Fox 1997: 59). Now all receivers in the country could receive TV Globo. The state was less charitable to other networks. Carvalho's Excelsior lost its licence in 1970, while Tupi went bankrupt in 1980. In contrast, between 1970 and 1980 Globo grew in size to three television channels and forty-six affiliates; the group also came to include a publishing house, a video-tape producer, an art gallery and Fundação Roberto Marinho.

As Benedict Anderson (1991) notes, the much earlier European building of an imagined community in Europe had its basis in the press and literature. But, in Latin America, the culture industry – which in Horkheimer and Adorno's sense was national – involves, unlike in Europe or the USA, not primarily newspapers and telephony, but electronic broadcasting. In the second stage of the culture industry as described above, for example, there was a rapid growth in national markets. Ownership of TV sets spread quickly (if not to the same levels as in Europe): in 1980, at the height of this second stage in Brazil, there were 97 TV sets per 1,000 inhabitants; in 1996, there were 204 (Fox and Waisbord 2002: 12). In Latin America, then, the building of an imagined (national) community takes place via radio and television, that is, Latin American imagined communities are primarily televisual imagined communities. Culture-at-a-distance (Thompson 1995) in Latin America is neither primarily print-based (newspaper readership is low), nor is it interactive or communicational (telephony was notoriously slow in developing). It is instead a question of sounds and images. Only with the Internet does this seem to be changing, but the Internet is part of a third stage, the emergence of *global* culture industry.

This third stage is born in a wider economic policy shift from import substitution to neoliberalism. With few exceptions, early Latin American television and radio followed the US model of private ownership. The telecommunication operators, on the other hand, were state owned, on a European model. In the age of the global culture industry, this is reversed: now, the previously state-owned telecommunications sector has become more vulnerable to takeover by foreign capital than has television. This takeover has happened through a combination of foreign direct investment, and the selling of equity. It has involved borrowing in fixed income securities – in bond markets from foreign banks – to the point that foreign operators commonly have become majority equity holders. In recent years, this foreign investment has mainly been European,[8] yet overall, in Brazil and elsewhere in Latin America, the total value of assets held by US firms is still substantially higher than that of European countries. At the same time, a *clientelistic* media regime has developed in many Latin American countries, with little public accountability. Broadcasting licences are given out directly by government ministries – by the Minister of the Interior in Mexico, the Minister of Posts and Telecommunications in Argentina and the Minister of Communications in Brazil. Licensing and regulation are closely tied to political favours handed out by the government of the day. Politicians or ex-politicians, for example, at the turn of this century owned 94 of 302 Brazilian television stations (Fox and Waisbord 2002: 10). This absence of broadcasting independence stands in contrast with the arms-length regulatory regimes developed in North America and Northern Europe. Yet alongside and intersecting with such clientelism is a growing regional transnationalization in which key geopolitical players – notably Mexico and Brazil – produce content and export it to the region as a whole whilst simultaneously acquiring interests in the media in smaller Latin American countries.[9]

Thus this third stage sees, on the one hand, European and US inroads in national telecommunications and non-terrestrial broadcasting in Latin America, and, on the other, an internal Latin American geopolitical economy in terrestrial TV. In the first case there is European and US technology (and finance);[10] in the second, Latin American content. In the former development, the role of banks, such as Citigroup and Spanish banks alongside the operators, whether in telephony, cable or satellite, is increasingly important; in the latter, there is highly developed and regional national content, including music and television production such as soaps, as well as advertising. This distinction between technology and content, however, is increasingly complicated. The national newspapers *Estado de São Paulo* and *Folha de São Paulo* have, for example, acquired mobile operators (Fox and Waisbord 2002: 14). The largest ISPs (Internet service providers) are, first, UOL, a joint venture of Folha and broadcaster Abril, and, second, Terra, owned by Globo. In the absence of a national telecommunications champion (as in most Western cases), the newspapers and broadcasters have moved into broadband connection and mobile telephony. Their ability to do so is a consequence of their control of national content production: the huge and increasingly high-production-value studios of Globo and Televisa. Indeed, in many ways the Brazilian cultural economy remains the most national of all Latin American countries, just as, in some ways, the USA is the most national of Western countries. The USA exports a large number of programmes. It is the most immune to foreign ownership of the media and to the mass circulation of foreign content, in part because of its huge internal mass market. Brazil, with a population of 182.8 million in 2006, also has a huge internal mass market. Grupo Globo is not quoted on any foreign stock exchanges. It enters into the global culture industry by virtue of being national, of having a national market.

This is not of course to say that United States broadcasting companies have not been powerfully involved in the setting up of the broadcasting industries in Brazil and much of the rest of Latin America. Indeed,

Mexico's principal early media entrepreneur Emilio Azcárraga began his career as a distributor for RCA (Radio Corporation of America). RCA itself was originally in the equipment business – radio receivers, gramophones, records – but swiftly moved into broadcasting. In Brazil and Mexico in the 1920s radio was run by enthusiasts who set up small private stations, but the US commercial model quickly came to dominate in Latin America. Azcárraga founded the station XEW in 1930. By 1938, the company had fourteen affiliates. The idea was to build a commercial broadcasting network based on advertising revenues, and while there was competition between the press and radio for advertising revenues in Latin America, there was only one winner – radio (and later television). The press has still never reached any sort of levels of mass circulation. Because of its large internal market, Brazil is one of the largest advertising markets in the world.

RCA, as equipment producer, established the radio network NBC, the National Broadcasting Company. NBC and the other major American network at the time, CBS (Columbia Broadcasting System), used advertising dollars to produce programming. So, for example, from the 1930s Roberto Marinho's Globo and Radio Bandeirantes were producing *radionovellas* (soaps), the precursors of the popular television, *telenovella*. Radio, then as now, was also an incredible promotional device for the record industry. It helped sell both record players and records. Film stars too appeared on radio, alongside comedy, sport and news. In the 1940s and 1950s, programming – in Spanish and Portuguese – produced by the US networks began to flood in. Advertisements often sold US products; Latin Americans bought US radio receivers and record players. At this point (US-owned) CBS set up Cadena de las Américas while (US-owned) NBC established Cadena Panamerica, with affiliated stations throughout the region. President Getúlio Vargas controlled Rádio Nacional, which co-produced programmes with NBC and CBS (Fox 1995: 530).

From 1960, ABC (the American Broadcasting Company) began to invest in Latin American television, acquiring 43 per cent of Venezuela's Venevision. At the same time NBC owned 20 per cent of Venezuela's Channel 2, while a coalition of Time-Life and CBS controlled Channel 8. In Mexico, the commercial radio networks affiliated with NBC and CBS had begun to push for commercial television from as early as 1945. President Miguel Alemán Valdés, in office from 1946 to 1952, was faced with the choice of the British public-sector model versus US commercialism, and opted for the latter. Later, his son became president of the private TV-broadcasting giant Televisa. Other licences went to those who were already newspaper or radio broadcasting magnates. Two of the most important TV channels went to Rómulo O'Farril from the newspaper *Novedades* and to the ubiquitous Azcárraga, of radio networks and magazine publishing success. O'Farril and Azcárraga joined to form one company in 1955: Telesistema Mexicano, which from the beginning produced programming for export to other Latin American countries. By 1959 Telesistema was a de facto network, operating some twenty stations (Fox 1997).

Television grew more slowly in Brazil. It was initially seen as an elite and urban phenomenon. Radio and newspaper owner Assis Chateaubriand was given the first television broadcasting licence for TV Tupi in São Paulo in 1950, followed by a station in Rio de Janeiro. They were soon followed by other channels, such as TV Paulista, TV Rio and TV Excelsior in Rio and São Paulo. The licences for these channels were awarded as direct political favours. With the arrival of video technologies in 1959, Brazil's largest station Diários Associados could for the first time film its productions and transmit simultaneously on all its affiliated stations. Diários Associados dominated Brazilian television until the mid-1960s and the simultaneous rise of military power and TV Globo (Fox 1995: 534–5). In Argentina, as in Brazil, legislation prohibited foreign ownership of channels. Foreign capital instead moved in as part owners of the channels' production companies, with the CBS/Time-Life alliance becoming especially important. One major channel produced programmes in association with ABC and a second with NBC. After the Second World War, Juan Perón nationalized the previously pro-Axis radio networks, forcing the previous private owners to sell the companies to the government at reduced prices. Perón's overthrow by the military in 1955 seemingly paradoxically opened the doors to legislation to allow foreign investment in television. Peronist artists and writers were banned from public expression and Mexican and US productions began to replace Argentinean content.

By the early 1970s in Latin America, US television series and films made up about half of what was shown on television and in cinemas. US wire services provided 60 to 80 per cent of international news, including news from other Latin countries. In both broadcasting and telecommunications, foreign firms have provided Latin America with an infrastructure. In television and radio, this was provided by RCA-NBC, Time-Life/CBS and ABC. They provided the equipment, the content, the expertise, the transmitters, the receivers and the advertising model. In telecommunications, much more recently, it has largely been the Europeans – Telefónica, France Telecom, Portugal Telecom and Telecom Italia – who have provided the infrastructure. Indeed on 17 October 2002, ten days before the election of President Lula, Telefónica Móviles and Portugal Telecom announced a merger to create South America's largest mobile telephone operator in Brazil, with thirteen million subscribers. Overall, heavy losses have been suffered by infrastructure investers, especially by France Telecom and Telecom Italia.

In between these two periods, however, there were major attempts to make Latin American media comply with national development programmes. In Mexico there was partial nationalization, although the two largest private networks merged in 1973, formed the Televisa conglomerate and successfully fought against incipient nationalization. This was a similar strategy to that adopted by Globo in Brazil. When threatened with the setting up of a parallel public broadcaster, these private broadcasters out-did their government's demands in terms of patriotism. By 1986 – the beginning of the downturn of import substitution – Televisa owned four national Mexican channels. By 1990, 20 per cent of Brazilian congressmen (part-)owned television or radio stations or major local newspapers. These outlets now typically form part of a national network, and sitting on top of most of these networks is Grupo Globo.

Brazil's media sector continues to be one of the most concentrated in the world. It is unique in the prominence of family ownership of the big three firms: the Marinho family of Globo, the Civitas family of Abril and the Frias family of Folha. In May 2006 Globo TV still held 76 per cent of television market share for prime time broadcast and 55 per cent of total TV market share. They produced some 80 per cent of their own prime time content. Folha have the highest circulation São Paulo daily paper (320,000) and the largest Internet service provider (Universal Online). Abril's dominance is more in magazine publishing – with 54 per cent of magazine circulation and 58 per cent of magazine advertising revenues – though they are a power in cable television. Despite their continued massive market share, Globo's debt increased over the years. This is true of the debt of all the large Brazilian media companies. The big three had by 2004 run up the large majority of a sector debt of US$3.2 billion. This was as a result of large losses on cable investment and, in addition, to the devaluation of the Brazilian currency, the *real*. Some 80 per cent of media sector debt was denominated in dollars.

One strategy for dealing with this debt was the selling off of underperforming units. Thus, in 2004 Globo was able to sell Net Servicos, its loss-making cable arm (with $318 million of defaulted debt), to Telmex, Mexico's ambitious telephone giant. The 2002 legislation, enabling 30 per cent foreign ownership of domestic media, also seemed to offer a way out. This legislation came from the more neoliberal government of Fernando Henrique Cardoso. But the socialist-leaning Luiz Inacio Lula da Silva, who succeeded Cardoso in October 2002, has not thought of reversing these laws. In the just mentioned Globo-Telmex deal, various proxy-ownership devices were used to make sure that Telmex did not have a 30 per cent de jure share in the cable company, though its de facto share was some 60 per cent. The first foreign acquisition of a part of a Brazilian media company was when the Los Angeles based Capital Group took a 14 per cent stake in Abril for US$50 million. Then in May 2006, Africa's largest media group, Cape Town-based Naspers, paid $422 million for a full 30 per cent stake in Abril S.A.[11] In between, Portugal Telecom took a 22 per cent stake in Folha-UOL. Folha underwent restructuring to form a holding company in 2005, at which point they bypassed Abril to become the country's second largest media firm. The restructuring was also necessary for any future IPO on the Sao Paulo exchange. After not a single IPO in 2002–3, 2004 onwards has seen a large number of new listings of major Brazilian firms. But these firms are, for example, in the cosmetics and the finance sectors, which are not family-dominated as are the media firms. The Frias family, for instance, still holds 78 per cent of Folha.[12] Globo's bedrock revenues come from television advertisements and sales of TV content. Improvement of advertising revenues and sales in this, along with a debt restructuring including divestiture of weaker businesses, led Moody Investor services in February 2006 to upgrade Globo's foreign currency corporate family rating.[13] There has not been a flood of foreign investment in Brazil's media since the 2002 legislation, nor a rush to encourage the firms to IPO. There is a marked reluctance for foreigners to invest because of the tenacious control that the leading families seemed determined to preserve.

In newer media, Brazil compromised, and by March 2006 there were some 14.1 million active home Internet users and 25.9 million total Internet users. At the end of 1999 the number of total users stood at only 5.8 million.[14] At the end of 2005 there were 85 million Brazilian mobile phone subscribers, making the country fifth in the world. With mass subscription, annual revenue per unit has declined: though total revenues have increased to $13.6 million at the end of 2005. Of this only $1 million comes from data transmission of which 70 per cent is SMS. Surveys show that there is a widespread and strong interest in other downloadable content such as music and video, etc. But incomes are too low and prices too high to pay for this.[15] Of the BRIC (Brazil, Russia, India, China) economies, Brazil would seem to be the worst bet for newer media investors. In Russia, individuals have much greater purchasing power. India and China have 6–8 times Brazil's number of consumers. And content, for example games, is cheaper in China. Brazil is trying to promote itself as a sort of laboratory of savvy new media users in the 14–35 age range. But then every country wants to be a loss leader for investors.

The history of the Brazilian film industry is in some ways a counterpoint to the just described history of broadcasting, though with a more marked influence from Europe from the beginning. Luiz Severiano Ribeiro was one of the first exhibitors, beginning to show films in 1917. Atlantida, the first big popular production company, was founded by an associate of Ribeiro. The other early production company was Vera Cruz. This was founded in 1948–54 by an Italian industrialist who had previously invested in Brazilian theatre. There were few home-grown filmmaking talents for the company to draw on, and technicians and directors were initially imported from Italy, France and England. Although Vera Cruz was the first attempt to build an 'industrial cinema' in Brazil (interview with Inacio Aranjo), it remained basically an art film studio, specializing in production, with little expertise in distribution and showing very little understanding of cinema's industrial process. The hierarchical industrial vertical integration of the Hollywood majors began typically from exhibition and distribution and worked back into production (as it were, from the 'back end' forward), whereas European cinema was much more production-centred, focusing less on the interface with the consumer. The generation of imported technicians and directors thus contributed to the formation of a generation of Brazilian counterparts. Vera Cruz remained a 'cinema of foreigners'. Cinema Novo (founded by Walter Lima Jr) initially attempted to emulate the 'industrial model', and turned its attentions explicitly towards the market. Nevertheless, its content was heavily influenced by Italian neorealism: key central figures had studied in Italy with the director Roberto Rossellini in the early 1960s, and were influenced by the French *nouvelle vague*.

In the mid-1970s Brazilian films captured 40 per cent of the domestic market: some 120 films per year were made. But virtually no films at all were made in the early and mid-1990s. From 1990 to 1992, not a single Brazilian film was produced. In 1993 and 1994 only two and five films respectively were released. A new beginning was heralded, as in 1995, 1996 and 1997, seventeen, twenty-two and thirty films were released, while in 1998 forty films were in production.[16] From 1990 to 1994 the box office share for Brazilian films was 0.1 per cent. In 1995 this had grown to 4 per cent (out of 3.2 million admissions), including a number of adaptations of Brazil's most popular romantic novels, by authors such as Jorge Amado (Susana Schild, <www.filmfestivals.com/rio/creamcro>).[17] The temporary disappearance of the industry was due to a radical cut in government fiscal incentives for companies to invest in film under the neoliberal Collor government. This was partly repaired by the Audio-Visual Law of 1993, whereby firms were allowed to put up to 3 per cent of the corporate income tax they are obliged to pay into film. This contributed to a minor renaissance, with Carla Camurati's *Carlota Joaquina, princesa do Brasil* the first film to break the million barrier with 1.5 million admissions.[18] Under Fernando Henrique Cardoso in 1994, further positive incentives were introduced. In 1995 Fábio Barreto's *O Quatrilho* was nominated for an Academy Award for Best Foreign Film. Whereas Hollywood film comes direct to Brazil through the vertically integrated US major studios, Brazilian films must use much the same routes out as European films use to enter, that is, screenings in Cannes, Berlin and the other major festivals (about which, see below).[19] There were two Brazilian films in the competition at Cannes in 1996. The renaissance of the Brazilian (and Latin American) film industry was confirmed by Walter Salles' *Central do Brasil* (*Central Station*) which received Academy Award nominations for Best Foreign Language picture, and a best actress nomination (for Fernanda Montenegro). It won awards in Berlin and San Sebastian in 1998. This happened just before the release in 2000 of *Amores*

Perros and in 2001 of *Y Tu Mamá También* in Mexico and *Nine Queens* in Argentina, and in 2002 in Brazil, *City of God*.

Under the dictatorship, church and military censorship had meant that films by Jean-Luc Godard and other members of the avant-garde could not be shown. The independent cinemas, including Ademar de Oliveira's chain and Station Botafogo, began to emerge in 1985–6. Ilda Santiago formed Grupo Estação with Adriane Retter, Marcelo Mendes and Nelson Krumholz, starting with one dilapidated cinema in 1985. Now Grupo Estação has fourteen cinemas in Rio de Janeiro, eight screens in São Paulo and four in Belo Horizonte. Yet despite this renaissance, one of our interviewees told us: 'For us [Brazilians], Hollywood ... [is] the truth, it's the real cinema. Brazilian cinema just doesn't do well. It's to do with a [US] publicity machine that works very well, which is consolidated. Is it possible in Brazil to make a film like *Titanic*? You see the rapport, *Titanic* or any number of Hollywood Films, it is truth. ... I think the real world for us it's the USA. The US is the Brazilian dream. ... Our rapport with the real is culturally not in cinema, but in football, a thing which expresses Brazil really well. Music in Brazil is also a thing that is very strong.' He continues: 'Even among poor Brazilians, music has penetration: it sells. ... From the beginning of the century this music *populaire*, it comes from Rio. It has poets: poets who work in music. If there is a democracy in Brazil it is in music. The creation of music runs very deep, whereas cinema does not run very deep.'

Global Microstructures: *Trainspotting*

André Sturm runs the small independent distribution company called Pandora. We interviewed him in his São Paulo office in 1998. Sturm had purchased exclusive rights to distribute *Trainspotting* to theatres in Brazil. He did not buy them directly from Film Four but from 'a guy from Argentina', 'who bought all the rights to Latin America' before 'the film was even started, when it was in preparation'. 'The [Argentinean] guy knew about *Shallow Grave* ... and he has a very good relationship with Film Four.' Sturm had had the same idea: 'I saw *Shallow Grave* too.' *Shallow Grave* was released in 1994. Like *Trainspotting*, it starred Ewan McGregor, was directed by Danny Boyle, and was scripted by John Hodge, with Brian Tufano as director of photography. Effectively acting as an advertisement for *Trainspotting*, *Shallow Grave* had not done well commercially in Brazil. For Sturm, this was because the distribution was mismanaged by Columbia, a company that does some independent film distribution in the country: '*Shallow Grave* lost money in Brazil because Columbia doesn't know how to handle a movie like that. They buy this kind of movie sometimes and kill them.' 'You have here in Brazil some very good movies come through Columbia: one week though and it's gone.' 'With a movie like that you have to work. You have to call the right news journalists to see the movie. You have to plan *where* you release, *how* you release.

You make contact with the exhibitors. Sometimes we have to bring out the movie with one print and then add more prints. Sometimes... we've had to open a little bit bigger. With *Trainspotting*, we started with twenty-two prints.'

Typically paying less than US$45,000 for the theatre rights to a film, Sturm's previous biggest business success was Kieslowski's *La Double Vie de Veronique*, for which he bought the exhibition rights in 1991 for US$5,000 and which 'did $100,000 in admissions'. Sturm says he paid something like a quarter of a million dollars for *Trainspotting*. The price was higher than it might otherwise have been because he bought after Miramax had acquired the film for US distribution, after the UK release and after the screening, party and publicity in Cannes 1996. 'So this [Argentinean] guy was reselling Brazil and Mexico, where he doesn't have his own distribution. And he wanted $500,000 for the movie. We [Pandora] didn't have that to pay ... we never do these crazy things.' 'People paid, for example, $1.5 million for *Donnie Brasco* and lost a lot of money.' Instead, Pandora entered into a partnership with a video company, Alpha Films. 'We sometimes buy together; we buy rights together. I do the theatre operations, he does video operation and we split the profits.' Alpha is predominantly a mainstream video company, doing 'action films', but 'they do one quality video per month, supplied by me'. The money came from 'a kind of reserve that we [Pandora] were keeping'. Alpha put up 60 per cent and Pandora 40 per cent. And 'there's a bit of an auction and the Argentinean guy raises the stakes again. Then we said our limit is $250,000–$300,000 and we told him you have four hours to say "Yes" and if not, we are out and he says "OK, I give you the deal".'

While the negotiation with 'the Argentinean guy' is the focus of the story being told here, Sturm recognizes that the interests of his company are not defined in this single relationship alone, but simultaneously in relation to all the other players in the field. With *Trainspotting* 'we thought it would be important for us to handle [the film], even paying that crazy price. Even if we don't make all our money back it will be important for the company, for Pandora as a brand'. Indeed, now, 'I get a lot of buzz, a lot of publicity when I go to the market: they say, "Oh, he had *Trainspotting*".' In this particular deal his principal competitor was the firm Lumière which 'did a very stupid thing' (by withdrawing from the market). 'They [Lumière] are very strong', and 'are really in a different, bigger market: they buy Miramax movies or big independent films with John Travolta or Brad Pitt.' Other key players include 'of course the majors', that is, the Hollywood majors who do their own distribution. Then there are two or three national companies which are also big exhibitors, although they 'are not exactly independent because they're massive with 180 screens.' Then 'there are some video companies'. A recent rise in the prices of rights in independent films due to this emergent video market has meant that many of Sturm's most direct competitors have closed down in the past eighteen months. However, there are another three or four companies which do independent distribution, but they 'buy very, very small movies for about $10,000'. For Sturm, this is a 'wonderful market, because I am buying the films I want for the prices I think I can pay.'

As we noted in chapter 2, many analysts assume that the global flows of cultural products are organized either in hierarchies or in *networks*. But our study suggests that their movements, while often structured in terms of horizontal associations, as are networks, are coordinated as *microstructures*, a term we have adapted from the work of Karin Knorr Cetina on finance markets (Knorr Cetina and Bruegger 2002). In outlining what she means by microstructures, Knorr Cetina develops a framework put forward by the phenomenologist Alfred Schutz. In his studies of the interaction order, Schutz turns the spotlight from the subject as actor to the subject as observer of a mediating object. His argument is that intersubjectivity is produced in the series of 'interlocking of glances' that occur in the contemporaneous observation of an object such as, in the example he puts forward, a bird in flight. In Knorr Cetina's case, the mediating object is not a bird but rather the on-screen market, which comprises prices and other information that are continuously moving, displayed and updated. In her study, 'Traders do not face each other, but face the screen.' Traders thus have 'micro-viewpoints that are pitched at the level of the local and the situation as the prime social reality and are extended to larger settings' (ibid.: 908). We extend further this suggestive analysis.

In this book, the object of intersubjectivity is neither a bird nor the transparent, functional computer described by Knorr Cetina, but rather is an opaque cultural product. It is, however, an object in movement. Just as the computer screen is constantly refreshed by knowledge, the objects we are following are continually caught in processes of translation and transposition, collection and dispersion, differentiation and integration. We further extend Knorr Cetina's analysis, however, by suggesting that the interaction order identified in this way does not only *not* have to be produced face-to-face (that is, it does not have to rely upon co-presence). It also – in our analysis – does *not* have to be contemporaneous, that is, it does *not* have to happen all at once or all at the same time for everyone. Knorr Cetina revises the notion of situation such that interaction can be disembedded from local settings, and space may be separated from place. We would further suggest that a situation may be separated from the here and now and that an event may be separated from the immediate. Indeed, perhaps what we describe here is not a situation but an *object-event*. What remains vital in both understandings, however, is what Knorr Cetina describes as 'response presence'. For us, as for Knorr Cetina, this includes the orientation of participants towards the observation of a common object-(event); the reciprocity of these orientations (although this reciprocity is not necessarily symmetrical); and an interlocking of the temporal dimensions of these orientations. Let us illustrate these points in relation to the object *Trainspotting*.

Trainspotting was a successor project to *Shallow Grave*. The driving force was producer Andrew Macdonald, Scottish grandson of cinema mogul Emeric Pressburger. Macdonald, Danny Boyle and screenwriter John Hodge collaborated on *Shallow Grave*. Hodge was an Edinburgh physician whom Macdonald persuaded to write the film's screenplay as early as 1990. *Shallow Grave*'s production company was Figment Films for Film Four (<www.filmfestivals.com/sanseb96>). Boyle too was not originally a film industry figure, but an internationally renowned stage director. The very low-budget *Shallow Grave* was the highest grossing British film in 1995. Its worldwide box-office take was $20.5 million (although only $3 million of this came from US box office). The largest markets were in Britain and France (<www.the-numbers.com/movies/1996>). After *Shallow Grave*, Macdonald received offers to work in Hollywood, which he declined to start work on *Trainspotting*. *Shallow Grave* was more than half a decade from conception to realization, *Trainspotting* only about twelve months. Macdonald had come across the Irvine Welsh stories a year after their 1993 publication and stage production. Hodge built a plot line around one of Welsh's main characters. He had completed one-third of the script by November 1994, for which Film Four gave backing. The second draft was completed in February 1995 (Hodge was to go on to win a BAFTA award for the best screenplay). Film Four agreed further funding the following month. In April 1995, the film went into pre-production. It was shot in Glasgow in four weeks starting on 22 May 1995. The film was not invited to Cannes that year, but was marketed there.

The UK release was in February 1996. It was distributed by Polygram Filmed Entertainment, Europe's largest film company, itself grown out of the world's largest music company. (At this time, Polygram's parent company was Phillips, but it was bought by Seagram in 1998.[20]) Boyle and Macdonald decided to save the film for 1996 Cannes and not show it in the Berlin Film Festival. But Cannes director Gilles Jacob 'loathed the film' and would not have it in the competition. Instead, Macdonald and Film Four negotiated a 'Special Screening Out of Competition' for 0:30 am on a Monday night. According to Bill Van Parys of *US Magazine* ('Ewan McGregor', August 1996) it 'was the hottest ticket in town. Mick Jagger, Chrissie Hynde, Oasis, Blur and Elastica turned out to fete the movie sensation and McGregor'. Miramax's US release followed two months later. It was at this moment that André Sturm bought rights from the 'Argentinean guy', who had owned them since just after Film Four had guaranteed backing.

Trainspotting was made for $2.6 million. It was the highest grossing British film of 1996. Its UK box office take in 1996 was $15 million, making it the fourth highest UK grossing British film at that point in time. It opened in 357 theatres on 19 July 1996. The opening weekend take was only $262,000, but box office receipts grew and peaked at $1.4 million for the week of 2 August, when it moved to number thirteen in the American charts. It played and played in the USA, until December 1996, by which time it had grossed $16.5 million. Compare this with the profile over time of the much-hyped follow-up, *A Life Less Ordinary*, which opened in 1,208 US theatres, took $2.0 million its first weekend, and then quickly disappeared, grossing in total only $4.3 million. This latter, more expensive, film lost an enormous amount of money, grossing only $9.0 million at the box office worldwide. *Trainspotting*'s worldwide box office was $72.2 million. According to the 2000 European Audiovisual Laboratory Report, *Trainspotting* and *Il Postino* were the two top European films from 1996–9 in regard to number of times broadcast on unencrypted channels. The Report notes that the films boosted the market shares of the channels showing it, especially in Portugal, Italy, Switzerland and Belgium. It estimates that the number of viewers watching *Trainspotting* on television in the UK and Belgium was three times the box office, in Portugal and Spain twice the box office, and in Switzerland and Germany equal to the number seeing it in film theatres (<www.obs.coe. int/about/oec/pr/european_films_ontv>). While this is a great success in British terms, it is salutary to note that *Trainspotting* had only the ninth best box office in the UK in 1996: the top eight were all Hollywood films, number one being *Independence Day* at $49 million. The three highest grossing ever UK films at that point were *The English Patient*, *Four Weddings and a Funeral* and *The Full Monty*, all of which grossed worldwide more than three times *Trainspotting* at $200–250 million. The world's then highest ever earning film, *Titanic*, puts this success even more in perspective. That film took $1.835 billion worldwide – some twenty-five times that of *Trainspotting*: $600 million in the USA, and $119 million and $138 million in Britain and France respectively (*The Numbers*).

What the biography outlined here suggests, however, is not only that the object itself is transformed in its movements, but also that buyers organize their bids in relation to the object as it is transformed and transforming. This set of relations – distributed in time and space – is what comes to constitute the global microstructure of the markets of the culture industry. The price that both 'the Argentinean guy' and Sturm had to pay was linked to their capacity to judge the potential of the film before its ultimate success (at the box office). They did so in part by looking at its 'back history', in part by considering their relations with competitors and other players in the field in the present and in the future, and in part by considering its potential relation with the audience. Because he thought *Shallow Grave* was good, Sturm was after *Trainspotting* in Cannes the year *before* it was released. Yet the rights for Latin America had already been sold by then. 'The Argentinean guy had bought it for a very good price.' The film was then bought by Miramax for US distribution after its successful UK release (that is, as an enhanced object), but before 1996 Cannes, at which point '*every*body was looking for the movie'. Yet Cannes festival director Gilles Jacob despised the film. Why was this? Perhaps because, as David Aukin, Channel 4's then Head of Drama said, although it 'isn't really about drugs ... it's a buddy movie ... the subject matter may have been too strong for the official selection at Cannes' (<www.filmfestivals.com/cannes96>). Buyers thus not only look back, to assess, for example, the accumulation of rights by an object, but also have to look forward, to the final market, to critics and to the attachment of consumer markets.

US critics compared *Trainspotting* to Stanley Kubrick's *A Clockwork Orange*. Both are anti-social-realist films dealing with subjects – gangs, drugs and violence – normally dealt with via social realism. Both are stylized and fast-paced. Both are independent films that shocked the critics and sometimes the audience. But in contrast, *Trainspotting* was always more an object – a thing – of youth culture, more popular culture than it was cinematic from the very beginning. As discussed in chapter 2, Polygram put large sums of money into a sophisticated marketing and branding strategy, including posters, a soundtrack, and the phrase 'Believe the Hype!'. In Brazil, the film was released by Pandora in 'big mainstream cinemas'. Sturm says: 'I got eight cinemas in Rio ... through the biggest Brazilian circuit, all in city centres.' 'I contacted [the CEO of Brazil's largest chain of exhibition houses]; I talked to his assistant. He said, "OK, send me a poster". Two days later the assistant calls me and says, "Send me a print: he is interested. When do you want to release the film?".' In São Paulo, 'I work also with mainstream cinemas, a chain, Alverada. Alverada at the same time had Belles Artes ... the best cinema in São Paulo. The chain belonged to Gaumont, the Paris circuit. I'd worked with a Belles Artes guy. I went to him and said, "Now, I need more cinemas" and he gave me five salles.' The rights to the soundtrack of the film were owned by Polygram in Brazil, as in the UK. So 'they helped me [Sturm]. We did promotion together. When I released the movie, they gave me CDs and I did some kind of promotion with radio.'

But the thingification of a film such as *Trainspotting*, its descent into the social field, is not something that can be entirely managed, and is not always commercially successful. Sturm suggests that *Trainspotting* was not the success that 'we [Pandora and Alpha] expected, because the drug thing became very strong in the media here ... and did create a kind of negative thing'. 'Here in São Paulo we started to do pre-screenings: Saturday night at ten or eleven pm.' Then, a month before the release, 'there was a guy, like 55 or 60 years old, a lawyer or something. And he made an official petition to a judge not to allow the film to be released. This was wonderful because it became a huge "scandal" and made huge publicity for us. It got into the press and they start to say, "How terrible can it be?" The judge was a woman. She called me and said, "Please, I want to see the film before I make my decision. Can you do a special screening for me?" "Of course", I say. And then the newspaper ran their interview with her. And so it was ten days of "What's going to happen? The judge is going to forbid the movie ... allowed ... not allowed". And the guy of course becomes famous. He is very happy because people interviewed him. And he didn't *see* the movie. He just read it is about drugs, so he said it is a movie that makes young people take drugs ... and the guy didn't see the movie. It was very funny.' Despite – or perhaps because of – the extra publicity, the success of the screenings was uneven though: 'Like in São Paulo the film went very well. But in some cities like Rio, which I thought was a very modern city, [it did not]. And it was a disaster in Manaus. Belem was better than Manaus. Manaus was, I think, the worst: we did something like 400 tickets in a week. On the other hand, in Brasilia it was a huge success.' *Trainspotting* did well in São Paulo, he says, 'because the critics gave it strong support, loved the movie'. Sturm 'did interviews with the director by phone: we brought over [actor] Ewen Bremner'. In Rio, by contrast, there were 'poor reviews'. 'It didn't start well and there was not the word of mouth to make the film go.' In 'other cities we had, "Don't go, terrible boy, drugs, drugs, drugs"', though there were 'positive reviews in [the capital] Brasilia'.

Sturm also suggests that in Brazil *Trainspotting* appealed not so much to young people, 'but the twenties to forties'. He concludes that there is, 'a different geographic logic [in Brazil to that in Europe] ... low[er] class people don't have this subculture thing'. Instead the film was successful within the Brazilian independent film culture. The film was nominated for Best Adapted Screenplay (John Hodge) and Best Film Editor (Masahiro Hirakubo) for the 1997 Movie Brazil Awards. 'On balance', Sturm says, 'we didn't have what we expected but we did a very good job. We had about 150,000 admissions; the average ticket is $4. So $600,000. In video we did about 10,000 units at about $55 each, almost exclusively to shops.[21] Video revenues of about $550,000 brought total revenues to $1.15 million, which 'only recouped our money' because of heavy 'costs of advertising print and video release'.

Bruno Wainer is a buyer at Lumière, the company that did not bid for the film against Pandora. Interviewed in July 1998, he said: 'Nothing happened in Brazil with *Trainspotting*. An excellent film – *j'adore ce film*, but it was very closed for the Brazilian market. The *Trainspotting* phenomenon in England was not reproduced.' 'Here we only had less than 100,000 viewers [Sturm said 150,000]: small in comparison to England and Europe.' 'It showed in many cinemas because the exhibitors too much believed the distributor [that is, Sturm]. The distributor convinced ... commercial cinemas were convinced ... [there was] a big campaign for it; but still the film didn't make it.' In Wainer's view, 'the film was *mal lancé* in Brazil – the film went directly to the commercial circuit. The distributor *a lancé* the film like it was a commercial film for a normal public.' The public 'rejected the film as too violent: drugs and all'. 'It wasn't a film that grew. The film began big the first week. By the second week in 50 per cent of the *salles* it was out: by the third week it only played in one cinema.' This was a 'bad strategy'. In contrast, with the licence to exhibit *Delicatessen* 'we [Lumière] began small and ended with 150,000 admissions; or *Captain Fracasse* 150,000 or *Reine Margot* – 150,000. *Central do Brasil* for its part made 1.1 million admissions. *Trainspotting* began with twenty-two prints. No more were ordered. *Central do Brasil* starts with thirty-five copies. By the seventh week eighty copies were needed.'

Global Microstructures: Wallace and Gromit

As much as anyone, Zita Carvalhosa was responsible for bringing Wallace and Gromit to Brazil. In 1998, she was director of the São Paulo Festival of Short Films (Festival Internacional de Curtas Metragens). Aardman films, as independent films with BBC backing, move across territories via, in part, the festival route. *Toy Story*, in contrast, is the product of – and moves as an object of – a major global company that works through hierarchical distribution and licences. Carvalhosa had seen *The Wrong Trousers* in January 1994 at the Clermont-Ferrand Festival, the world's number one venue for *courts métrages*. It was at Clermont-Ferrand that she first made contact with (a representative for) Aardman producers.

A few months after Clermont-Ferrand, Carvalhosa went to Bristol. Of all the films shown in her São Paulo Festival in August 1994, *The Wrong Trousers* – which was in the Festival's 'Programme del'Ouverture' – had the greatest success. Indeed, Carvalhosa organized a section of the festival around Aardman. 'Aardman was unusual', she observed, 'because short films, they don't usually have an immediate impact with the public.' The Aardman film was 'a new sort of humour', very 'underplayed', as Mariana Mirosawa who reviewed the video for *Folha de São Paulo* said: 'There was a story, it was narrative, and for animation this is not very common.' Brazilians were already familiar with the work of Nick Park through *Creature Comforts*, which had been shown in 1993. The setting in this short film is an English zoo, in which the characters – from more temperate parts of the world – comment on the English weather. 'There is this character, this personage', notes Carvalhosa, 'it's a Brazilian, it's a panther, and she says, "I need space. I cannot *live* in this place". Carvalhosa continues, 'They [Aardman] invited me to come to England for a festival ... I spent a day in Bristol, had lunch with Nick Park.' 'Then we invited him [Park] to come to Brazil for the festival.' He was unable to come, 'because there was at the same time a homage to him at Hiroshima' (one of the world's biggest animation festivals). The Brazilian animation festival, Anima Monsi, also held an Aardman programme in 1997. 'English short films are the most professional in the world.' 'Aardman always', Carvalhosa notes, 'had a very definite policy: well-made, promotion. ... They create characters, but above all styles. It seems to be the characters that win empathy from the public, but in fact it's the way it's made.'

Carvalhosa is a major figure more generally in the Brazilian culture industry. Apart from running Superfilmes, a major production company, with André Klotzel, she is President of the Associação Cultural Kinoforum, an association that organizes two festivals per year, on shorts and documentaries, and produces publications. Klotzel is President of the Brazilian Association of Courts Métrages. He produced and directed many films and is also a screenwriter. Born in 1959, Carvalhosa came to London at the age of 14 when her mother was doing a PhD. She worked at the ICA in London in the mid-1970s and studied in Paris from 1978 to 1982, starting in social science but shifting to cinema. With Klotzel and three other friends, she started Superfilmes in 1983. With an elite French education, she did not start as a technician or an assistant director, but instead pursued a private sector (production) and organizational (third sector)/state role simultaneously. She was Senior Curator at the Brazilian Museum of Image and Sound for ten years. It was there that she began to organize the São Paulo Short Festival (from 1989). At the beginning of the 1990s (in the 1980s there were eighty feature films made per year in Brazil, in 1991 there were two) she 'made a living otherwise', and focused primarily on the museum and the festivals. Superfilmes at that point in time only made shorts. Klotzel, Carvalhosa and their colleagues began working on *Emerald Forest* with John Boorman in 1985. Between 1985 and 1998 they produced twenty-three shorts and nine feature films, including *A Marvada Carne* (*Damned Meat*, directed by Klotzel), which showed at Cannes and twenty-two other festivals in 1985 and played to 1.2 million box office admissions. Carvalhosa and Superfilmes have also produced animation from Brazil's most esteemed animator, Cao Hamburguer, for example his *Girl of the Screen*.[22]

At festivals, Carvalhosa suggests, the objects are less a question of selling as of *showing*. 'Festivals', she says, 'are important, 'cause if you make it, *show* it! I like showing better than making. Before I liked making (producing) better.' 'But there are lots of people who make yet only a few who show.' For Carvalhosa, Nick Park and Cao Hamburguer, are 'very strong and very sure of themselves. They know very well what they are doing. They do not *sell* their product ... they are not going to make concessions.' 'Selling ... they have nothing against. But it's not their thing. He [Park] finds other people to work for him. For Wallace and Gromit, the commercial dimension is secondary: they are cultural characters.' 'It wasn't Aardman that started [the commercial distribution of Wallace and Gromit]. They were *discovered*. It was others who asked them to get larger, because they had a good product.' Aardman 'is a very, very good *production* company. First comes the good product.' 'They already had won two Oscars when they entered the markets. ... When they did the programme with us they did not have commercial interests.' *Toy Story* is 'completely different. ... [It is] something constructed from the word go to be a great global success.'

Carvalhosa has a team of four at the festival who have worked together for a decade.[23] A festival, she says when interviewed in July 1998, is 'a meeting place more than a market. It is *not* a market. There are relations that develop here, because the people are here. There's not a lot of business. Me, I'm not very good at business, it's not my idea of life. We have a production company which is very good, but ... .' Carvalhosa says, festivals 'are a whole circuit of film exhibition. ... There are two types of festival. ... First, festivals where you present so they can have access to distribution. And second, festivals which are a way of *showing* films.' 'For Brazilians it is a chance to *see* films. For the producers of short films it's a way to show films to others, so these films can make a career in the international circuits of short films.' For example, 'Me, I make a film, not to make money. Or I would have made other films. I don't go for the American model. I make films so that they can be seen. I want to show films I've produced and all the other films I think are good.' (For example, Carvalhosa produced a short (seven-minute) film, *A Alma do Negócio* (1996), directed by José Roberto Torero, which sold to Canal Plus, CDF, Polish and Australian television, yet even Canal Plus here paid only $130 per minute.) You never 'produce a short film that is in deficit. It must be paid in advance. Shorts are always linked to the public sector. Features in Brazil are also always supported by the public sector, [but] need to show up in markets to justify themselves.'[24] Animated short films are not a market product, but a product of innovation, she believes. 'Wallace and Gromit are part of a circuit that is not commercial. It's a circuit that is about novelty. It [the festival] is a place of discovery, where old and new directors try to make something different. Short films are a place where you try out different things.' 'You go into it, into the game. You may be discovered, maybe not, but you're always playing with the idea that you've got to make it differently. *Trainspotting*, it's like *Sex, Lies and Videotape*. Now and then something different emerges into the global production of cinema. And people always are engaging with this different thing.' Markets, including markets for cultural goods, are a distribution of stabilized microstructures. But before an inventive cultural object can gain such market stability, it must emerge as an 'object-event'. And this happens, typically, not in markets, but in spaces of showing. In other words, the microstructure here is organized by an object-event which is not transparent like the computer screen, but rather an opaque object of display; it has its own space and time, it draws people in.

Biographies of People: Industrial Love

André Sturm was born in 1966 in Porto Alegre, a southern, non-tropical Brazilian city with a large Germanic population. He studied business administration at the Fundação Getúlio Vargas Escola de Administração de Empresas de São Paulo. This is 'the most important business administration school in Brazil. It has a strong economics department.' Sturm is

from a professional family: 'I didn't want to be a doctor or lawyer or engineer so I went to business school. My father wanted me to go to Vargas
because Universidade de São Paulo is "full of communists". ... It really is.
Don't go there. But I had [eventually] to go there: because my school
[Vargas] was very rigid and formal and I wanted to go to university.
[There, however, it was] communism: it was bad.' But, 'I always liked
movies. In my first year I was completely disappointed. At the start of the
second year there was a small Cinéclub. ... There was one guy only taking
care of the club. ... And I decided to go there and see what is this
Cinéclub, and I start working there and I have a lot of initiative ... so in six
months I was the guy at the Cinéclub, and I take care of programmes,
everything. So I found something completely different because when you
think of films, you always think about producing. Nobody knows this
profession of distribution and exhibition: unless you are inside you never
heard about that. ... So I really get involved and start to meet all the people that work in the other Cinéclubs. And the Cinéclubs actually did
become important in the city. I organize a lot of events.'

Sturm said that by the mid-1980s the Cinéclubs were not quite as political as they used to be. In the 1970s, they were really an arm of the
Communist Party, which, at the beginning of the '70s, decided to give
some of its people an education. The Party decided to go to the Cinéclubs
and organize because, under the dictatorship until 1985, it was the only
type of association allowed to exist in Brazil. It was the only way, said
Sturm, to put people together and say bad things about the government.
But: 'I was involved because I liked movies. They were involved because
they liked politics. The National Organization of Cinéclubs was a very
left-wing organization.' Sturm says that he had no interest in normal politics, but he was involved in CinéClub politics. He became director of the
National Organization. At the time, 'the 16mm places were really very
left directed until really '88 or '89. The dictatorship finished and people
were no longer interested in going to bad places, bad projection, bad
chairs, to see *Frankenstein*.' The 'older generation left. I had a terrible
fight with them. Because I was never left-wing in my life. I'm not a fascist
but I'm not gauche. When you're 18, in the university, and, "I'm sorry, I
don't agree. I don't like it". So it became a problem: "Now he must be
from the CIA; he's a spy for the FBI". ... I wanted to do CinéClub work better and to get movies, the prints. It was really funny. I heard things unbelievable in the time: like Cinéclubs are the first step of socialist revolution in Brazil.' Some ten or so years later, he continued, the younger
generation, people between 16 and 22, are completely apolitical, not even
interested in the right to vote. Nelson Cunhos, from the Communist
Party, was President of the National Organization of Cinéclubs. 'Now he
has changed. If you talk to him today he will laugh.'

After finishing university, aged 22, Sturm decided he 'wanted to have a
wonderful theatre to show wonderful movies'. In 1988 he spent a whole

year looking for a place, a theatre: 'a closed theatre, an old theatre. I only twice went to bid, but could not close a deal.' Money, he said, was not a problem. Money was the solution to a problem. He realized it was a bad idea to do the theatre because there would be no films to show. At that time there was no distribution of good films in Brazil. So he realized that he must have the films before he could get the cinema, and he decided to go to the Berlin Film Festival in 1989 to see how it works. 'I was there and think I must know how is this business of film, buying films, so I meet people and I close three deals. Then I come back and open a company because I didn't have a company.' The company was Pandora. Because he was young, some people wouldn't talk to him, 'but some people liked me and trusted me and signed. ... You don't have to pay in the same moment. You sign deals and after the contracts come, you send back and then I went after the money. I couldn't go to banks because we had 30, 40 per cent inflation each month. My father lent me $4,000. And then I started. I pay one movie, I bring one movie, release one; I pay another, I get some money.' By 1998, at the time of our interview, Sturm was showing about fifteen films per year and he was vaguely thinking of going into production. In 2002 the film *Sonhos Tropicais* was released by Pandora, starring Carolina Kasting, directed by André Sturm. It won first prize in the Recife Film Festival and also featured at Rio and Curitiba.

Born in 1960, Bruno Wainer broke into the Brazilian film industry at the beginning of the 1980s, as a production manager, and an assistant director. We interviewed him in the Rio offices of Lumière, Brazil's largest independent distribution company, although he works 70 per cent of his time as director of distribution for Severiano Ribeiro, Brazil's largest exhibition company. In 2002 Ribiero had 185 screens, 20 per cent of the market share in Brazilian exhibition. Brazil is the sixth largest film market in the world – after the USA, France, Germany, Britain and Italy. In 1995 there were 1,400 screens in Brazil. Eighty prints (copies) is considered a major release. Ribeiro has a major distribution operation too. Wainer and Frenchman Marc Beauchamps came together to run Lumière. They met in 1986, both aged 25, both assistant directors on a Franco-Brazilian co-production. Wainer says, '*Nous, moi et Marc, nous sommes du cinéma. Nous venons du cinéma, nous travaillons dans le cinéma depuis dix-sept ans*' ('We, both Marc and I, are both in cinema. We come from cinema, we have been working in film for seventeen years.') It is important to Wainer that, 'Miramax and the Weinsteins chose to work with Lumière as their Brazilian distributor'. For Wainer, it was one film, Miramax's *Pulp Fiction*, that changed everything. *Pulp Fiction* 'cost $10 million, made $200 million'. By this time, Miramax had already been acquired by Disney. The Weinsteins '*sont tres doués pour ça* [have a great talent for this]; they buy, they co-produce, they put everybody under contract where there is talent. They have a very clear policy. They don't want to become a major; they want to be a *très grande boite indépendente* [a very large independent company]' Asked why the Weinsteins were happy at Disney, Bruno said: '*Parce qu'ils sont juifs; moi je suis juif – alors je peux le dire s'ils* [because they are Jewish; me, too, I'm Jewish, so I can say that if they] are there its because it's a super *bon* business, super because it gives them complete financial independence. What more could they want? They have all the money in the world to produce what they want. They must make *un profit fou!*'

Lumière also integrated backwards into production: their first film was *Little Book of Love*, released in 1996. The average Brazilian production costs about $2 million to produce. *Book of Love* was made for $900,000, and took 400,000 admissions (about $1.6 million) at the box office alone: '*400,000 entrees pour un film de $900,000. Putain, c'était superbe.*' Lumière split the $4 per ticket with the exhibitors and thus took $800,000, then 'the video sales pay the cost of commercialization. You begin to see the revenue with television sales, and with international sales you start to make a profit.' What really counts, says Bruno, is box office: 'you make your money in the box office; television you know more or less, video too: the only place where you can hit the jackpot is in the theatres: you can do two million admissions.' What he is referring to here though is the money to be made from distributing films in Brazil that are made outside Brazil: *The English Patient*, for example, cost Lumière $600,000 for Brazilian rights; *Up Close and Personal*, $850,000 for all Latin America.

The English Patient was Wainer's largest coup, made possible because of a personal connection to Saul Zaentz, the producer of the film. Zaentz also produced *Amadeus, One Flew Over the Cuckoo's Nest, The Unbearable Lightness of Being*[25] and a Brazilian film, *At Play in the Fields of the Lord* (1991, directed by Hector Babenco), on which Wainer was a production manager. 'So I knew the guy and I knew his story and all. And one day [in 1996] I'm at Cannes. There was our video partner who comes in with a flyer of that film [*The English Patient*] and I said, "Ah ... it's the Saul Zaentz film. Christ, it's the great producer and it's not been snapped up. ... And I turn around and there's Saul Zaentz at the next table! ... Saul, he looks at me, but he didn't recognize me at once. But ... "Ah, Bruno, how are you? ... What are you doing?" "Look, I'm with these guys who want to buy the film." "Listen, if you want it, it's yours." No problem. So paf! We buy the film. But my video guy doesn't want it: "There's no casting. Who is Ralph Fiennes? Who is Kristin Scott Thomas?" I said, "No, no. We buy. We buy. We buy." And it made 1.5 million spectators. This paid our whole $600,000. The video guy didn't have film culture.'

In 1998, Wainer told us, Lumière was in the market. It had Miramax sewn up. 'Lumière is central to Brazilian cinema, because I worked fifteen years of my life in Brazilian cinema and all the Brazilian producers know me with the alliance that we have with Ribeiro's distribution operation. We did *Central do Brasil*.' Yet, he admitted, this is not big business. The Brazilian distribution and exhibition industry is insignificant in comparison to, for example, Globo. In 1997, total box office for cinema exhibition in Brazil was only $200 million. In Britain $119 million was spent at the box office on *Titanic* alone. Yet Wainer is not tempted by television: 'Me? I'll tell you. I'm 37, I'll be 38 years old and I discovered one thing: *mon truc* [my thing], it's the cine-screen. You know there is someone who takes care of television. I don't even like *selling* to television. My thing is the cinema, this screen. *C'est comme ça. Mon truc.* I've been doing this since I was 17. I start as a technician and now as a distributor. Cinema is what I like to do and cinema is where people, the people I have the best relations with are. I don't have good rapports with television executives. Marc [Wainer's business partner], he has good networks with television.'

Ademar de Oliveira is probably Brazil's largest independent exhibitor. At the time of interview, he had ten *salles* in São Paulo and five in Rio de Janeiro.[26] We interviewed him in his impressive Espace Unibanco in Rua Augusta near São Paulo's Avenida Paulista. The space is very much like that of the Parisian independent exhibitors of the 1970s, with bookshop, bar and café. Like so many of his generation, Oliveira's first foreign language was French. (Sturm, and the new generation, is Anglophone.) But why is the cinema called Espace Unibanco, the name of one of Brazil's major banks? 'Because I borrowed from banks to transform this space – $1.5million. And $10 million in Rio.' Yet although the majority owner of his cinemas seems to be Unibanco, Oliveira is given total independence to programme and run the cinema. He came to São Paulo in the 1970s to go to university to study sociology. His ambition was to be a sociologist. Instead, he wound up in the Cinéclubs. After studying at university he worked in a small independent cinema in São Paulo's Bella Vista with a hundred seats. Oliveira did the organization there; he also ran a 'schools go to cinema programme' and learnt 35mm projection. In 1980 there were two or three hundred members of Cinéclub Brazil. In the early '80s, still under the dictatorship, Oliveira came to Rio where he was founding director of the 'L'agrupamento de ciné clubiste': The Cinéclub in the Associaçao Brasileira de Imprensa. In the 1970s, he notes, 'the Cineclubs were a political instrument'. And at the time, Oliveira himself was very left-wing. From 1980 to 1985, with the gradual redemocratization of politics, the clubs turned their emphasis (or at least he turned his clubs) to 'cultural training'. His major commitment is to cinema education. This was already his role in the Bella Vista cinema and it was the direction in which he took the Rio de Janeiro Cinéclub movement in the 1980s.

It remained the focus of Oliveira's continuing education programme in the chain of São Paulo and Rio cinemas. Every morning there is a session of 'schools go to cinema', involving 90,000 students per year, from small children to university students. Unibanco contributes to this, for which they get an income tax write-off. Oliveira also brings out the film education publication, *Jornal da Mostra*.[27] Under the dictatorship, Oliveira noted, it was only possible for most people to see US films; a 're-educa-

tion' process in European cinema has been necessary for a new generation. There then emerged, especially in the Brazilian middle classes, a
large audience for art cinema: a 'demand for an alternative film education'. Oliveira was a journalist from 1970 to 1978, and in his educational
mission he is aided by the Brazilian press, which is 'very open to all films
that are not American'. Oliveira was also the main organizer of the Rio
Festival (Mostra Rio) – a festival without a competition – from 1987 to
1997. *Trainspotting* had its '*avant-première*' in the Mostra just before its
opening in July 1996 (simultaneously with the Miramax opening in the
USA, two months after Cannes).

Film exhibition in Brazil has changed in recent years, Oliveira says.
Warner and UCI opened up large numbers of theatres. Before that, the
two Brazilian exhibition giants, Ribeiro and Paris Films, had the largest
market shares. Alpha, *Trainspotting*'s video distribution company, was an
offshoot of Paris Films. The Ribeiro chain in some locales entered into a
joint venture with UCI. The American chains spread with the proliferation of shopping centres from the early 1990s. The independent cinemas
are almost all based in city centres. In São Paulo, apart from Oliveira's ten
screens, there are ten other independent screens. A number of figures in
the industry have wanted to buy Oliveira out.

Marco Aurélio Marcondes was also involved in the CinéClubs movement. On finishing university in 1977 he 'built a little company of distribution, just for Brazilian films'. At the same time (1977–82) he worked in
distribution for 'the state arm of the movie industry'. In the second half
of the 1980s, after the dictatorship, he joined an independent exhibitor
and distributor, Artfilms, which was owned by an old family. It distributed and showed only European films. The company owned thirty theatres, and were especially present in Rio. From this position, Marcondes
moved into production, bringing out nine films. These were popular
films, with audiences up to five million, financed by Artfilms and
Columbia. With the collapse of production in the early 1990s, Marcondes
set up a distribution company with Ribeiro, called Severiano Ribeiro e
Marcondes – of which he owned 30 per cent. This company, which also
distributes video for Miramax, Channel 4, Canal Plus and others, was
taken over by Lumière in 1997, and Marcondes started at Globo Films –
just as Globo Films itself was starting. By the end of the twentieth century, Globo, as noted above, was the fourth largest TV network in the
world, with revenues of $5.5 billion – in comparison with, for example,
ABC's $2 billion in Brazil in 1997. Globo's intention was to build a film
business both in distribution and production. When we interviewed him,
Marcondes was producing a $5.5 million film to be released at Cannes in
1999: he raised the money outside Globo, from VW, banks and credit card
companies.

'Routes. Routes. Routes. Routes. Routes. Routes. Routes':[28] Anthropophagy

The last of the Brazilian interviewees introduced above, Marcondes, described a new age of Hollywood cinema as beginning in the early 1980s. This period saw the emergence not only of video but also of the multiplexes, frequently located in shopping malls, next to restaurants or bowling alleys. Cinema became a leisure experience. This was also for him the generation of the 'UCLA people', especially Spielberg and Lucas, and the point at which Hollywood started matching its US admission figures with export figures. In Marcondes' understanding, as film became more global, it became part of a branded leisure culture and bought increasingly into new media.

But the cauldron of contemporary Brazilian culture, argued another interviewee, the film critic Inacio Araujo, can be traced back to another source, to what was known as the *anthropophagy* of the 1920s and '30s. Something along the lines of 'anthropophagy' may have made a major return in Brazil, in Argentina and in Mexico in the global renaissance of Latin art and cinema beginning in the very end of the 1990s. Anthropophagy and the cannibal was the theme of the 1998 São Paulo Biennale.[29] At stake in this is not so much a culture of diaspora or hybridity as of *métissage*. Diaspora and hybridity are substantives, whereas *métissage* is a process. Yet the Brazilian *mestiçagem* and Spanish *mestizaje* are a very distinctive process: a process of production of a special type of mestizo culture through anthropophagy. Anthropophagy has its roots in Dada, in Francis Picabia's magazine *Cannibale*, published in Paris in 1920. Picabia, a friend of Marcel Duchamp and a presence at the famous New York Armory Show in 1913, and *Cannibale* were integral to the Paris Dada movement. Picabia – with his twists and turns from symbolism to para-Cubism to Dada to surrealism and after – was perhaps, even more than Duchamp, France's (protean and) prototype modernist. In Brazil the ideas of *Cannibale* and anthropophagy informed São Paulo's 'modern art week' in 1922. This was the epoch of radio and the new literature of modernism. The literary figures Mário and Oswald de Andrade stand out from this era: the figures of 'anthropophagy'. This is a movement of 'the absorption of the sacred enemy' (Oswald de Andrade): the cannibalism of European and US culture in Brazil. Two fundamental texts appeared in 1928. One was 'Macunaíma' by poet, essayist, musicologist and modernist theorist Mário de Andrade. This text spoke of a reappropriation of indigenous folklore: of a 'hero without qualities' and a 'hero of our people', split between the forest of the interior and the São Paulo metropolitan carnivalesque. The second and perhaps better known text is *O Manifesto Antropofágo* by novelist and playwright Oswald de Andrade.

In this manifesto, Oswald de Andrade writes: 'Only anthropophagy unites us ...The world's only law. ... Tupi, or not tupi is the question' (Tupi is a language spoken by some of Brazil's indigenous population): 'We want the Caribbean revolution. [Cannibalism, meaning the eating of human flesh, is derived from the word cannibal, a Spanish mispronunciation of Caribs, a term used to describe natives from the Caribbean islands.] Bigger than the French Revolution. The unification of all efficacious rebellions in the direction of man. Without us Europe would not even have its poor declaration of the rights of man.' It continues: 'I asked a man what Law was. He replied it was the guarantee of the practise of the possible. This man was Galli Matias. I ate him.' And further: 'But those who came were not crossed. They were fugitives from a civilization that we are eating, because we are strong and vengeful like the Jabuti.' He argues for '[t]he permanent transformation of Taboo into totem' and '[a]gainst social reality, clothed and oppressive, categorised by Freud – the reality without complexes, without madness, without prostitution and without prisons of matriarchy of Pindorama'. The manifesto is signed: Oswald de Andrade, and dated 'In Piratininga, Year 374 of the Swallowing of Archbishop Sardine'.

In Freud's *Totem and Taboo*, the brothers not only killed the archaic Father, but also ate him. This father – who sexually had all the women – was not yet 'the law'. 'The law' is born with the emergence of the symbolic, initially in the rites of totemism. Andrade's interest is in the symbolic and 'the law' in Europe and the West. In European modernity – for Andrade as for much of contemporary cultural theory – the law and the symbolic are constituted around the figure of Freud's Oedipal father. Andrade's 'cannibale' is thus to eat the law, literally to consume the symbolic. Such a cannibalism, an anthropophagy, is at the source of the mestizo culture of difference. The monolithic identity of the European Oedipal father is cannibalized to produce mestizo difference. In the work of Georges Bataille, and in another sense in Slavoj Zizek, a culture of excess, that is, a culture of the real, is abjected, and in some instances defecated, from the symbolic. In anthropophagy this consumption, this consummation, goes further than what is proposed by Bataille. The symbolic becomes less the subjectivity of abjection than literally of introjection. In this eating, there is a guarantee of the practice of not just the exceptional, but 'the impossible' (compare this with the notion of the possible in the previous chapter). The transition from taboo to totem is anthropophagy. What was a European taboo becomes a mestizo totem. In the West, for Andrade as for Freud, the emergence of totem from taboo (endogamy) signalled the transition from nature to culture. In anthropophagy, the mestizo transgresses culture itself. It is telling perhaps that there is a renewed interest in anthropophagy at the turn of the twenty-first century in the age of global culture industry. In global culture industry more generally, what was culture is transgressed, is cannibalized by industry. The symbolic is cannibalized by the real.

9 Conclusion: Virtual Objects and the Social Imaginary

Introduction

With globalization, culture becomes fully industrial. Culture and the culture – or creative – industry shifts from a logic of representation to a logic of things; media shift from the register of representation to that of objects. It is this shift and how these objects flow that has been the subject matter of this book. There is a shift from culture as a regime of representation to culture as a *system of objects*. There are three steps to this change. First, culture literally escapes the register of representation to reconstitute itself in the register of things. Second, the cultural object, once removed from the realm of representation, constitutes itself as a system: a system whose virtual or deep structure generates a series of actual forms. Third, the system and its actual forms enter into flows that we encounter, that we experience as the public, as the users, the audience, the consumers of this culture. This experience is not just of the object (it is not just subject-object), it is an intersubjective encounter, which is at the same time a process of exchange, involving what we understand as a social imaginary. These are the three points around which we want to structure this conclusion.

A central argument of this book is that in their transformative potential, the objects of global culture industry are *virtual* objects. As virtuals,
they are potentials that generate a succession (a series or flow) of actual
forms. In other words they are virtuals that actualize in a great variety of
ways. They are not *dead* labour like Marx's classical commodity. As potentials that generate a process of forms, they are very much *alive*. These
potentials are structural processes that generate the cultural forms we
encounter. But, as we shall also stress in this conclusion, it is the consumers, audience or users of global culture industry who do a great deal
of the deciding what these objects and these processes are. The 'we' at
stake in this intersubjective encounter is constituted in a *social imaginary*,
the 'middle region' of our sense-making apparatus. We make sense of the
world through intuition and perception, our 'lower' faculties, and
through the 'higher' faculties of rational understanding. Between these
two levels – and forming sometimes harmonious, sometimes contradictory connections between them – is the imagination or the *imaginary*.
The imaginary very importantly comprises memory: in the case of the
social imaginary it is a collective memory. It is this social imaginary that
in some part determines the empirical products – the actual forms – of
global culture industry. This social imaginary is, however, itself structural and indeed processual, itself undergoing constant modification.
Our argument is that the deeper processes of this social imaginary form
a structural relationship with the generative potential of the objects of
the global culture industry. There is a relationship of 'structural coupling' between the virtual objects of the global culture industry and our
social imaginary. Thus the social imaginary itself is a central agent, and
partly responsible, for the deeper and structural transformations of the
global culture industry.[1]

It is also our argument – through the book and in this conclusion –
that the global culture industry is at the same time deeper *and* more
superficial than classical culture and the classical commodity. It is
deeper in that, unlike classical culture and the commodity which are
actuals or forms, at stake now are virtuals, or deeper structural processes
that generate forms. It is also more superficial, in that unlike in classical
culture in which form takes on the rounded, harmonious features of
classical beauty and art, today's cultural objects are encountered
through the flatness of an interface, of a decorated, ornamental or geometric surface, and in this sense have as much to do, say, with design,
which is industrial, as with art, which is properly cultural. Finally,
through the book and below, our argument is that though all of this
opens up a wonderful world of invention for both producers and the
social imaginary of users, at the same time what we are dealing with is
capital accumulation. We are dealing not just with invention but also
with power: the power of global and imperial capital. We are dealing
with a capitalism that has begun to base its accumulation less on the

abstract, homogenous labour of actuals, and more on the generative and invention-based potential of virtual objects. We are dealing with the power of what is becoming virtual capitalism. If the national manufacturing order can be characterized as actual capitalism, then this global cultural order is virtual capitalism.

From Representation to Thing

Let us stress, at the risk of repetition, that we do not want to argue that culture never was representational. We are not making an ontological argument about the 'being' of culture. Our argument is that culture was primarily representational and now in large part is not. The older representational paradigm of culture incorporated much more than just realism. The emergent culture of the object breaks at the same time with realism and the critique of realism, that is, there is a fundamental break with the entire regime of representation. Thus Picasso and Matisse, in art, and Clement Greenberg, in criticism, carry out the critique of the Renaissance regime of realist representation and promulgate the flatness of the picture plane. Yet this critique of realism still occupies its ground in relation to representation. In contrast, Marcel Duchamp's move into conceptual art instead avoids the problem of representation altogether. Duchamp in this sense moves into the register of the object. Or in film, Jean-Luc Godard breaks with the classic realist Hollywood film by putting the focus on the cinematic apparatus. This too is the critique of representation. But as such, it is a critique of the regime of representation. It deals with a 'crossed-out' ~~representation~~, much as the philosophy of Jacques Derrida deals with a crossed-out signified. It remains in the regime of representation. Classical culture industry works in the commoditized regime of representation. Global culture industry does not stand in a position of critique to this. Global culture industry escapes into another space altogether: the realm of the object.

The shift from representation to objects can be seen in strongest relief in this book in our discussion of animation in chapter 5. Narrative here exemplifies the order of representation of the classical culture industry that we encounter in the novel, drama or cinema. Something else happens in cartoons. The narrative is disrupted by the intrusion of an abstract surface (or perhaps better the surface of an abstract space). Norman Klein likens the effect of the intrusion of this abstract surface to Cubism, and its facet planes of cubes, cones and spheres that intrude into the previously representational surface of the picture plane. It is the surface of an 'abstract space' that disrupts the metric and two-dimensional space of narrative representation (DeLanda 2002): a non-metric space, a non-metric surface. Yet this surface is very much a question of the graphic, a question of line. Its privileged place is the non-narrative and graphic storytelling of cartoons. This is because the real live actors of normal cinema cannot follow the logic of the line, cannot stretch and shrink with plasticity – what Sergei Eisenstein called the 'plasmaticity' of the cartoon character.[2] Real-live actors in cinema have what Deleuze and Guattari (1999) would call 'bodies with organs', that is, they are organisms that are already formed. Cartoon characters have plasmatic, 'molecular' bodies that can follow the line of the graphic rather than the much more formed and molar nature of narrative. Daffy Duck can stay Daffy Duck, Bugs Bunny can stay Bugs Bunny as they metamorphose. They stretch and shrink and squash; sometimes they literally explode, but they stay who – or perhaps better, what – they are.

Representational culture is both pictorial – as in Renaissance perspective – and narrative. The metamorphosing abstract surface of today's cultural objects intrudes upon both pictorial and narrative representation. It intrudes upon the integrity of narrative. It does so by disentangling the integrity (and the identity) of the main character(s). Narrative storytelling is driven by the motivations of the protagonist. Narrative, whose roots are in the novel, *le roman*, flows from the internal subjectivity of the protagonist(s), from their motivation and their character: from the identity of their character (Ricoeur 1990). The reader of the narrative thus knows the character's motivations: we know his or her purposes, his or her goals. What cartoon graphics does – what its stretching lines, facet planes and abstract surfaces do – is to disrupt the integrity of the narrative by intruding upon the integrity of the subjectivity that is driving it.

Henri Bergson's comparison of drama with the comic is instructive here. Bergson's comic works like the automata of the cartoon: according to a logic of not 'life', but instead mechanism. Unlike the motivations of the live character in drama, the comic character behaves according to habit, to repetition. In his *Matter and Memory* (1991), Bergson contrasts mechanistic matter with vitalist memory. Bergson's comic is matter without memory. The comic, like matter, works through cause and effect. Life, and narrative drama, for Bergson comprise memory that is constituted in the interval between cause and effect, between reaction and action. The comic is cause and effect without interval. There is a depth to narrative, to the novel, which contrasts with the surface-like nature of the cartoon and the comic. The human has depth: the machine is all surfaces. For Vladimir Propp (1970), characters in the novel work from a principle of depth and motivation from within. In fairy tales, characters operate instead according to function. Fairy-tale characters, like cartoon characters, are thing-like in their repetitive rule following. Characters in the novel and drama have the human freedom to find their own rules. In narrative drama and the novel, it is the story that drives the medium. In the cartoon and fairy tale it is instead the medium that drives the story. The novel and narrative occupy the irreversible time of the singular subject. This subject comprises the depth of memory, whose trace underscores this irreversibility. The comic in contraposition occupies the reversible time of mechanism. The dramatic character is introduced in a situation that is tied to the story: he or she is not separate from this. The comic character, Bergson notes, may be introduced in any situation whatever as if disembedded from the story and its irreversible time.

The thing-like nature of the comic and cartoon operates in a register of not action but gesture, not motivation but punctuation or notation: of not narrative drive but explosion. In each case, the unconscious and mechanical gesture, the explosion, the punctuation reveals something that the comic does not want revealed. What is revealed is the character's own mechanism. To be social is to operate according to motivation and rule-finding flexibility. The comic and cartoon character in this sense are *unsocial* (or post-social, Knorr Cetina 2000). It is the lack (or failure) of identity or purpose or motivation of the comic that strikes the viewer: the disconnections of character. This intrusion of mechanism embarrasses and disrupts the life-narrative of agents. Giddens (1990) spoke of the 'ontological security' of subjects ensconced in a coherent life-narrative. Gerhard Piers (1953) referred to its disruption in terms of shame. In such shame, you are caught outside of the identity you put across. This intrusion into narrative is unsocial because the coherence of your life-narrative must intersect and work with the life-narratives of others. It is in the comic that we betray what Bergson calls the 'middle regions of the soul'. Not the upper regions where we are in control, comparing, judging and shaping coherent self-identities through our life-narratives, but the habitual, conventional middle regions where we resemble each other and are a bit like puppets.

In *Toy Story* and the Wallace and Gromit animated features, it is not the narrative but the graphic that is what defines (characterizes) the object. John Lasseter of Pixar describes how his career began with a short film that has since become a Pixar logo: a brief animated sequence of a lamp. Nick Park starts with a drawing of Wallace, or one of the other characters. It is then storyboarded; the figure precedes the narrative. Once the abstract surface of cartoon logic, this logic of the mechanism of things, makes its breakthrough, it is unstoppable. And animation, already in the register of things, is ideal for the merchandising of things. The things that are the best for merchandising are those that are able to stand outside a narrative. In *Toy Story*, Sheriff Woody drives the narrative, in which he grows up, becomes a man by recognizing that he is a toy and as such is substitutable, replaceable. Whereas Woody is the toy that acts as if he is a human-like protagonist, Buzz Lightyear is the thing that thinks he has a life. Buzz is the machine disrupting the Woody-driven narrative. Buzz will not admit he is a toy, will not develop and move towards reason as Woody will over the course of the narrative. He mechanistically repeats that he is a Space Ranger; that he can fly; that he is on a mission. 'To infinity and beyond' is his motto, almost his trademark. And who sells the toys? Who sells the merchandising? Not Woody, but Buzz. 'To infinity and beyond' is the denial of narrative, which has to do with Woody coming to terms with Andy growing up.

The same is true with Wallace and Gromit. Only here it is Gromit, the dog, who is reasonable and takes on the human qualities as the motivated protagonist of the narrative. And it is Wallace who takes on the mechanistic qualities of the intrusive thing. It is Wallace's comic potential that intrudes into the sensible Gromit's drama. It is the comic and cartoon logic of this thing-likeness, this intrusion of the thing into the narrative that propels these cultural objects into merchandise, into games, ringtones, key rings, alarm clocks, T-shirts and screensavers, and a whole wider system of objects outside of the film. All this has to do less with a logic of text and reader, as did the classical culture industry, and more with a logic of play. It makes the film *Toy Story* just one instance in a wider commercial system of objects. Buzz becomes a 'property', which is given only initial exposure in the film. That is, one aspect of animation, its graphic, mechanistic aspect, is already in the commercial system of objects and is at odds with the narrative of the film and the integrity and the identity of character. There is a resolution to this contradiction. It happens largely outside the film, and is in favour of the commercial system of objects. And in relation to this sytem, the object itself acquires a life. The mechanism deplored by Bergson becomes Deleuze and Guattari's '*machin*ism'. We are faced with vital machines: the machine no longer as a cause-and-effect linear system, but as a non-linear, self-organizing and vital system. It is this that is at stake in the system of objects of the global culture industry.

The Cultural Thing-itself

Theodor Adorno suggests that with the 'mass product' and culture industry, there is the commoditization of the 'thing itself'. The thing-itself is for Adorno 'the internal organization of the object itself, its inner logic'. Epistemology and science address not things-in-themselves but things-*for*-themselves. Art, and correspondingly ontology, is about things-in-themselves. The principles of the culture industry can be seen perhaps most clearly in contradistinction to what might be called 'science-industry'. If technology is the industrialization of science, the culture industry is the industrialization of art. 'Kantian' science is about things-for-us or appearances: that is phenomena. A number of thinkers have juxtaposed Goethe to Kant in this context. 'Goethean' art is about things-in-themselves: it relates to essences or noumena. Science is about the outer logic, the extensive logic, the connections between and external organization of these phenomena. Art, for its part, addresses Adorno's 'internal organization' of the object, 'its inner logic'. Science, from very early in the history of capitalism, gave us, through technology, through research becoming effectively R&D, through findings becoming uses, the standardization of things-for-themselves, that is the mass production of science products. In late capitalism we have again through technology, in an age of mechanical production, the standardization of things-*in*-themselves, the mass production of art products. Science lends itself to the industrial principle, in that it always aims at greater universalism, so that the statements its findings lead to can embrace an ever greater range of particulars. Art, in contrast, always wants to make the one-off, the singular. It never wants to make statements that embrace universals. Thus from nearly the beginning we have capitalism as 'science-industry', and this is about the industrialization, in mass terms the standardization, of universals. Only in late capitalism – on any scale after the Second World War and on a much greater scale after the end of the Cold War – do we get the culture industry or the industrialization of singularities. Science wants to find universals in nature, while art wants to create singularities. The principle of science transfers directly from Galileo and Newton to Adam Smith's possessive individualism to the principle of the commodity. This commoditization of the universal happens easily; indeed it is the transfer of classical scientific principles to the economy. Yet there is a major gulf between taking the findings of the universal into the economy and the creation of singularities. There is always a tension in the culture industry, always a tension between standardization and difference. The homogeneity of the commodity finds itself sliding into the heterogeneity of difference. At stake in the global culture industry is something that is neither exactly singularity nor commodity, but difference itself. Difference in an age of globalization, of flows, is always abstract difference. Appadurai (1986) contrasts the concrete singularity and rootedness of the gift and use value with the abstract generality of the commodity. But such abstract generality or abstract equivalence applies only to classical science-industry. At stake in today's global culture industry is less the concrete inequivalence of gift and use-value, than abstract difference. When we speak of difference we mean not concrete singularity, but abstract difference. Concrete singularity precedes the commodity: abstract inequivalence succeeds it.

Walter Benjamin always insisted against Kant that experience was not, as in science, only of the empirical, but also of the transcendental. Science is about *findings* in the empirical, while art is about *creating* the transcendental, or creating a prism onto the transcendental. Thus science-industry is about implementing findings in the making of prototypes, while the culture industry is about the standardization of creation. The culture industries are always the *creative industries* (McRobbie 1999). Science has findings, art has creation or *oeuvre* (work). Science is about findings in *nature*. It is about judgements. We recall our discussion of Freud's juxtaposition of comparison and mimicry. Comparison addresses standards in regard to natural phenomena. Natural phenomena or facts as they appear in nature come under regularities or universals. Art is more in the realm of *mimicry* than comparison. For Goethe, the artist imitates nature in his or her creativity. For Kant, nature is physical, while for Goethe it is also metaphysical. Science is about finding regularities in the phenomena of nature. Art is about creating singularities like nature creates singularities. Art is in a relation of mimicry to nature.

Goethe and later Benjamin counter Kant and science's physicality with art's metaphysics. Both reach back behind Kant to Baruch Spinoza. In Spinoza's metaphysics of single substance – in contrast to Kant's two-substance critique – this substance is both natural and divine. Goethe takes up the side of nature in his theory of creation. Nature is creative; it creates unique things: singularities. Benjamin (1991) takes up the side of the divine. He derives his theory of creation from the Old Testament's Genesis. God created man, who in the Garden of Eden spoke a metaphysical language: a language of the proper name and singularities. This is the stuff of art, of aura. This metaphysical language is destroyed in the Fall and again destroyed with the rise of the commodity and mechanical reproduction. In its place rises a debased and instrumentalized physical language that Benjamin calls 'semiotic'. Where is there now a place for the transcendental? In the interstices, now and again, in the commodity's homogenous time, there are small glimpses of the metaphysical: of Benjamin's 'messianic time'. This is *Schockerlebnis*. It is not the *Erfahrung* of Kantian science; nor is it the enduring *Erlebnis* of Goethean art. *Erlebnis* now only pokes its head through *Erfahrung* in shocks. These shocks are *the event*, both for Benjamin and for us in this book. The problem in the global culture industry is that capital has not only taken the production of difference and brought it under its wing as the principle of power, it has also largely captured the event. The event is a breakthrough of difference into the homogenous temporal logic of the commodity. The event is generated from a transcendental, and even this has come under the logic of capital. For Goethe and Benjamin, creation is *schaffen*, *Schöpfung*. The word *Kreativität* did not exist in German in the time of Goethe, or for that matter of Benjamin. With the growth of the culture industry, the word *Kreativität* is everywhere (Bröckling et al. 2003). *Kreativität* is the industrialization of *Schöpfung*.

In this book we have drawn on similar ideas from Deleuze. Deleuze shares Goethe's vitalist metaphysics and Spinozist influence. In Deleuze, Goethean creativity becomes invention, generation and construction. This is inscribed in Spinoza's idea of *potentia*, that is power as creative force that is counterposed to *potestas*, or power as domination. It is *potentia* – at the same time life (in French, *puissance*) – that is involved in creation only to be trumped by the *potestas* of the culture industry (Negri 2000). Creativity as *puissance* becomes creativity as *pouvoir*. In science-industry, power is external and extensive and epistemological. In culture-industry, power as domination is transitive and intensive and becomes ontological.[3] Goethe's processual idea of creation is paralleled in Deleuze's philosophy of the actualization of the virtual. Goethe's focus is on the process of creation: Deleuze's is less on the virtual or the actual than on processes of actualization and virtualization. Goethe speaks of this often via the example of a plant and the flower in nature, which unfold. Originally compressed, they unfold in their creativity. Deleuze also uses the language of the fold and of unfolding. Goethe's transcendental or intensive moment is compressed: it is plastic. He is influenced by the precursors of molecular biology in the work of Geoffroy St Hilaire. His molecular bodies solidify as they unfold. This sort of molecular body is also at the heart of Deleuze and Guattari's, also virtual, 'body without organs' (1999). Yet Deleuze's transcendental – much like the mathematical metaphysics of Leibniz's calculus – is more mathematical than linguistic (DeLanda 2002).

The transcendental for Goethe and Benjamin is linguistic; for Leibniz and Deleuze it is mathematical. For Deleuze in *Difference and Repetition*, virtualization is a process of differentiation as in differential calculus. And actualization is a process of differenciation, which is also integration in integral calculus. Differentiation as in calculus is compression: it is moving from the metric extension of the actual to the non-metric intensity of the virtual. This differentiation is de-differenciation. For Deleuze invention runs both ways. For Goethe it is mostly a process of unfolding from the folds. For Deleuze it is unfolding in differenciation (actualization) but also folding. Thus he will be more interested in how a body with organs can become a body without organs than the inverse. He is more interested in how underneath the movement-image there is the virtual of the time-image than the reverse. Because Deleuze's ontology is rooted less in art than in mathematics, he is able to collapse the transcendental and the empirical in a way that Goethe cannot. Thus Deleuze's metaphysics is a 'transcendental empiricism'. Unlike Goethe's opposition of the machine and the vital, Deleuze and Guattari give us vital machines. Indeed, in Deleuze and Guattari's terms the generation of the actual is machinic, from the *potentia* of desiring-machines. Thus Deleuze breaks with the cultural pessimism of Goethe and indeed Adorno. His 'standardized thing-in-itself' becomes also the difference generation of the culture machines. He captures the tension in the global culture industry between *potentia* and *potestas*. For Goethe's and Adorno's cultural pessimism of the transformation of *potentia* into *potestas* is Deleuze and Guattari's optimism of invention where *potestas* becomes *potentia*.

Play: Ontology and Mimicry

There is another piece to the puzzle of the shift from representation to the object: *play*. The narrative and representational social imaginary lies in the *reader* or *audience*, while the *player* engages the culture of things. For Hans-Georg Gadamer (1976), we can experience a cultural entity either, on the one hand, epistemologically or, on the other, ontologically. In an epistemological encounter, we relate to the entity from its outside:

as a thing-for-itself. In an ontological relationship we relate to it from its inside: as a thing-in-itself. The reader or audience of classical culture industry would in this sense stand in an epistemological relation to the cultural entity (the 'text'), while in the global culture industry the user or public stands in an *ontological* relationship. The Kantian engagement with the object in which we can never know the thing-in-itself, but only its appearance, is for Gadamer supremely epistemological. In it, the experiencer is outside of the thing that he/she experiences. It is Husserl and phenomenology that give us knowledge through ontology. In phenomenological knowledge we experience the thing-in-itself. Moreover, epistemology presumes that the experiencer is separate from and in a different world from the object with no intentionality or attitude towards it. For Husserl (1983), knowledge is already intentional, already of an object. That is we are in the world with the object ontologically, with an attitude towards it.

One way of getting ontological with the object is in play, in the particular type of attitude, the special type of intentionality involved in play. In play, we descend into the world with objects. We deal not with a text but with an *environment* of cultural objects. For Gadamer, the account of play appears at the very outset of *Truth and Method* (2004). Play is for Gadamer the door that opens the transition from nature to culture.[4] When we play, we are already cultural. This is a question of ontogeny and phylogeny. A child playing is more than merely 'natural', though still preconventional. Play may give a model for convention, perhaps partly though imitation, through 'mimicry'. But convention is not yet conception. Gadamer's *Truth and Method* juxtaposes epistemological and positivist 'method' to ontological and hermeneutic 'truth'; play, for Gadamer, has a lot more to do with 'truth' than with 'method'. Play and other activities, cultural and true, come increasingly under the hegemony of method over the course of Gadamer's masterpiece. Our method or methodology in this book, as we described it in chapter 1, is a question of an attempt at getting ontological in the world with the objects. Gadamer was scathing about his historicist predecessors in the hermeneutic *Geisteswissenschaften* like Wilhelm Dilthey. Dilthey (2003), in an initial move – with Goethe and against Kant – moved out of the epistemology of the *Naturwissenschaften* into the historical space of ontology. But in a second move, Dilthey epistemologized method and systematic classification, thereby for Gadamer sacrificing truth. Our modus operandi has been not to revert to the systematic classification of Dilthey or for that matter to Weberian ideal types. It has been to follow the object rather than once again withdraw into epistemology and classification.

A version of truth versus method, ontology versus epistemology, is found in Roger Caillois's (2001) writing on play. Caillois criticizes Johan Huizinga's *Homo Ludens* for its focus on the overly methodical, what Huizinga (1955) calls 'ludic', notion of play. To the ludic's binding rules, its arbitrary imperatives and purposive conventions, Caillois opposes *'paida'*, whose principles are the non-principles of divergence, turbulence, free improvisation, carefree gaiety and impulsive exuberance. Caillois gives us four types of play, one of which is the rather heavily rule-bound 'agon' and another is the more antinomian 'mimicry'. Huizinga's *Homo Ludens* emphasized agon: Caillois's ontology identifies a metaphysics of mimicry. In the global culture industry, these two types of play return and come into competition, though mimicry perhaps gains dominance over the more utilitarian rationality of agon. For Gadamer, play, by definition, cannot be purposive: for Caillois, it should not be. For both Gadamer and Caillois, we play non-purposively. Indeed, culture itself is primarily non-purposive. Gadamer – and also Jacques Lacan – were influenced by philosophical anthropology, in which culture develops in the 'lack' created by man's poverty of instincts. Where animals are first purposive, the human is not. He or she plays; he or she is emotional. What the global culture industry does is use play and mimicry, use this emotionality – this affect – for the accumulation of capital.

The infantilism of mimicry is central, as we noted in chapter 5, to Sigmund Freud's understanding of the comic. When we encounter a phenomenon we can deal with it in two ways. Either we can imitate it or we can compare it with other phenomena. The first of these types of activity – imitation – is, for Freud, characteristically infantile: the second, comparison, is mature. Comparison involves standards: adult and solid norms as the basis of judgement. The norms that make comparison (and indeed classification) possible are also the basis of sociability. In comic imitation we betray ourselves as childish. We are operating from the intermediate regions of our minds: we are pre-conventional.[5] If we betray and expose ourselves through comic imitation, however, we may preserve ourselves through the more adult mode of comparison. In imitation, our sense of self, Caillois notes, is undermined. At the same time, he continues, we are free from the worry of self-preservation. Thus comedy for children works through characters' not being able to control functions that they themselves (the children) have just learnt to control. In *Toy Story* it was often the fathers of the film's child viewers who engaged in mimicry, and their break with narrativity is registered in the cash registers of the object's merchandisers.

The social imaginary of Swatch collectors we spoke of in chapter 6 is also a community of playfulness. This social imaginary consists less of story than of game. *On joue un jeu.* We play a game. *Wir treiben ein Spiel.* Yet we play outside the rules of a game. We mimic outside of agon. This tension in play between agon and mimicry is seen in Nike's branding in the use of the figure of Michael Jordan. Whereas Swatch is self-confessedly a non-utilitarian emotional product, Nike is caught between the logics of utility and emotion. Michael Jordan is a player in the agonistic, rule-structured and purposive game of basketball, in a similar sense that Nike shoes are built for utility, with, for example, aerodynamic features. Yet Nike branding works perhaps less through identification with basketball rules than through long-term emotional bonding with Michael Jordan and other athletes such as Tiger Woods. Further, the identification with Michael Jordan is less with his rule-boundedness than his violation of laws: for example, of the law of gravity in his time–space defying movement. Here he is like a cartoon character, as Spike Lee describes him, 'up in space, up in the air. Explosive, all the horizontal creative passing angles, hanging in space' (Lee 1997: 20). Like Michael Jordan, like Air Jordans, the goddess Nike is light as should be the goddess of speed and victory, the goddess of the event that intrudes into ordinary rule-bound time. She glorifies the spot at which time comes to a temporary halt. Michael Jordan, the living hangman, and the goddess Nike, are moments at which the abstract surface breaks through. Brazil and Ronaldinho give you the moment of magic, not the application of rules of agon. Basketball has a rule whereby if you are in the air when the last second ticks and the gun sounds, you can still get away your shot. Time stands still literally as you hang in the air. You are like the goddess Nike 'in the time of no-time-at-all'. *Just Do It*, just do it like Jordan. 'Doing it' is not about standards, it is not about comparison and judgement. It is immediate: it is about mimicry. Don't think, don't compare. Go for it. Just Do It. Be the abstract surface. Metamorphose. This is 'ilinx', joy in movement, one of Caillois's modes of play.

The Object as Ornamental Surface

There seem to be two types of cultural or media theory today: two ways of understanding contemporary culture. In the first, media and culture comprise a set of depthless surfaces: of simulacra, of fleeting and superficial images. Culture is reduced to a skin, an interface, an ornament or a decoration. The author and indeed the subject lose their depth and are instead a discursive constitution. Meaning is hollowed out and deferred and becomes just a superficial play of signifiers, a mere pastiche. This is the first sense in which postmodernist culture has come to be understood, from the mid-1980s, in the writings of not just Baudrillard and Fredric Jameson, but also those of Derrida, Barthes and Foucault. A second and opposing understanding came in the second half of the 1990s. In this understanding, culture is inventive, it generates differences, and is complex and mutating. It is fractal and topological. It self-constructs from a vector plane. There is a depth of creative substance. In new media it is no longer the surface of the interface that Negroponte (1996) had us believe was the be-all and end-all, but the computational 'back-end' that counts; comprising algorithms and compressed non-metric spaces that generate – like a 'difference machine' – the culture we encounter. It would seem that contemporary culture and today's media could be either one or the other: that the two types of postmodern culture stand in opposition to one another. The seven cultural objects of this book, the seven biographies described here, comprise *both* aspects: they are a surface integument, that is, simulacral, and at the same time endlessly generative of invention. They are ornamental surface and structural depth. In each case our objects are also systems: they are systems with deep, though changing, structures. These structures generate forms, which take the form of interfaces, integuments, skins. These simulacral surfaces in their global movement couple with their environment, at the same time constituting or at least modifying the latter, which then simultaneously modifies and mutates the fractal space, the topological space at their core. As vital generative depth, they are more alive than the commodity, indeed more alive, more charged with energy, with *puissance*, than the work of art itself. The work of art needs the agency of the artist – it needs a relationship of *poieisis* with the artist – in order to unfold in what for Heidegger (1994) is a process, a becoming, of *phusis*. The technical object, the objects of technological culture, that are the products of global culture industry, as it were unfold themselves – they reflexively unfold generating form even in the absence of artistic *poieisis*. At stake in this book has been a sociology of the object. Here the technical object of global culture industry is caught between the two classical objects – on the one hand the work of art and on the other the commodity. But 'caught between' in a very unusual sense, because these objects are held together in a tension of polar contradiction. As generative process, they are more packed with vitality, even more ontological than the work of art. As simulacrum, as ornamental surface, they are emptier, more superficial, more dead than the commodity.

This can be seen starting not just from art but also from architecture. Let us begin to address surface. In order to do so, it is instructive to consider design: both as surface of ornamentation (simulacra) and as generative virtual system. The Roman architect Vitruvius, writing in the first century BC, spoke of three dimensions of design or architecture: *firmitas, utilitas* and *venustas. Firmitas* refers to structure, or load-bearing qualities; *utilitas* to use; and *venustas* to beauty. The load-bearing qualities or structure become the province of the engineer. *Utilitas* becomes a matter for the plan, the programme of the building, and its horizontal space of action. *Venustas* or beauty becomes the question of form, of the outer walls of the building. *Venustas* is less a question of structural support or indeed infrastructure (base), less a matter of action (*utilitas* and plan/programme), than a question of *perception*. Thus the building and the designed object are experienced through action (use) and perception. The architect and the designer are most of all concerned with *venustas* or form. This was featured in the Beaux-Arts tradition that trained architects coming out of Paris and spreading through the world from the mid-eighteenth century. Design meant form. Structure was left to the engineers. Utility or function would follow. The great materialist architectural theorist Gottfried

Semper, in his critique of formalism, ends up giving us a theory of just this above-mentioned ornamental surface. Semper resolves the problem of form into a question of surface. He refused to take Greek antiquity and hence classicism as his paradigm. He noted that in architecture the question of *venustas*, of beauty or form, was a matter neither of load-bearing structure, nor of plan or programme of action. It was instead a question of *the wall*. Visiting the Great Exhibition in London in 1851, he fixed on the exhibit of the Caribbean Hut. The walls of the hut were thin; their material was textile; they were decorated with ritual patterns, with weaving. The walls were there for looking at, for perception. These ritual yet decorative walls were for Semper the origins of *form*. They are in the place of Vitruvius's *venustas*. These walls are at the origin of the Greek columns, stone columns. Through an evolution of what Semper calls *Stoffwechsel*, or materials-change, they shift from textile to stone and take on the more sculptural dimensions, the three-dimensionality of classicism (Hvattum 2004). This form is not the three-dimensionality of sculpted classical columns, but two-dimensionality; not stone, but textile; not beautiful, but *decorative*. Indeed, decoration here comes to be at the root of beauty, rather than being a debased transformation of the latter. Beauty, the transcendental essence of art, becomes resolved into the empirical facticity of design. The transcendental judgement associated with art becomes resolved into the empirical experience of *taste*. It is just as much design and empirical taste as art and metaphysical beauty that are at stake in global culture industry.

With Semper we are fully prepared for Robert Venturi and Denise Scott Brown's 'decorated shed'. For it is not art, but design, and in particular design in the paradigm of the decorated shed that is at the heart of what form is in the global culture industry. *A medium is a structure and a surface.* In Venturi's (1977) *Complexity and Contradiction*, the volumetric density of classical form is reduced to decoration on the outside of a shed. Venturi's post-modern critique of modernism was not primarily that we should look at form instead of function. In Venturi there was an implicit send-up of function in reducing plan and utility to the shed, a place to store garden tools. More important, though, was the flattening of beauty, the flattening of the wall into decoration, into ornament. Form becomes ornament in the decorated shed. It is still to be perceived (not used); it is flattened as in Semper's hut into two dimensions: into a thinness, in which it becomes an integument, a skin, like, indeed, the interface of a medium. And we are of course insisting that global culture industry objects are both interface and generating structure.

When Rem Koolhaas and Hans Ulrich Obrist spoke with Venturi and Scott Brown in *Mutations*, they compared their two early books about urbanism: Koolhaas's *Delirious New York* (1977) and Venturi et al.'s *Learning From Las Vegas* (1977). Koolhaas says that *Delirious New York* is about urban substance: the sort of processual, structurally mutating and generating substance that we have been addressing under structure. In contrast, Venturi said that *Learning From Las Vegas* was about urban *form*. The decorated shed flattens classical form; so does *Learning From Las Vegas*, in which neon and signage carry out a similar flattening of form. With neon and signage, form comes to resemble the media. The cityscape flattens into an interface, a mediascape, or often a 'brandscape'. The built environment flattens into a media environment, a brand environment. Built object space becomes culture-industry space.

Scott Brown says that this thinking came from her association with the Independent Group in London in the late 1950s. The Independent Group included artists Richard Hamilton, Eduardo Paolozzi and Lawrence Alloway, who coined the term 'Pop Art', and architects Rayner Banham and Colin St John Wilson. They broke into the public eye in a major way in the 'This Is Tomorrow' show at the Whitechapel (1956), in which the public saw Hamilton's trademark 'Just What is it That Makes Today's Homes So Different, So Appealing?' Hamilton, who incorporated the tradition of Marcel Duchamp, is the linchpin of what transforms conceptual art into media and culture industry. Here the three-dimensionality of form – whether classical or modernist – is flattened into the two-dimensionality of pop. This two-dimensionality, Hamilton said to the contemporary curator Obrist in an interview in 2005, is not so much visual art as 'visual culture'. Hamilton's suggestion was that art starts working less in the more volumetric and beautiful media of sculpture and painting and more in the two-dimensional media, the flattened media of contemporary visual culture. Duchamp takes discarded found objects. These are objects that were designed. They are not found in nature but in culture. Duchamp chooses more or less utilitarian artefacts like urinals and wheels. Warhol and Hamilton, for their part, draw on more ornamental artefacts like furnishing and Campbell soup cans. In Hamilton and so much other work in Pop, including of course Warhol, art becomes design. There is a convergence in such flattened media forms in the biographies of all of this book's cultural objects.

In the biographies of our objects of global culture industry, there is a flattening-out: an emptying-out of use-value. Nicolas Hayek thus established Swatch in a move from utility to accessory. Yet the function of *utilitas* remains. We still *use* the watches. There is still the function of *utilitas* but it is subordinated to *venustas*, or *venustas* flattened to the 'style' of the accessory. There is still – as there was in Semper's Caribbean hut – a meaning function, but (S)watches are no longer to be durables that are given for (hearth) ritual events such as graduations, weddings or anniversaries. Instead, they punctuate the 'little rituals' of everyday life. Swatch is, as Hayek insists, an emotional product, but at stake are little emotions. The biography of the object as system was somewhat different with Nike. At the start, Nike, with its waffle method of aerating rubber soles, was product- and engineering-driven. Nike was for utility, for sport, to run faster and jump higher, not for fashion. Indeed, Reebok was first into the Swatch-like idea that trainers could be a fashion good, an accessory, while Nike still in the mid-1980s, and with some success, was technology-led. It was at this moment that Phil Knight decided that Nike would become 'a marketing company'. Yet Nike would never be an out-and-out fashion shoe like the leisure shoe-type trainers from Prada and Hermes. Nike is still as much sport-event as fashion-oriented. Even its market-led-ness is focused on something like *utilitas*. You want not just to be seen playing basketball in Nikes: you want to *play* basketball in Nikes. Yet engineering and 'loadbearingness', or at least structure, is now meant to be *light*. This is partly symbolic, partly for utility. Again, there is a move to *venustas* as decoration, as ornament.

The brand or the cultural object-system itself is this integument, skin, interface, but also a deeper generative, constructive and creative structure: a compressed structure. The brand itself is non-metric: yet it generates a series of actuals, that is, the range of products in which the brand surfaces. Brand managers talk about the breadth of brands, brand extension, the duration of brands. The core, or the virtual, of the brand is not extensive, but intensive. It is a fold that unfolds into the extensive, the qualitative and the predicative. What are Nike's predicates? The products, services and promotions are what we encounter. They are metric and actual. Yet the brand forms on a vector plane: a plane of immanence, a non-metric fold, even a non-metric Bourdieuan type field in which it is in competition for non-metric, compressed space.

One last point about design and specially architecture, then. We experience architecture from inside a technology, which we inhabit, so to speak. That is, we perceive it from inside, not from the surface, though we perceive this too, but also from, as it were, the bowels – what Adorno saw as the intrinsic interconnections – of the thing-itself. At stake is a medium that first flattens and then stretches (pops up) back into three- or multidimensionality, just like the characters in animated objects we studied. In this context we perceive ontologically. We are at – we inhabit – the core of the thing-itself. So we perceive in the flattened medium, the browsing depth, of the Internet, and in the interior of many installations in contemporary art. This is very different from the more 'epistemological' experience of the reader, the recipient or the audience of texts and other representations. Now culture is more like design: we experience it more like the inhabitants of designed spaces. We experience culture now first through use, second on its surfaces and third from the inside.

Trademarks: Structural Coupling and the Social Imaginary

As we noted in chapter 7, there has been a shift in intellectual property law to an increasing role for trademark law, alongside copyright, in the global culture industry. This is of note because, in legal thinking, trademark does not mark something as the work of an author, even a collective or distributed intelligence author. It is not the mark of something an advertiser or branding expert makes; it is something that is located inside and outside the production process: in the social imaginary of (and about) consumers. Now the social imaginary comprises not just the sign or signifier (the graphic mark 'the Swoosh', the name 'Swatch'), but also the signified, which is immaterial. This signified is the identity or 'soul' of the company: of, say, Nike, Prada or Apple. It is particular Nike products that this signified is associated with – it is particular actualized products that are encountered – but it is Nike more abstractly, itself a concept, that is at the core of a brand's place in the social imaginary. Similarly certain shapes and colours and sounds are associated in the public domain with a set of Apple's products. The colours, shapes and sounds, as well as the iPod, the iMac and the iBook, are actuals. The brand that is associated with them and generates them is a virtual.

In this book we have extended the idea of the social imaginary (Castoriadis 1987; Parameshwar Gaonkar and Lee 2002) to include the social imaginary of *the consumer*. And here the use of the notion 'distinctive and distinctiveness' in trademark law is interesting. A mark or sign must be recognized as different from other signs in the public domain for it to be subject to trademark. It is the distinctiveness of the mark that is at stake in legal judgements, for the legal recognition of distinctiveness is the basis of the exclusion of other trademarks from the particular folded space a mark occupies. Thus it is distinctiveness, difference, that is the source of value: the brand's source of generation of surplus value. This distinctiveness is held legally to exist outside of particular products themselves and to reside in the imagination, or rather in the relation between a product (or a series of products) and the imagination. Trademarks thus occupy a compressed space, a space of difference in itself. The empirical flow of things that we encounter is partly generated from this virtual space of marks. However, these marks do not have extension, they do not *represent* an object: they constitute its core. They constitute a logic of things, congealed in the figure of logo. The public encounters actual difference, but at the same time they *experience* the virtual, the core of the thing. Marshall McLuhan (1997) described the media networks of the global village as a sort of 'outering' or externalization of the human sensorium. In a similar sense, the marks of the brands are an outering of the social imaginary. This compressed virtual constitutes brand value. Brand value is value in surplus above the contributions of capital and labour-power in the products, the actuals generated by the brand. At stake in the global culture industry is a partly virtual regime of capital accumulation. And the basis of this is less the producer than a relation with the social imaginary of the consumers themselves.

We can imagine the set of topological marks that make up the thing-in-itself as like the intensive structure of a cultural object in duration.

But they are also becomings: they are in constant change. How does this work? The cultural object, we have been suggesting, is at the same time a structure and a form. It is dynamic; that is, it circulates and moves through, or perhaps better as flows and fluxes. Its movement, we also suggest, is in part a matter of a series of engagements with its environment: with its users and other features of its environment. These engagements are a series of 'structural couplings'. This is a concept often used by Niklas Luhmann (1999), drawing on the work of Humberto Maturana and Francisco Varela (1979), whose context is molecular biology and cognitive neuroscience. In molecular biology, in the case of an organism as system, a genotype would be analogous with what we have called structure and a phenotype with form. Through particular couplings of phenotypes with their environment, there can be changes at a structural, genotype level. In neuroscience, the neural networks would be structure and consciousness (or mind) form. The system couples with its environment via its form, yet it couples structurally too with systems as structures (in this case neuronal networks). These neuronal structures coupling with systems in the environment (including cultural structures), result in changes not just in forms of consciousness but also in the deep structures of the neural networks (Neidich 2003). The same would apply to topology (structure) versus typology (buildings) in architecture. Here we also find evolutionary paradigms: the coupling is very often a co-evolutionary activity. In this book, what we are looking at is a series of structural couplings of objects with their environments or social imaginaries. During these couplings, intensive features of the object take on very strong associations with actual products in these social imaginaries. In a number of these cases there will then be new marks added to the topological structure of the object (as, for example, in the generation of Air Max products or the Hangman, the silhouette figure of Michael Jordan which marks a series of Nike products), which in turn will take on different shapes as a part of topological constellation of marks. Thus there will be structural change in the object: in this sense the brand, and the cultural object in its core, is a becoming.

What is the public, the consumer, the user, experiencing? They are not experiencing homogeneity, but difference. This is the difference of the rapid succession of products that Georg Simmel had a century ago alluded to in his essays on the proliferation of cultural styles. As we noted before, at stake is not experience as *Erfahrung*, which is the encountering of regularities, of homogeneity, but *Erlebnis*, the experience of difference. Wilhelm Dilthey challenged Kantian epistemology with his ontologization of experience as life, in his idea of experience as *Erlebnis*. This was taken further in Husserl's phenomenology, and especially his phenomenology of inner-time consciousness. For Husserl (1964), whereas outer-time consciousness was the experience of identities, of homogenous Newtonian clock-time, inner-time consciousness was the experience of differences. What made it possible for one thing to come after another in inner-time consciousness is the difference of that next thing. If the *Erlebnis* of inner-time consciousness is not internally differentiated, then it does not count as *Erlebnis* at all. Also challenging Kantian *Erfahrung*, Benjamin was in effect more pessimistic than Husserl: more aware of the deadening domination of outer-time consciousness in his contemporaneous capitalism. So for him the time of *Erfahrung* was dominant, except for the odd moment when difference forced its head through in the shocks of *Schockerlebnis*. In this sense, for Benjamin *Erlebnis* is also *Ereignis*: experience is also the event.

Although phenomenology and hermeneutics had challenged experience as equivalence and homogeneity, these ideas were still working within the realm of representation. What happens in the contemporary age as we leave representation? What happens, as Katharine Hayles (1999) describes, is that experience as presence and absence gives way to experience as pattern and randomness. Experience thus becomes no longer representational, but *informational*. Experience is informational from the point of view of the cultural object and that of the psychological, social and cultural forms – individuals, communities – with which the object couples. It is Niklas Luhmann who most tellingly makes this step. In his youth, Luhmann studied the temporality of Husserl's inner-time consciousness, in which, as noted above, experience is the experience of difference (Arnoldi 2002). He followed Husserl in assuming that consciousness is always intentional. Unlike the Kantian or Cartesian subject, for whom consciousness is separated from its object, Husserlian consciousness is intentional in the sense of being in the world with and attached to objects. Even in classical phenomenology, consciousness is – unlike in epistemology – already *coupled* with the object. Intentionality is coupling, but it is a coupling that presumes a transcendental and foregrounds representation. In his later work, Luhmann, drawing on Maturana and Varela, translates this to systems that experience difference as information. As Varela says, when systems couple, system A experiences system B as information (Varela et al. 1993). System A is here making pattern out of noise. How does system A do this? From system A's history of past structural couplings. This history constitutes a deep structure, an 'in-itself' for system A. It is this core, this 'memory' that makes a pattern out of the noise. This will be different for systems C, D, E and F because each will have a different memory. So system B *communicates*, as Varela says, a 'state' of itself, which for system A is information. And system A does the same in regard of system B. What are these deep structures, these memories, these histories of structural couplings? From the point of view of the cultural object they are the constellation of its marks: the distinctiveness of its trademark structure.

Both systems A and B take in information: for both, information is difference. If it is not different, it is not information and there is no experience. What is experienced on both sides – by object and by subject – is difference. The object experiences the subject only as difference and vice versa. This is also Bateson's information as a 'difference that makes a difference'. Such difference makes a difference in two ways. It does so first as virtualization. Here, encountering the changing branded object makes a difference to the social imaginary. Information is taken in through virtualization and this changes the deep structures of the social imaginary. And the object encounters the subject too as a difference that makes a difference to its virtual. That is, system B makes a difference to system B in a process of virtualization. And vice versa. The second way that information here is a difference that makes a difference is through a process of actualization. Here, the compressed core of the cultural object is a difference-in-itself (Deleuze 1994): a structure-of-trademarks that generate a series of actuals that exist as actual difference or differences-for-themselves. Here too, this time a virtual difference makes an actual difference. This is internal to both the object and the collective subject, whose social imaginary is its difference-in-itself.

There is one last step here in the dynamics of experience in the global culture industry. It has to do with signs. Our suggestion is that we experience trademark, or the structure of trademarks, as *icons*, as described by Charles Sanders Peirce (1978). Now Peirce's theory of signs is a sort of bridge between Saussurean and Benjaminian theories of language. Whereas Saussure (1966) gives a theory of signs that works in the realm of the extensive, Benjamin's works in the intensive. Whereas Saussure's idea of the signifier is fully in the realm of the physical, Benjamin's is paradigmatically a *metaphysics* of language. Whereas Saussure operates in the realm of equivalence, indeed of linguistic equivalent exchange (as Baudrillard noted when he equated Saussurean sign-value with Marxist exchange-value), Benjamin wants to operate in a linguistic theory of the name in a realm of inequivalence and the singular. Saussure's signifier is the universal that captures all the particular referents: Benjamin's sign is the singular. Peirce captures both points of view: physical and metaphysical, extensive and intensive. For example, Peirce's 'symbol' and 'index' are more fully physical and extensive, while Peirce's 'icon' is more metaphysical and intensive. Symbol and the index are perceived, the icon is not perceived but only experienced. The icon is a virtual. An object's iconology – its intensive ordinates of movement – is its mark topology.

The icon is not to do with the aesthetic – and here is where Benjamin breaks with Nietzsche – but rather the religious: they relate to the middle regions of the soul. The higher regions of the soul approach the ultimate reason that is in for example Leibniz and Spinoza, the divine. The closest 'man' can approach this divine is in metaphysical reason, in mathematics and poetry. The icon and the religious work on a much lower level. For Hegel (1998), as we know, religion operates in the middling realm of reason and the mind, far below that of philosophy. It works on the level of icon painting, in medieval Russia, as for example portrayed in Tarkovsky's *Andrei Rublev*. McLuhan's theory of the media too works less through semiology than iconology. We are not in media as citizens, as abstract reasoning individuals: instead we are *communicants*. The icon and culture and indeed light-throughness of the media have as their model the stained-glass windows on medieval churches, where culture is fully graphic to illiterate peasants. These signs are much less symbols or indexes than icons.

For Peirce (1978), the sign stands to someone for something in some respect. The sign creates in the mind of that someone another sign that is the 'interpretant' of the first sign. In this sense the public take as information that which the sign communicates to it, as described above. Yet, Peirce's argument continues, the sign stands for something, its object, but not in all respects, but only in that it refers to an idea that is the ground of its representation. This ground would seem to be the icon. Or more precisely, the sign would be iconic to the extent that it referenced this ground. Deleuze, in *Cinema I* and *II*, uses Peirce's semiotics to speak of the sign and the image in cinema. Deleuze opposes the (Saussurean) semiotic understanding of cinema. For Saussure, the referent or the object will be external to both signifier and signified, and it is static. In contrast, Peirce's sign and his idea of the image are not external to the object (that is, they are not representational), and are dynamic or mobile. In Deleuze the movement image or the cinematic shot or surface does not represent the object but is a 'mobile section of duration of the object'. For Peirce, the image is a set of logical relations in continual transformation in relation to the ground. The icon then is the ground for an infinity of movement-images ('To infinity and beyond'). The iconology of a cultural object is a set of 'intensive ordinates' of movement, generating a series of actual, though often not actualized, shots, or products. Thus the movement-image is the thing-itself caught in movement as a continuous function. The thing-itself here is indeed the time-image, the iconology of the object.

The Surface Imaginary

In his studies of the 'mass ornament', Siegfried Kracauer (1995) does not simply see the turn to the surface that he held to be characteristic of mass culture as a symptom of a world lacking the meaning which could give it substance (Levin 1995: 19). Instead, Kracauer insists that from the perspective of a new philosophy of history, the surface acquires new meaning.[6] Thus, mass is not to be understood in opposition to surface, but each in relation to the other; surface is not outside or on top of mass, but is rather a vector of the movement of mass. To illustrate this thinking, Kracauer pays special attention to the mass forms of his day: the hotel lobby, arcades and bestsellers as well as cinema and photography, the media practices that 'display an elective affinity with the surface' (quoted in Levin 1995: 20). In this work, he focuses on the penetration of culture by *ratio*. Thus, he says, 'The ornament, detached from its bearers, must be understood *rationally*' (ibid.: 77; emphasis in original). He goes on to describe this reason in terms of 'Euclidean geometry' and the 'elementary components' of physics, such as 'waves and spirals'. As Thomas Levin rather wonderfully puts it in his introduction to a collection of Kracauer's Weimar essays: 'Suspending the traditional opposition of (merely decorative) applied ornament and functional structure (a discussion familiar to him from his ten-year stint as an architect), Kracauer here casts the geometry of the mass of the Tiller girls as both an ornamentalization of function and a functionalization of ornament' (ibid.: 18). Kracauer describes the reason at work as providing a (mathematical) logic that organizes the mass; this is the logic of a 'linear system', training 'the broadest mass of people to create a pattern of undreamed-of dimensions' (ibid.: 77).[7] He sums his argument up by saying that 'The mass ornament is the aesthetic reflex of the rationality to which the prevailing economic system aspires' (ibid.: 79).

In our study of the global culture industry, the surface is also of importance and we suggest that this surface – like that described by Kracauer – is also to be understood in relation to the rationality to which the prevailing economic system aspires. However, we have not described this logic as either Euclidean or linear. Instead, we suggest it may be understood in relation to the mathematical (and philosophical) understanding of the manifold,[8] a very particular (way of understanding) surface. In classical mathematics, a geometrical object such as a curved line or a surface may be described by the rate at which some of its properties change, such as, for example, the rate at which its curvature changes between different points. In the early nineteenth century, a curved two-dimensional space was studied by embedding the surface in a three-dimensional space with its own fixed set of axes (in which, conventionally, time might be represented as extension in space); then, using those axes, coordinates would be assigned to every point on the surface; finally, the geometric links between points determining the form of the surface (and its dynamic properties) would be expressed as algebraic relations between the numbers.[9] But the mathematician Carl Friedrich Gauss developed a method that allowed the study of the surface without any reference to a supplementary embedding space/time. DeLanda writes:

Gauss developed a method to implant the co-ordinate axes on the surface itself (that is a method of 'co-ordinatizing' the surface), and, once points had been so translated into numbers, to use differential (not algebraic) equations to characterize their relations. As the mathematician and historian Morris Kline observes, by getting rid of the global embedding space and dealing with the surface through its own local properties, 'Gauss advanced the totally new concept that *a surface is a space in itself*'. (2002: 12)

Another mathematician Bernhard Riemann, took a step further in the study of the surface as a space in itself, taking on the more general problem of N-dimensional spaces. Riemann was able to move mathematics into a realm of abstract spaces with a variable number of dimensions by providing a way to study them without the need to embed them in a higher-dimensional (N+1) space. This development opened up the study of space so that it could consider the manifold, understood here as the space of possible states that a physical system can have. As DeLanda notes, '[this] way of posing spatial problems would, a few decades later in the hands of Einstein and others, completely alter the way physicists approached the question of space (or more exactly, of spacetime)' (DeLanda 2002: 12).

The analogy we draw here is that the cultural objects we have described in this book display certain of the characteristics of the manifold outlined just above. So, for example, we suggested that certain surface characteristics of these objects – the use of colours, of line and gesture, of catch-phrases and graphic design – are the intensive ordinates of movement. They are points at which the surface is coordinatized. This coordinatization does not take place in relation to an externally fixed space (N+1), but is rather made in relation to a space of possible object states. What we have described as intensive ordinates – the logo, the icon, the catch-phrase, the goal, the gesture, the painted face, the movement of an eyebrow, the graphic line – are points of the object's surface. The movement they describe is not extrinsic to the object; the logic of the thing-in-itself as conceived by Adorno is now compressed into the logic of the thing-for-itself. It follows from this that the global is not used here to describe the movement of discrete units in fixed time and space (it is not that objects are made and then distributed, as either commodities or gifts); rather the notion of global describes how it is that objects in movement make (and, as we have seen, mark) time and space. And the global spacetime they bring into being is not (only) to be understood in terms of extensivity, of distance travelled in space and time; it is not (only) metric. Rather, it is a space of possible states in which lines may be stretched – and myriad other transformations carried out – while the object remains invariant.

In the accounts of the biographies of the seven cultural objects presented in this book, the logic we identify is still that of capital. And as in Kracauer's era, this is the capitalism of the 'entire contemporary situation', but as such, it is now a disorganized capitalism (Lash and Urry 1994), a global capitalism of difference and disjuncture (Appadurai 1996). And whereas Kracauer, Adorno and Horkheimer understand the logic of the mass product of the mid-twentieth century in terms of identity, standardization and calculation, that is, an abstract logic of equivalence, the logic of the mass product – the biography of the global cultural object – we describe here is that of difference; it is the object of a logic of a differential geometry. Calculability has been introduced at another level of abstraction, another organization of exchange, contributing to the emergence of a global culture industry coordinated in terms of an abstract logic of inequivalence of global flows of disjuncture and difference. This is indeed what we understand as the mediation of mass in movement, the mediation of things. And whereas Kracauer might argue that what is required is not *less* rationality but *more* (capitalism 'rationalizes not too much but rather *too little*' (1995: 81)), what we have argued is that what characterizes the global culture industry is a non-metric rationality that is not concerned with calculations of 'less' or 'more' (with the calculation of quantity), but instead describes a state of becoming both more and less at the same time (that is, the calculation of quality). It is the merely possible and the all-too-real.

The Global Culture Industry

All this said, it remains for us to return to how we started this book: to the biographies of cultural objects. We want in particular to reconsider how they circulate or move from *person to person*, because how we experience the object, that is, subject-objectivity, is always also a question of intersubjectivity. This brings us back to our methodological starting point, and the ideas of Arjun Appadurai (1986) on the circulation of objects. What we are looking at are different types of *exchange* in this intersubjectivity. Appadurai, in his work on the social life of things, is interested in, on the one hand, the concrete singularity of the gift in exchange and, on the other, the abstract homogeneity of the commodity as an exchange-value. Here, the contrast is between gift-value and exchange-value. Both these types of value emerge through not production, but exchange. The particular type of intersubjectivity involved defines each. And all cultural-thing-biographies, all circulation of cultural goods, are a question of intersubjectivity. The subjects may be collectives, corporations or individuals: they may or may not be attached to technologies. Thus this book about objects has needed to investigate relations between subjects, not just intersubjectivity, but exchange. This is exchange of whatever type that involves relationships or a temporality of, as we described in chapter 7, relations of 'giving and getting', 'buying and selling'.

At stake in the *global* culture industry is perhaps neither singularity nor the commodity, but something else: a different mode of exchange. This third mode of exchange which is neither gift- nor commodity-exchange is most apparent in the movement of collectibles and merchandised goods. The commodity is about equivalence, about the exchange of equivalents (and it is in this organization of exchange that the life of labour-power is, as it were, killed). Both the classic gift and exchange in the global culture industry are about the exchange of *in*equivalents (in these organizations of exchange, labour power acquires a life; see Mauss 1976; Bourdieu 1977). For the moment, let us call these three types of exchange (1) gift-exchange, (2) commodity-exchange and (3) media-exchange. In *Outline of a Theory of Practice*, Bourdieu describes a particular regime of value: one that stands in contradistinction to the regime of value of the commodity and of modern capitalism. In this book he is dealing with a regime of value based on the concrete inequivalence of gifts; in his later book, *Distinction* (1984), a second regime of value emerges: one of the abstract equivalence of not only economic capital (that is, the commodity), but also the abstract equivalence of social capital, cultural capital and symbolic capital. In global culture industry, however, we think there is a move to a regime of giving and getting that is once again temporal but rooted in not concrete but *abstract inequivalence*, or difference. This is what we are describing here as media-exchange.

Commodity-exchange is primarily spatial – not just in Bergson's sense of taking place in a spatialized time, but also in a literal space of the market. As Bourdieu writes in *Outline of a Theory of Practice* (1977), the exchange – the buying and selling – of commodities happens (in theory) at the same time, in no time at all. This rules *time* out of the equation. In contrast, both gift- and media-exchange are very largely temporal. Bourdieu addresses this in a critique of Lévi-Strauss. The notion of structure in Lévi-Strauss (1999), unlike that in Durkheim, is rooted in modes of gift-exchange. In Lévi-Strauss's typology, exchange provides the determinants of social behaviour, setting up a set of extensive social coordinates, within which action takes place. Bourdieu's departure is not so much his shift from structure to action or to practice: it is that he breaks with Lévi-Strauss's neo-Cartesian spatialized and extensive ordinates for temporality. Lévi-Strauss's structure is spatial, Bourdieu's practice is temporal. Practice takes place in the interval between getting and giving, although there is nothing voluntary about the reciprocity. This is the stuff of Bourdieuan *practice*: such practice is largely purposive but also a question of the orientation of the habitus. But this type of exchange may also be contrasted with what we are describing here as media-exchange. In this organization of exchange, capital effects an entry into the in-between of giving and getting, buying and selling, and attempts to occupy the gap, the interval. It is no longer organized in terms of spatialized time, the time of discrete units (clock-time as the standard unit of measurement of labour power), but is rather organized in terms of a discontinuous time, in which exchange is ongoing, and logos punctuate a flow of disjuncture and difference.

Take, for example, the phenomenon of the 'little gift' that we mapped in describing the movement of merchandised goods, promotional goods, football shirts and collectibles. Very often, perhaps in the majority of cases, a person will not get these things for his- or herself, but for someone else. So a university student will be given for his birthday by his flatmate a West Bromwich Albion shirt. Or you will give your girlfriend –

who you know is a collector – a Wallace and Gromit figure. Sometimes such an object is a matter of authenticity. It requires an origin, a place, event or relationship (or all three) of origin, pre-existing the object. This origin is a mark of authenticity. The good then becomes a trace or 'index' of the individual, event or place. Or consider the classical giving of heavy and valuable watches for weddings, graduations and other meaning-laden transitions: births, deaths and engagements. This is a ritual function, in which the good may also become a symbol. Typically, the gift consecrates an event (birth, death, wedding), a social bond (marriage, a child, a life) or a place. The point about the little gifts of the not-so-authentic lightweight and plastic watches is that we give and receive them *all the time*: on holiday, birthdays, seasonal festivities, anniversaries, passing shops, weekend excursions. They are a much more continual – a continuous – punctuation of everyday life.

The classic gift consolidates, like a monument, it *consecrates*: today's little gift – the 'free gift', treats, promotions or items of merchandise *punctuate*, like the logo between programmes punctuates the flow of programming (Williams 1974); it interrupts, it agitates, it insinuates (obsequiously). This giving and getting confirms a different sort of *lien social* (social bond). This social bond it creates is not, as in the classic gift, lifelong and enduring. Nor do we have the emptiness of market- and commodity-exchange, which is a sort of destruction of the social bond. With the giving and getting we describe as characteristic of the global culture industry, we have instead a social bond of weak ties. The classic gift describes an economy of proper place: of patrimony, fixed domestic capital, an economy of the hearth, of inheritance and reproduction. This contrasts with the placelessness, the non-place of the commodity economy. The *difference* economy does not operate in the register of either place or non-place. The classic gift and the commodity economy make sense of the world in terms of presence (place, here), on the one hand, and absence (non-place, there), on the other. Global culture industry's economy of difference makes sense instead as pattern and randomness. The giving and getting of cultural objects in today's global economy of difference is the way we encounter the noise of the flows. It is the way that we put pattern into this noise.

This sense-making activity always takes place from a point of view. Yet, as we just noted, this point of view is from the *inter*subjectivity, the social bond of exchange. In the global culture industry, we are, as it were, in a relation of structural coupling with the media environment at the same time as we are structurally coupling with one another. We encounter the flows in regard to long-term, and binding though symbolically attenuated, relationships. But we encounter the flows in regard to relationships. We encounter the flows in twos and threes and more: in the cuddly toys bought for sons and daughters, the visits to cinema and art galleries (and their shops) with partners, the football tickets and shirts shared with friends. The classic gift also involved this: but usually in regard to the making of a single stable place, for a few heavy and well spaced-out events. Now that place is a place of flows and constantly changing; we travel from place to place, and we gift-give in an almost endless succession of little events. *Grand mort v. petits morts!* These now are no longer life-events, but punctuations of everyday life.

At stake is an economy of time also in that there is no longer only the spatial organization of supply and demand in the market in which the right price will produce the required supply. Instead, there is a time pressure. Promotional goods in, for example, cereal packets are one-offs. Children desire every one of the plastic figures of the characters of the film *The Incredibles* in their Happy Meals™ at McDonald's, but they can only do this if they eat there at least once a week over a specific five weeks. Or consider the 500 pairs of retro Nike trainers acquired on e-Bay and then sold on in the UK as the only such pairs in the country, for a limited time only. What is the calculus for this sort of value? This is no longer either a gift or a commodity regime of value, but a differential regime of value. It is value as defined by distinctiveness, yet value as temporally determined by the role, say a watch, plays in an open-ended series of which it is but a single item. Here the little gift is a unit of information. It is a difference that makes a difference. But only a little difference.

Newtonian time for Bergson was spatialized partly because we did not live it but were separated from it, abstracted from it. We are separated from clocks because they are outside ourselves. The proper temporality of the gift as described by Bourdieu is a time with which we are entangled, but so too are we snared in the global culture industry. Yet the two types of entanglement – separated by the commodity interval of disentanglement – are very different from one another. To be entangled in the authentic and singular logic of proper place is far different than being snared in the logic of flows. Bourdieu's habitus was purposive: its goals are set by the insult and counter insult of revenge or events and givings saturated with heavy meaning. Activity between the punctuations of the global culture industry will have more to do with the non-purposive activity of play, often with chance or or adventure. We are locked less into ruleboundedness than mimicry. If purpose was locked into the restricted economy of reproduction of the classic gift economy, then play opens out onto a general economy of waste and the chronic over-production of the economy of difference. In this space of excess, Bateson (2000) notes, play constructs a 'metacommunicative frame' to organize such activities. The global culture industry – through giving and getting – take place inside this frame, but also makes it possible that we can be drawn outside the frame of purposive, communicative rationality to out-do ourselves and be out-done.

Notes

Chapter 1 Introduction: Theory – Some Signposts

1 See more recent work on culture industry, including Angela McRobbie (1998, 1999), Du Gay (1997), Hesmondhalgh (2002) and Bennett (1995).

2 This, of course, was a central thesis of Georg Simmel (1997).

3 This is on the whole a relatively recent phenomenon. Indeed, Hollywood's revenues from outside the USA have only superseded revenues from within the past decade, and Nike only developed an explicit global strategy from 1995.

4 See Hardt and Negri (2000).

5 Indeed over 50 per cent of foreign direct investment in Latin America over the past decade has been in telecommunications.

6 Nike pays more than $40 million to associate its logo with Tiger Woods.

7 We are indebted on this point to John Urry (2003).

8 Singularities are special types of monads. They are monads with windows and doors. We are grateful to Maurizio Lazzarato for this point.

9 In *Simulacra and Simulations*, Baudrillard's idea of hyperreality seems to be a question of such cybernetic power.

10 In this environment, signs become 'signage'. See the interview of Robert Venturi and Denise Scott Brown with Rem Koolhaas and H.-U. Obrist in Koolhaas (2001).

11 Peirce writes, 'An Icon is a sign which refers to the Object that it denotes merely by virtue of characters of its own, and which it possesses, just the same, whether any such Object actually exists or not' (1978: 102).

Chapter 2 Method: Ontology, Movement, Mapping

1 We are aware that what we are doing is not ethnography in a conventional sense, not even a multi-site ethnography. Yet to the extent to which Deirdre Boden infused this study, it does have a certain ethnographic spirit in the sense of a microsociology. The method that we are proposing and have used is more a cartography than an ethnography.

2 *Trainspotting* was made for US$2.6 million; it was the biggest grossing British film of 1996. Its UK box office take was $15 million in 1996, making it the fourth highest UK grossing British film in history at that point in time.

3 *Trainspotting* opened on 19 July 1996 in the USA. The opening weekend take was only $262,000, but it grew to $1.4 million for the week of 2 August, when it moved to number thirteen in the American charts. It continued to play for a relatively long time, until December 1996, by which time it had grossed $16.5 million.

4 In this instance, the 'we' was Deirdre Boden and Celia Lury.

5 Deleuze in his cinema books takes this further. Phenomenology presumes that consciousness selects an aspect of the object through what is described as a ray of light from consciousness to the object. This object however is an extensive object, much like those in the classical culture industry. In global culture industry the light is already inside the object itself (Alliez 1995; Rodowick 2001). In global culture industry we are dealing with what McLuhan (1997) called 'light-through', not 'light-on' media. Thus in classical culture industry image comes from consciousness and the cultural medium takes the place of matter. In light-through global culture industry, the medium becomes image-matter.

6 For Gabriel Tarde, the fundamental relation of what Simmel would call sociality was affect: affect is comprised of, on the one hand, belief and, on the other, reflection; see Lazzarato 2002.

7 Note that this limit on self-organization is not a question of causality or determination. Indeed, reflexive singularities will open themselves up to external transformation through communication and connection. Such an opening is a chance to escape, or for *dérive* (in the Situationist sense), from both the external determination of mechanism and the incarcerating solipsism of pure self-organization. Here is where we part ways with Luhmann. We think that contemporary capitalism is based on a shift from mechanistic to self-organizing systems, and the main battle is not between mechanism and self-organization (or reflexivi-

ty), but between more or less closed and more or less open self-causing systems. For a system to survive, of course, it must be operationally closed. The systems we address are thus more ephemeral and en route to formation or decay in comparison to Luhmann's.

8 This is of course an oversimplification to make a point. It draws on the highly valuable ideal-typical contradistinction of vitalism and mechanism in Prigogine and Stengers's *Order out of Chaos* (1984). Positivism in social science is not fundamentally Newtonian. Its function-alist assumptions in Durkheim are of course more Darwinian than Newtonian. The same is true in Parsons, whose *Social System* (1955) and subsequent works took on a number of cyber-netic assumptions as well. Functional causa-tion is very different from Newtonian causa-tion (Cohen 2001). For both Durkheim and Parsons there needs to be an important dimension of self-modification, so that social systems preserve their identity and do not drift into entropy. The other main type of pos-itivism encountered in social science is in the various guises of multivariate analysis. This statistical positivism breaks of course with Newtonian causation for a probabilistic uni-verse, one of Brownian motion, of thermody-namics, of quantum mechanics. Norbert Wiener was operating in such an environment (Hayles 1999). The point for us is that Durkheim's and Parsons's systems are exten-sive in that their components are institutions and organizations. They were writing in an extensive era of capitalism and modernity. Durkheim's and Parsons's systems were also operationally closed, as is Niklas Luhmann's *Die Wirtschaft der Gesellschaft* (1999). Yet the components of Luhmann's systems are com-munications and thus intensive. In this sense, it is Luhmann and Deleuze and Guattari who provide a paradigm for this study. All are deal-ing with intensive systems in today's regime of capitalist accumulation. They are opposite sides of the same coin, however. Luhmann's autopoietic systems are operationally closed and provide a framework to think how domi-nation and closure work in relation to this book's cultural objects and much more widely. Deleuze and Guattari's open machinic assem-blages (or rhizomes) give a framework to think of invention, of political possibility.

9 See Multiplicity (2003) and Rogoff (2000).

10 We are grateful for discussions of psychogeog-raphy to Nicolas Firket of AMO in the Office of Metropolitan Architecture (OMA) in Rotterdam.

11 We are indebted to Manuel DeLanda and Axel Roch for discussions of topology and opera-tionally open systems as emergent systems. We are indebted to Il Chang, Rob Shields and Maria Lakka for discussions on the virtual in cinema.

12 We are indebted to discussions with Catherine David for an idea of cartography that chal-lenges notions of volumetric space. One of the first places where cartography as method was introduced is in Guattari and Rolnik 1996.

13 We take on board Deleuze and Guattari's dis-tinction in *What Is Philosophy?* between event and exhibition. As cultural objects and their interrelations affect operational closure, they tend to become exhibitions; as they open, they can be events.

14 In the case of Euro '96 the object at stake is, in everyday terms, an event. In more sociological terms, if the object is classically understood as located in the realm of necessity, as an event it occupies that of contingency.

15 This is the European nations' championship involving, for example, England, Italy and Spain and not the Champions' League, the European club championship involving, for example, Real Madrid, Manchester United and AC Milan.

16 From our point of view, branding and multi-channel television are, alongside the Internet and mobile phones, 'new media' (Lury 2004).

17 While Manchester United plc is clearly now a private good, the Football Association's rights in the England team are also rights in a *public* good (as are their rights in the FA Cup). The sort of public value at stake is not economic value. It has more to do with individual and especially collective identity than with eco-nomic value. One of the functions of UEFA and the FA in their role as regulatory bodies is to ensure that such public goods do not decline in value. The reworking of the public, the pri-vate and the voluntary is encountered in a number of our cultural biographies.

Chapter 3 Football Biography: Branding the Event

1 See Horn and Laing 1990.

2 Interview, Elyce Taylor, East-West Records, 22 July 1996.

3 See Liz Moor (2003) for further discussion of branding and music events.

4 Interview (Bird & Bird), intellectual property lawyers for FA in Euro '96, July 1996.

5 Interview, Rick Blastley, MMP, 19 July 1996.

6 Interview, Taylor.

7 Ibid.

8 Interview, Andy Strickland, 18 July 1996. Both *90 Minutes* and *Goal* have now closed.

9 Ibid.

10 Interview, Michael Hodges, *90 Minutes*, 19 July 1996.

11 Interview Gavin Hills, *England Magazine*, 22 July 1996.

12 Interview, Adam Brown, Football Supporters' Association, 14 May 1996.

13 Interview, Hills.

14 Ibid.

15 Interview, Hodges. In June 2006, Thrills was writing music journalism for the Independent-Online Edition.
16 Ibid.
17 Ibid.
18 Ibid.
19 Interview, Philip Cornwall, *When Saturday Comes*, 17 July 1996.
20 Ibid.
21 Interview, Hills.
22 Interview, Ralph Robinson, Media Communications Workshop, 23 July 1996.
23 Interview, Hills.
24 Interview, Cornwall.
25 Team was a firm that broke away from ISL. See below.
26 Interview, Hodges.
27 Interview, Gavin Hamilton, 17 July 1996. By 2006, *Four Four Two* was still being published, while *Total Football* and *Goal* had both disappeared from the market.
28 Hills continued to write for *The Face* for much of the 1990s, becoming very much the voice of a generation, before dying in a tragic accident.
29 Interview, Hills.
30 See chapter 8.
31 Interview, Marc Butterman, Director, Operations Department, Football section ISL, 16 April, 1997.
32 Interview, Fraser Peet, Director, Marketing and Public Relations Department, Football Section ISL, 16 April 1997.
33 In 1998 the EBU's (European Broadcasting Union) contract – it paid only £24 million for Euro '96 – ran out. The contract went out to auction in 1996. Bidding against the EBU, IMG and NewsCorp, ISL acquired the rights from UEFA and FIFA. In retrospect, it would seem that FIFA and UEFA might have asked for a higher price for the broadcasting rights. But no one at FIFA, 'had any concept of just how far the popularity of TV international football would accelerate over the last 10–20 years'. 'Football was as unfashionable as you could possibly get in the '70's. It was terrace fighting. It was very hard to find sponsors' (interview, Peet). At that time sponsorship was frequently local and only comprised the boards on the pitch; there was no exclusivity.
34 Interview, Peet.
35 Interview, Keith Cooper, FIFA, Geneva, 6 February 1997.
36 Ibid.
37 The first systematic sponsorship ISL package for the Olympics was in 1988. The IOC had learnt from the Los Angeles Games in 1984. In previous Games 'the local organizing committee had gone considerably into deficit. In the LA Games the hosts sold masses of sponsorship, in a very disorganized and unpoliced way. They made a killing. The IOC learnt from this and centralized marketing rights, selling them to ISL.' In the package developed there are four tiers of sponsorship, the top being $70 million, 3–4 times more expensive than the top Intersoccer sponsorship, yielding together for ISL some $300–400 million, from which again they pay a large part to the IOC for original rights purchase (interview, Butterman).
38 Interview, Butterman.
39 Interview, Peet.
40 Interview, Glen Kirton, FA, May 1996.
41 Interview, Butterman.
42 Interview, Peet.
43 Interview, Butterman.
44 Ibid.
45 Ibid.
46 Ibid. ISL was declared bankrupt in May 2001. ISL was founded in a partnership between Dassler and the Japanese advertising agency Dentsu. Dentsu also is engaged in sports marketing and originally owned 49 per cent of ISL. In 1996 their share was reduced to 10 per cent. The model was that ISL would buy global broadcasting and sponsorship rights, and Dentsu would auction these rights in Japan. In 2000-2001 ISL tried to move into new sports, and badly overpaid for global rights. During the early months of 2001, ISL desperately and unsuccessfully were in search of a white knight. A court in Zug, Switzerland declared ISL bankrupt on 21 May 2001. Dentsu provided bank guarantees for a portion of ISL's debts and paid out $42 million. FIFA took on in-house the purchase and sales of sponsorship and broadcasting rights for World Cup 2002 in Japan/Korea. FIFA assured Dentsu that they would honour ISL's remaining commitments. Dentsu easily absorbed the $42 million loss. They earned $150 million for World Cup media rights in Japan as well as $40m in for sponsorship rights from Toshiba, NTT, Fuji Xerox, Fujifilm and JVC (see *Media*, June 2001; also see <www2.gol.com/users/kilburn/dentsuisl.htm>.
47 Interview, Peet.
48 Interview, Cooper.
49 The governing bodies must tread a fine line between maximizing revenues and remaining in charge of a public good. The British FA, having developed itself as a marketing organization under Adam Crozier, was in December 2003 mostly in the headlines in its public function as enforcing doping rules. In 2004, it was beset by scandals. See the discussion of the Brazilian FA in chapter 8.
50 Interview, Peet.
51 Ibid.

Chapter 4 Art as Concept / Art as Media / Art as Life

1 Nairn became Director of the National Portrait Gallery in 2003.
2 According to Simon Ford (1996), the earliest usage of 'young British artists' was for the British Pavilion of the 1996 Venice Biennale.

He also records other names for the grouping including the 'neo-conceptual bratpack' by Sarah Greenberg, (*Artnews*, September 1995), 'The Brit Pack' by Patricia Bickers (*The Brit Pack: Contemporary British Art, The View from Abroad*, 1995), and the 'Britpop' artists by Waldemar Januszczak (*The Sunday Times*, 3 December 1995).

3 Bruce Mau's contemporary work for Zone Books and his work with Rem Koolhaas is illustrative of this: it draws attention to print media as information on a page. It seems to us that such site-specificity (on a page) is part and parcel of a certain technologization of art. In the age of the global culture industry, science and art become technologized. Site-specificity is the way in which this happens in the arts. To become part of the global culture industry, art must and does become site-specific.

4 Jill Ritblatt is wife of John Ritblatt, Chairman and Chief Executive of British Land, Britain's second largest property company. In 2003, the Board agreed that their son, Nick, would be Chief Executive, provided that John Ritblatt stepped down from being Chairman (Times OnLine, 9 December 2003).

5 See the debate on minimalism and conceptualism in *The Duchamp Effect*, an edition of *October* with contributions from Benjamin Buchloh, Rosalind Krauss, Sarat Maharaj and Thierry de Duve.

6 The notion of value and institutional meltdown was central to a conference on art and urban space in East London, developed and convened by Sam Whimster in 2001.

7 Art & Language was a conceptual art group of artists and antics founded in Coventry, England, in 1968, whose leading figures were the artists Michael Baldwin and Mel Ramsden and the critic Charles Harrison.

8 O'Doherty wrote a series of essays in *Artforum* in 1976, developing a notion of the white cube. He was one of the first critics to address the crisis in post-war art and sought to examine the assumptions on which the modern commercial and museum gallery was based. These essays are (re-)published together as *Inside the White Cube: The Ideology of the Gallery Space* (2000).

9 The YBAs were not the first artists to move east. A number of artists moved to St Katherine's Docks, Butler Wharf and Hackney in the 1970s and 1980s, often driven by a need for space prompted by a desire to make large work. This move was facilitated by the artists' housing association movements, Space and ACME. Rachel Whiteread's 'House', in Grove Road, Hackney, can also be seen in this context.

10 Situationism literally means such a 'site-ism', whether the site to which a *dérive* moves is in physical or mediatic space.

Chapter 5 The Thingification of Media: Animism and Animation

1 As a genre of animation, clay animation developed only slowly, largely because it is labour-intensive in comparison to the industrialized cel-animated cartoon form that gained dominance in the middle of the twentieth century. Clay animation gained some recognition in the 1970s and 1980s, with Will Vinton's Oscar-winning *Closed Mondays* (1974) and the trademarking of Claymation in 1981 (Wells 1998: 58–9).

2 Interview, Liz Kaynes, Aardman Animation, 17 March 1997.

3 Caillois argues that Huizinga considers play at only the latter end of the continuum he identifies.

4 All three of the Wallace and Gromit shorts – *A Grand Day Out, The Wrong Trousers* and *A Close Shave* – were commissioned by Executive Producer Colin Rose at the BBC. Each of the three shorts is progressively longer, more complicated and more expensive. *A Grand Day Out* has only eighteen credits (including four 'additional model-makers, a film editor, camera and sound effects) and is ©National Film and Television School (NFTS). Nick Parks is animator and cinematographer for this first film, and cinematographer for the following two. *A Grand Day Out* was nominated for, but was the only one of the three films not to win, an Academy Award. *The Wrong Trousers* has thirty credits, *A Close Shave* has forty-five.

5 Indeed, it is possible to locate Buzz in relation to the history of animation in which the cartoon pays homage to the machine, what Klein calls '*machina versatalis*'. For Klein, cartoons are 'automata that struggle', they model experience in terms of the industrial machine. This is an ambivalent process. On the one hand, technology may be undermined, revealed as a gag, a toy; on the other, there is an inevitable glorification, in which the cartoon is an advertisement for the industry that made it. So while we might laugh because we know Buzz is not a Space Ranger, and cannot fly, we are impressed by the machine that keeps him in the air, the culture industry.

6 Model-makers construct a different Wallace mouth for each of the inventor's expressions.

7 Consider this extract from an online interview with Nick Parks:

Grover: In a recent documentary where I first saw your faces, I couldn't take my eyes from your mouth movements – identical to your creations. Since everyone in Aardman must master these idiosyncratic 'GromitGrimace' expressions in their work, and since these so obviously originated from your own mirror, my question is this: does everyone working at Aardman now move their mouth like yours?

Nick and Peter: Yes, it's part of the job description for any animator that they have to move their mouth exactly like me! [Nick]

(Nick Park and Peter Lord, live online, *Guardian Unlimited,* 14 July 14 2000)

8 This improved model has a cameo role in *Toy Story 2.* He too believes he is a Space Ranger, and is locked in Oedipal competition with his father, the evil Zorg.

9 In his study of fairy tales, Propp emphasized the importance of function rather than motivation for a character. He suggests that when a medium is abstracted down and nakedly visible ('once upon a time'), characters function purely at a surface level, at least in comparison to a novel. Indeed, they are largely free of novelistic uses of character – the temporal rendering of remorse, guilt and so on – instead they are to be understood in relation to *rules* which emphasize the medium, not the story. In reaching for the sky, in aiming for infinity and beyond, the characters from *Toy Story* display neither ambition nor hubris; instead, they act according to drawstrings.

10 There is an annual Brand Licensing show in London. In 2004, 2,500 properties were traded. Sales of licensed products were worth £7 billion in 2003 (Rickett 2004: 38).

11 Interview, Cathy McCarthy, Fording Union Media, 19 July 1997.

12 Ibid.

13 Ibid.

14 It cannot be an accident that combining the names of the two main characters in *Toy Story* produces the word 'buddy'.

15 Interview, McCarthy

16 Interview, Rob Wijeratne, International Licensing Manager for the BBC, 12 February 1997.

17 The most hit-upon site for Wallace and Gromit is the eBay site for collectibles. For *Toy Story* it is the Pixar and Disney sites.

18 Interview, Kaynes.

19 Nick Park was born in 1961 in Lancashire. He was a student at the National Film and Television School in the early 1980s. The story for *A Grand Day Out* was already formulated in Park's student project in 1982. He joined Aardman Animations in 1985, having already worked for two years on the claymation for *A Grand Day Out.*

20 Interview, Ian Grutchfield, Manager of Children's BBC Worldwide, 14 March 1997.

21 Interview, Wijeratne.

22 Interview, Grutchfield.

23 Interview, Wijeratne.

24 In order to show that 'games are not ruled and make-believe [but rather] ... ruled *or* make-believe', Caillois argues:

> Rules themselves create fictions. The one who plays chess, prisoner's base, polo, and baccara are played for real. As if is not

necessary. On the contrary, each time that play consists in imitating life, the player on the one hand lacks knowledge of how to invent and follow rules that do not exist in reality, and on the other hand the game is accompanied by the knowledge that the required behavior is pretense, or simple mimicry. (1961: 8)

Chapter 6 The Mediation of Things: *In Medias Res*

1 Adorno writes:

> The customer is not the king, as the culture industry would have us believe, not its subject but its object. ... The masses are not the measure but the ideology of the culture industry, even though the culture industry itself could scarcely exist without adapting to the masses. (1991: 85)

2 In contrast, while Adorno recognizes that '[o]ne will have observed that it is difficult, initially, to distinguish the preview of a "coming attraction" from the main film for which one is waiting', what he says about what it tells us 'about the main attractions' is that, '[l]ike the previews and like the pophits, they are advertisements for themselves, bearing the commodity character like a mark of Cain on their foreheads. Every commercial film is actually only the preview of that which it promises and will never deliver' (1991: 160).

3 This account of mass is further developed by Jean Baudrillard in his description of how it is that the masses 'envelop the media' and by Giano Vattimo in his account of the modern mass society as the society of generalized communication (1994). See also Terranova's account of the mass as a non-sociological category:

> The masses are not specific social classes, but more of a generalized dynamics that takes over when you take away all attributes, predicates, qualities or references from a large number of people. The mass, that is, is a lowest common denominator, not in the sense of a loss of quality but as a kind of pre-individual and collective potential to be affected. This is about the physical capacity of a large number of bodies to form a kind of passive mass – a receptacle for the affective power of images. (2004: 136)

4 In contrast, Adorno writes, 'the expression "industry" is not to be taken too literally. It refers to the standardisation of the thing itself – such as that of the western, familiar to every movie-goer – and to the rationalization of distribution techniques, but not strictly to the production process' (1991: 87).

5 In his discussion of the social lives of things, Kopytoff (1986) identifies two kinds of trajec-

tory of things, differentiated by scale and temporality:

(i) the life history of a particular object, as it moves through different hands, contexts and uses, leading to the identification of a specific 'cultural biography' of the object; and

(ii) the 'social history' of a particular kind or class of object, as it undergoes long-term historical shifts and large-scale dynamic transformations.

As he goes on to point out, these two types of trajectory are not entirely separate matters. The social history of things constrains the course of more short-term, specific and intimate trajectories, while many small shifts in the cultural biography of things may lead, over time, to shifts in the social history of things. However, while this model takes account of the ways in which an object may be transformed in time and space, it does not enable a consideration of the ways in which objects transform time and space.

6 Swatch's core markets are in Italy and France, but Swatch has embarked upon a strategy of global expansion, notably in India and China.

7 The Swatch Group Ltd acquired Groupe Horloge Breguet from Investcorp SA in 1999. This company was one of the oldest timepiece manufacturers in the world and now produces high-quality hand-assembled timepieces, situated in the highest price segment of the *haut de gamme* watch market.

8 However, in a later innovation, the technique was extended so that it could make use of metal.

9 In his use of the term 'new materials', Manzini does not merely refer to a limited number of 'artificial' materials, but rather to a set of qualities that are appearing throughout the whole range of materials, both old and new, 'natural' and 'artificial', and to their relationship to manufacturing. Of course there have always been 'new' materials, but while the introduction of new materials in the past may have led to temporary confusion as to a material's identity, Manzini's claim is that recent developments are such to create a situation in which it is expected that a material will have more than one identity.

10 Nevertheless, there was a very early decision not to include a regulating device (the 'Trimmer') although it was not known whether the absence of this component – which had always formed an integral part of practically every electronic quartz movement – would result in a loss of precision.

11 Along similar lines of brand extension, The Swatch Group entered into a 'marketing collaboration' with AOL TimeWarner in 2001. This collaboration was 'designed to utilize the strengths of each company in the areas of

media, entertainment, technology, sports, timekeeping and next generation Internet access devices' (Press release, 2001).

12 The Onitsuka Tiger Corporation was founded by Japanese entrepreneur Kihachiro Onitsuka, but later changed its name to ASICS Tiger Corporation and is now a $2.5 billion company worldwide.

13 In the sound-bites of political activism, comparisons are drawn between Michael Jordan's sponsorship fees with the hourly wage of assembly-line workers, and in trade and union investigations and reports by human rights organizations, Nike is regularly held up as an example of bad practice. Additionally, the brand has also come to be associated with images of production assembly lines under banners with the exhortation 'Just Do It', photographs of armed policemen outside Nike stores during anti-globalization protests and as part of a Doonesbury cartoon series.

14 As Marina Warner also notes:

From the 1880s onwards, the goddess of victory ratified innumerable claims, commercial as well as political. Nike/Victoria appears on trademarks, cigar labels, as a stamp of quality, a guarantee of authenticity. A cipher, she speaks to us – mutely but all the time and insistently – of winning through against the odds, and perpetrates the illusion that triumph is ours. (1987: 143)

15 The global 'athletic shoe' industry grew 2.6 per cent in the year up to 2005 to £8 billion. At the same time, the share prices of the big players – Nike, Reebok International, Adidas-Salomon and Puma AG Rudolf Dassler Sport – have risen by double-digit figures. Nike holds 34.1 per cent of this world market, more than twice as much as closest rival, Adidas, at 16.5 per cent. Reebok and New Balance are in third and fourth place with around 10 per cent each. The industry as a whole now sells more than 350 million pairs of shoes annually, with the majority of consumers being aged 18–29 (Davis 2005: 21).

16 In later years, the Nike strategy also involved – as in the case of Swatch – sustained intervention in new national markets and new sports markets beyond running and basketball, notably football and golf.

17 Despite its current dominance in so-called event-based marketing, reports suggest that the fluctuations of fashion have more consistently informed the performance of the brand in recent years.

18 FIFA sold the world television rights (excluding the USA) to the three 1990s World Cup tournaments to the European Broadcasting Union for £215m.

19 A later example of this was the £12 million kit deal Nike signed with Arsenal, which meant it played in a pre-season Nike tournament and

not in something like the Umbro Cup. More recently still, Nike signed a deal with Manchester United, the most consistently successful British football team since the early 1990s. It is itself a major brand.

20 The Commission also investigated charges of the 'trafficking' of under-age players to foreign countries, the connivance of diplomatic officials in forging players' passports and the vast fortunes that club presidents are said to have made from illegally selling players. Brazil 'exports' more footballers abroad than any other country (said to be about 10,000) (Bellos 2001b).

21 Jordan's original 1984 contract for Nike was for five years at $3 million per year, rising to $100 million over five years in the 1990s. Tiger Woods signed a five-year $40 million contract in 1996. His subsequent 2001 contract has been estimated at $100 million. Woods made an estimated $70 million in sponsorship in 2002 as compared to $6.9 million earnings on the tour.

22 For example, he directed a series of advertisements for Nike starring Michael Jordan and himself as the character he played in the film, *She's Gotta Have It*. He is a well-known basketball fan.

23 Cheryl L. Cole (1996) argues that as an 'All-American' figure, Jordan is both an effect and an instrument of modern power.

24 The 'Just' in 'Just Do It' may also be seen a sign of this animated, informated spatialization of time. It is a linguistic transposition of an athlete's figure suspended in the space of timeless time (Castells 1996), hanging in a frame in which gravity is absent, both absolutely relaxed and at the peak of exertion in a time that is so short that it can only just be imaged.

25 This interview with Franzão was carried out after the quarter-finals and before the semi-finals of the World Cup '98.

26 Ronaldo was called Ronaldinho, meaning little Ronaldo, until an even younger Ronaldinho came into the Seleçao.

27 They will be on-line, have satellite or cable TV and mobile phones, for example, and will have travelled abroad.

28 Interview, Ronald Radomysler, MD Drastona, June 1998.

29 Salim spoke neither French nor English and we did not speak Portuguese. His legal adviser who was present at the interview translated the interview.

30 He also identified the pivotal role of Teixeira, the son-in-law of João Havelange, a previous president of the CBF who had gone on to be president of FIFA. Prior to Teixeira's appointment in 1989, the single national team sponsor was Topper, but Teixeira negotiated sponsorship through the Brazilian sports sponsorship company, Traffic. Traffic itself bought rights to the Selecão's image. 'We sell to Traffic and Traffic has the right to negotiate

the symbols ... our logo.' 'The television rights to games and to friendly games we sell to Brazil TV.' Traffic had negotiated with Pepsi, which was team sponsor from 1991 to 1993; subsequently, it was Coca-Cola. Pepsi and Coca-Cola's level of sponsorship was about $4 million per year. Nike's is of a different order: $20 million.

31 The terms of a licensing agreement may vary considerably, and may reflect either the licensor's or the licensee's relative strength.

Chapter 7 Flow: The Practices and Properties of Circulation

1 In this understanding, as described by Michel de Certeau, there are two principal dynamics. The first is the accumulation of capital, of material and symbolic wealth, through the expenditure of effort, and the second is the care and development of the individual and collective body (through reproduction and inheritance) (1998: 52–6). As implied by Baudrillard, at least in his early work, the economy of the proper place works to reproduce and enhance these two dynamics in a productive and harmonious way. In this economy, property and propriety are brought together in the proper place. However, as de Certeau points out, this proper place is not the same as everyday life, for everyday life is more heterogeneous, and less legitimate – altogether less proper. It is not tied to *any* particular, organized regime of accumulation.

2 In the late '90s, the average price paid for a pair of sneakers was just over $30, but sales of Nike footwear and apparel alone amount to an average of $20 for every US citizen (Vanderbilt 1998: 3).

3 This restriction is by no means characteristic of all brands, many of which aspire to a total availability. A brand such as Gap can be said to come close to this condition. However, such total availability would mean that it would be closer to a genre than a brand. Generic status is in some regards a limit state for the brand.

4 In considering what might be involved by a mediation of things, the work of Georg Simmel is of obvious relevance. For Simmel, while any society is characterized by both an objective and a subjective culture, these cultures are not necessarily either symmetrical or analogous. Indeed, Simmel argues that in modern industrial societies objective culture has become autonomous from subjective culture. For Simmel, the gap between objective and subjective culture is always mediated, more or less successfully, by the practices of consumption. During the eighteenth century, for example, objective culture was developed in relation to the ideal of the *individual*, that is, in relation to the cultivation of a set of internal, personal values. By the nineteenth cen-

tury, however, objective culture is organized in terms of *education* in the sense of a body of knowledge and behavioural patterns. Importantly, although the individual may still define him- or herself in terms of learning, and the acquisition of an educated sensibility, he or she is at a distance from this body of knowledge. What is suggested here is that the organization of objective culture in terms of education, of learning and of taste, is currently being supplemented by that of distinctiveness: a proposal linked to the thinking of Simmel on style. This is a theme picked up and elaborated by a number of writers today. Thus, the contemporary anthropologist of material culture Daniel Miller puts it:

> [S]tyle has achieved a certain autonomy in contemporary industrial society, going beyond its capacity for ordering to become itself the focus of concern. ... In this new world, all architecture, furnishing, clothing and behaviour are intended to relate to each other in a visibly coherent fashion. This works to break down all frames into a universal order of good design. (1987: 129)

As Miller makes clear, objects can be more or less stylized. Style is not a fixed or universal property of objects, but is rather a consequence of the ways in which objects are related to each other within a particular culture. Style emerges from the process of comparing things – whether and how they are similar and different to other objects. These comparisons create distinctions within a system of objects, that is style. What has been argued here is that distinctiveness – as the mark of a style or a look – is the basis of value in the contemporary regime.

5 The notion of sign at issue here may be elaborated via a discussion of the semiology proposed by Charles Sanders Peirce (1978) and developed in the writings on cinema by Gilles Deleuze (1986, 1989). Semiotics as elaborated by Peirce is a study of signs which restores the immanence of movement to the logic of the image, sign and narration. It draws on a notion of the image in general – the Image – as a mobile material, as universal variation, the identity of matter with movement and light (Rodowick 1997). According to Peirce, the image is not a unified or closed whole, but rather an ensemble or set of logical relations that are in a state of continual transformation. That these logical relations are what constitute signs is made clear in his well-known definition of a sign as:

> something which stands to somebody for something in some respect or capacity. It addresses somebody, that is, creates in the mind of that person an equivalent sign, or perhaps a more developed sign. That sign which it creates I call the interpretant of

the first sign. The sign stands for something, its object. It stands for that object, not in all respects, but in reference to a sort of idea, which I have sometimes called the ground of the *representamen*. (1978: 99)

6 It seems to indicate an internal reversal within trade mark law: 'While unfair competition law is based on the prohibition against palming off one's goods as the goods of another, licensing itself is essentially a "passing off"' (Gaines 1991: 214).

Chapter 8   Culture Industry in Brazil: Image, Market, Display

1 A number of Brazilian cities – São Paulo, Belo Horizonte, Rio, Porto Allegre, Brasilia, Curitiba – are cabled.

2 For Buena Vista this Touchstone Hollywood Pictures productions; for Sony, Columbia-TriStar. Columbia was founded in 1924. In 1982 it was acquired by Coca-Cola. TriStar was founded in 1982. It merged with Columbia in 1987. Sony acquired the merged company in 1989.

3 Miramax was founded by Bob and Harvey Weinstein in 1979. It was acquired by Disney in 1993.

4 Rios also does acquisitions for HBO Venezuela.

5 Though this is true *eo ipso*: all licensing is by definition exclusive. In the licensing relationship there is often imperative coordination by the brand; if a licensee drops its quality, it frequently loses the licence. But brands need to choose the right licensee. There can be licensing for exclusive sales, exclusive distribution, production, and for merchandising products. Licensing is in a sense subcontracting with a rights arrangement.

6 There is a period of dictatorship (led by Vargas) from 1937 to 1945, and then from 1946 to 1955. There is a period of civilian government from 1956 to 1964, with the military returning to power from 1964 to 1984. The first free election after this was in 1990.

7 This company has held a quasi-monopoly position in broadcasting in the country ever since.

8 The big investment in the massive Latin American telecommunications growth in the 1990s came from the southern European telecoms, themselves recently privatized.

9 This combination of domination of home-content production plus export of content, clientelism and part-ownership of media in smaller countries in the respective region is paralleled in India, Egypt in the Middle East, Hong Kong in the Chinese speaking world and increasingly Nigeria in sub-Saharan Africa. It is more the rule than the exception in the world.

10 The exception is Telmex, a technology rather than a content company (that is, an operator),

which is a massive player alongside southern European telecoms like Telefonica in several Latin American countries.

11 *Business Wire*, South Africa, 6 May 2006.

12 *New York Times*, 6 January 2005.

13 Moody Investors Service, 6 February 2006.

14 Internet World Statistics, March 2006.

15 Moco.News, May 2006.

16 The average cost of making a film in 1997 was $1 million, estimates de Oliveira.

17 Schild is a leading film critic in Brazil. She has been Director of the Cinemateca at the Rio de Janeiro Museum of Modern Art.

18 This film was narrated in English by a Scotsman and spoken in Portuguese.

19 The first Brazilian film to achieve widespread international recognition was Lima Barreto's *O Cangaceiro*, which won a Cannes prize in 1953.

20 Bruce Barnard 1998, 'Lights, Camera, Action!', <www.eurunion.org/magazine/9809p. 18>.

21 'The majors sell to video shops at $80 per unit.'

22 Hamburguer, interview, 6 July 1998.

23 There are seven full-time people at Superfilmes, including Carvalhosa and Klotzel.

24 The ubiquitous André Sturm is the prime distributor for Superfilmes.

25 Zaentz owned the film and merchandising rights to all of J. R. R. Tolkien's work. Indeed, *Lord of the Rings* director Peter Jackson first was looking to do a deal with Miramax, which was working with Zaentz at the time. Miramax went to their patrons Disney, which would not come up with the production costs that Jackson asked for. Bob Shaye at New Line Productions did.

26 These five Rio *salles* do approximately 600,000 admissions per year.

27 *Mostra* means 'to show' in Portuguese.

28 In the 'Anthropophagite Manifesto', Oswalde de Andrade, 1928.

29 Suely Rolnik wrote one of the main catalogue pieces for the Biennale, taking up the anthropophagy theme. Rolnik, author with Felix Guattari in 1986 of *Cartographies of Desire*, was involved from the mid-1980s in introducing a variety of schizoanalysis that has had enormous success in Brazil. This is a sort of psychoanalysis whose goal, as in Deleuze and Guattari's *Anti-Oedipus*, is the destruction of the symbolic for a psycho-politics of the real.

Chapter 9 Conclusion: Virtual Objects and the Social Imaginary

1 Let us underscore at this point what might appear to some readers as a contradiction or at least an inconsistency in the argument of this book. At the outset we are describing a shift from a culture of representation to a culture of objects in global culture industry. Then about midway through the book we bring in the figure of the social imaginary. On many accounts,

such a social imaginary would constitute culture and indeed constitute or construct culture by means of representations. And this would be inconsistent with our focus on a culture of objects that is at the same time a culture of the real. First, let us say that our idea of a culture of objects and a culture of the real has little to do with classical realism. For us, classical realism is already in the realm of representation in the sense that it is about representations being in agreement with objects in the world. For us, the objects become autonomous, independent of the representations; indeed, in many cases, what were representations become objects. Ours is perhaps a radical 'objectualism'; it is in no way an objectivism in which subject or representation is counterposed to and in agreement with the object. Our objectualism is based on a radical and independent facticity of the object. However, this book is also not an exercise in constructionism. That is, it is about the culture of the real, but is neither classically realist nor constructionist. In realism, subjects and representations faithfully mirror objects in the world, in constructionism, subjects (or social collectivities) and representations construct or constitute such objects. For us, both the mirror-culture of realism and constructionist or other modes of representational disruption of such mirror-culture are characteristic of culture in national-manufacturing society. In global culture industry there is first a facticity of the object, an already-thereness that belies and precedes all constructions (Simondon 1958). Second, though most theorists may use the notion of the imaginary or social imaginary in the context of cultural constructionism, we do not. The social imaginary does not construct our global system of cultural objects. It instead *couples* with it: it 'structurally couples' with it, as we shall describe in more detail below. In the era of a more national culture, the social imaginary coupled with representational and narrative culture (whether realist or constructionist); now it couples with the global cultural system of objects. And this is in major part due to a change in the nature of the social imaginary itself.

2 The most general definition of 'plasma', which has the same root as plastic, is that which is to be moulded or formed.

3 We are grateful to Sebastian Olma for this notion of ontological domination.

4 Similarly, society is understood by Simmel as a play form of sociation.

5 We are indebted for these points to Yana Dolin.

6 Although in many other respects he does not move beyond the idealist opposition of essence and appearance, substance and surface.

7 This rationality is described by Kracauer as a 'murky' reason. He describes it as an abstract

rationality that has taken on mythic traits. Indeed, for Kracauer, geometric formations such as those of the Tiller girls are opaque because they are composed according to the dictates of a ratio that sacrifices meaning for the sake of an abstract unity of reified elements.

8 This account draws closely on the work of Manuel DeLanda (2002). He notes that N-dimensional curved structures, definied exclusively through their intrinsic features, were originally referred to by the term 'manifold'.

9 These are the elementary principles of calculus.

References

Adair, G. (1994) 'That's my toon', *Sunday Times*, 19 June.

Adkins, L. (2002) *Revisions: Gender and Sexuality in Late Modernity*. Milton Keynes: Open University Press.

Adorno, T. (1991) *The Culture Industry. Selected Essays on Mass Culture*. London: Routledge.

Alexander, J. (ed.) (1990) *Durkheim Sociology: Cultural Studies*. Cambridge: Cambridge University Press.

Alliez, E. (1995) *De L'Impossibilité de la Phénoménologie*. Paris: Vrin.

Anderson, B. (1991) *Imagined Communities*. London: Verso.

Appadurai, A. (ed.) (1986) *The Social Life of Things: Commodities in Cultural Perspective*. Cambridge: Cambridge University Press.

Appadurai, A. (1996) *Modernity at Large: Cultural Dimensions of Globalization*. Minneapolis and London: University of Minnesota Press.

Archer, M. (1996) 'No politics please, We're British?', *Art Monthly* 194/3: 11–14.

Arnoldi, J. (2002) 'Uncertain knowledge', PhD thesis. Goldsmiths College. London.

Back, L., Crabbe, T. and Solomos, J. (2001) *The Changing Face of Football: Racism, Identity and Multiculture in the English Game*. Oxford: Berg.

Bailey, P., Yearley, S. and Forrester J. (1999) 'Involving the public in local air pollution assessment', *International Journal of Environment and Pollution* 11: 290–303.

Barry, A. (2001) *Political Machines: Governing a Technological Society*. London: Athlone Press.

Barry, A. and Slater, D. (eds.) (2002) 'The technological economy', *Economy and Society* 31/2, special Issue: May.

Barthes, R. (1973) *Mythologies*. St Albans: Paladin.

Bataille, G. (2000) *La Part maudite precede de 'La notion de dépense'*. Paris: Eds de Minuit.

Bateson, G. (2000 [1972]) *Steps to an Ecology of the Mind*. Chicago: University of Chicago Press.

Baudrillard, J. (1994) *Simulacra and Simulation*. Ann Arbor: University of Michigan Press.

Baudrillard, J. (1996) *The System of Objects*, trans. J. Benedict. London: Verso.

Beck, U. (1992) *Risk Society: Towards a New Modernity*. London: Sage.

Beck, U., Giddens, A. and Lash, S. (1994) *Reflexive Modernization: Politics, Tradition and Aesthetics in the Modern Social Order*. Cambridge: Polity.

Becker, H. (1986) 'Photography and sociology', in *Doing Things Together*. Chicago: Northwestern University Press.

Beckett, A. (1998) 'The ecstasy and the agony', *Guardian*, 25 July.

Bellos, A. (2001a) 'Ronaldo faces jail over his Nike deal', *Guardian*, 11 January.

Bellos, A. (2001b) 'What happened to the beautiful game?', *Guardian*, 14 January.

Bellos, A. (2001c) 'How Nike bought Brazil', *Guardian*, 9 July.

Benjamin, W. (1991) 'Uber Sprache überhaupt und über die Sprache des Menschen', *Gesammelte Schriften, Band II-1*. Frankfurt: Suhrkamp, pp. 140–57.

Benjamin, W. (1992) *Illuminations*. London: Fontana Press.

Benjamin, W. (1997) *One Way Street*. London: Verso.

Bennett, T. (1995) *The Birth of the Museum*. London: Routledge.

Bennett, T. and Woolacott, J. (1987) *Bond and Beyond: Career of a Popular Hero*. London: Routledge & Kegan Paul.

Bergson, H. (1991) *Matter and Memory*. New York: Zone Books.

Bergson, H. (1999 [1911]) *Laughter. An Essay on the Meaning of the Comic*. Los Angeles: Green Integer Books.

Berking, H. (1999) *Sociology of Giving*. London: Sage.

Bhatt, C. (2004) 'Contemporary geopolitics and alterity research', in M. Bulmer and J. Solomos (eds), *Researching Race and Racism*. London and New York, pp. 16–36.

Bird, J. (1999) 'Minding the body: Robert Morris's 1971 Tate Gallery retrospective', in M. Newman and J. Bird (eds), *Rewriting Conceptual Art*. London: Reaktion, pp. 88–106.

Bolter, J. D. and Grusin, R. (1999) *Remediation: Understanding New Media*. Cambridge, MA and London: MIT Press.

Borger, J. (2000) 'This leading American business guru claims these trainers could spell the end of capitalism. Can he be serious?', *Guardian*, 29 September.

Bourdieu, P. (1977) *Outline of a Theory of Practice*. Cambridge: Cambridge University Press.

Bourdieu, P. (1984) *Distinction. A Social Critique of the Judgement of Taste*. London: Routledge and Kegan Paul.

Bourdieu, P. (1993) *The Field of Cultural Production: Essays on Art and Literature*. New York: Columbia University Press.

Bröckling, U. et al. (2003) *Menschenökonomie*. Hamburg: Verlag Hamburger.

Bull, M. and Back, L. (2004) (eds) *The Auditory Culture Reader*. London: Berg.

Buskirk, M. and Nixon, M. (1996) (eds) *The Duchamp Effect*. New York: October Books.

Caillois, R. (1961) *Man, Play and Games*, trans. and with an introduction by M. Barash. New York: The Free Press.

Callon, M. (1986) 'Some elements for a sociology of translation: domestication of the scallops and the fishermen of St. Brieuc Bay', in J. Law (ed.), *Power, Action, Belief. A New Sociology of Knowledge?* London: Routledge and Kegan Paul. Sociological Review Monograph, pp. 196–229.

Callon, M. (1998) (ed.) *The Laws of the Markets*. Oxford and Malden, MA: Blackwell Publishers.

Callon, M. (1999) 'Actor-network theory – the market test', in J. Law and J. Hassard (eds), *Actor Network Theory and After*. Oxford and Malden, MA: Blackwell Publishers, pp. 181–95,

Callon, M., Meadel, C. and Rabeharisoa, V. (2002) 'The economy of qualities', *Economy and Society* 31/2 (May): 194–217.

Caminiti, S. (1998) 'Ralph Lauren: the emperor has clothes', *Fortune* 137/9 (11 November): 80–9.

Carrell, S. (2003) 'Politically correct down to a T: the rise of ethical chic', *The Independent on Sunday*, 7 September.

Carrera, R. (1991) *Swatchissimo 1981–1991: The Extraordinary Swatch Adventure*. Geneva: Antiquorum Editions.

Carrier, J. G. (1998) 'Abstraction in Western economic practice', in J. G. Carrier and D. Miller (eds) *Virtualism: A New Political Economy*. Oxford and New York: Berg, pp. 25-48

Castells, M. (1989) *The Informational City*. Oxford: Blackwell.

Castells, M. (1996) *The Rise of the Network Society*. Cambridge, MA, and Oxford: Blackwell Publishers.

Castoriadis, C. (1987) *The Imaginary Institution of Society: Creativity and Autonomy in the Social-historical World*. Cambridge, MA: MIT Press.

Caygill, H. (1998) *Walter Benjamin. The Colour of Experience*. London and New York: Routledge.

Cohen, G. A. (2001) *Karl Marx's Theory of History: A Defence*. Princeton, NJ: Princeton University Press.

Cole, C. L. (1996) 'American Jordan: PLAY, consensus and punishment', *Sociology of Sport Journal* 13, pp. 366–97.

Cook, F. and Kabat, J. (1999) 'The Jordan years', *The Face* (31 August), pp. 88–93.

Coombe, R. (1998) *The Cultural Life of Intellectual Properties: Authorship, Appropriation and the Law*. Durham, NC: Duke University Press.

Cooper, R. (2001) 'Interpreting mass: collection/dispersion', in Lee, N. and Munro, R. (eds) *The Consumption of Mass*. Oxford: Blackwell Publishers, pp. 16–43.

Corris, M. (1992) 'Openings: Damien Hirst', *Artforum* (January), p. 96.

Crary, J, (1992) *Techniques of the Observer*. Cambridge, MA: MIT Press.

Davis, J. (2001) *Intellectual Property Law*. London, Edinburgh, Dublin: Butterworths.

Davis, J. (2003) 'Ethics girl', *The Independent on Sunday. The Sunday Review*, September 28.

Davis, J. (2005) 'Sneaker pimps', *The Independent on Sunday. The Sunday Review*, 10 April.

De Certeau, M. (1998) *The Practice of Everyday Life*. Berkeley: University of California Press.

De Duve, T. (1999) *Kant After Duchamp*. Cambridge, MA: MIT Press.

Debord, G. (1981) 'Introduction to a critique of urban geography', in Knabb, K. (ed.), *Situationist International Authority*. Berkley CA: Bureau of Public Secrets.

Debord, G. (1997) *L'Internationale situationniste 1958–1969*. Paris: Arthème Fayard.

Debord, G. (2002) *The Society of the Spectacle*, trans. D. Nicholson-Smith. New York: Zone Books.

DeLanda, M. (1996) 'Markets and antimarkets in the world economy', in S. Aronowitz, B. Martinsons and M. Menser (eds), *Technoscience and Cyberculture*. New York and London: Routledge, pp. 181–94.

DeLanda, M. (2002) *Intensive Science and Virtual Philosophy*. London and New York: Continuum.

Deleuze, G. (1986) *Cinema 1: The Movement Image*. London: Athlone Press.

Deleuze, G. (1989) *Cinema 2: The Time Image*. London: Athlone Press.

Deleuze, G. (1991) *Bergsonism*. New York: Zone.

Deleuze, G. (1994) *Difference and Repetition*. London: Athlone.

Deleuze, G. and Guattari, F. (1983) *Anti-Oedipus: Capitalism and Schizophrenia*. Minneapolis: University of Minnesota Press.

Deleuze, G. and Guattari, F. (1994) *What is Philosophy?*, trans. H. Tomlinson and G. Burchell. New York: Columbia University Press.

Deleuze, G. and Guattari, F. (1999) *A Thousand Plateaus. Capitalism and Schizophrenia*, trans. B. Massumi. London: Athlone Press.

DeLillo, D. (1998) *Underworld*. London: Picador.

Dilthey, W. (2003) *The Formation of the Historical World in the Human Sciences*. Princeton, NJ: Princeton University Press.

Dreyfuss, R. C. (1990) 'Expressive genericity: trademarks as language in the Pepsi generation', *Notre Dame Law Review*, 65, pp. 397–424.

Du Gay, P. (1996) *Consumption and Identity at Work*. London: Sage.

Du Gay, P. (ed.) (1997) *Production of Culture/Cultures of Production*. London: Sage.

Du Gay, P., Hall, S., Janes, L., Mackay, H. and Negus, K. (1997) *Doing Cultural Studies. The Story of the Sony Walkman*. Milton Keynes: Open University Press.

Dunning, E. (1999) *Sport Matters: Sociological Studies of Sport, Violence and Civilisation*. London: Routledge.

Edelman, B. (1979) *Ownership of the Image: Elements for a Marxist Theory of the Law*, trans. E. Kingdom. London: Routledge.

Eder, K. and Kousis, M. (eds) (2000) *Environmental Politics in Southern Europe: Actors, Institutions and Discourses in a Europeanizing Society*. Dordrecht: Kluwer.

Eisenstein, S. (1988) *Eisenstein on Disney*, ed. J. Leyda, trans. A. Upchurch. London and New York: Methuen.

Eisner, W. (1985) *Comics and Sequential Art*. Tamarac, FL: Poorhouse Press.

Featherstone, M. (1996) *Consumer Culture and Postmodernism*. London: Sage.

Finch, M. (2001) 'Life/Live: The French Perspective', <www.gbhap.com/cont.visarts/article/cval4/life-live.htm>.

Fine, B. (2002) *The World of Consumption: The Material and the Cultural Revisited*. London: Routledge.

Fleming, D. (1996) *Powerplay: Toys as Popular Culture*. Manchester and New York: Manchester University Press.

Ford, S. (1996) 'Myth Making: on the phenomenon of the young British artist', *Art Monthly* 194/3, pp. 3–9.

Foucault, M. (1976) *Histoire de la sexualité 1. La volonté de savoir*. Paris: Gallimard.

Fox, E. (1995) 'Latin American Broadcasting', in L. Bethell (ed.) *The Cambridge History of Latin America*. Vol. X: *Latin America Since 1930: Ideas, Culture and Society*. Cambridge: Cambridge University Press.

Fox, E. (1997) *Latin American Broadcasting: From Tango to Telenovela*. Luton: Luton University Press.

Fox, E. and Waisbord, S. (2002) 'Latin Politics, Global Media', in idem (eds), *Latin Politics, Global Media*. Austin: University of Texas Press, pp. 1–21.

Fraser, M., Kember, S. and Lury, C. (2005) (eds) 'Inventive life', *Theory, Culture and Society* 22/1 (Special Issue).

Frazer, J. (1993) *The Golden Bough*. Ware, Hertfordshire: Wordsworth Editions.

Freake, D. (1995) The semiotics of wristwatches', *Time and Society* 4/1, pp. 67–91.

Freud, S. (1938) *The Basic Writings of Sigmund Freud*, trans. and with an introduction by A. A. Brill. New York: Random House.

Frow, J. (2001) 'Invidious distinction: waste, difference and classy stuff', *The UTS Review* 7/2 (November), pp. 21-31.

Frow, J. (2002) 'Signature and brand', in J. Collins (ed.), *High-Pop: Making Culture into Popular Entertainment*. Malden, MA and Oxford: Blackwell, pp. 56–74.

Gadamer, H.-G. (1976) 'The phenomenological movement', in *Philosophical Hermeneutics*. Berkeley: University of California, pp. 130–81.

Gadamer, H.-G. (1993) *The Relevance of the Beautiful and Other Essays*. Cambridge: Cambridge University Press.

Gadamer, H.-G. (2004) *Truth and Method*. London: Continuum.

Gaines, J. (1991) *Contested Culture: The Image, the Voice and the Law*. London: BFI Publishing.

Garnham, N. (1990) *Capitalism and Communication*. London: Sage.

Gell, A. (1998) *Art and Agency: An Anthropological Theory*. Oxford: Clarendon.

George, R. (1990) 'Some spatial aspects of the Hollywood cartoon', *Screen* 31/3, pp. 24–44.

Giddens, A. (1990) *The Consequences of Modernity*. Cambridge: Polity.

Guattari, F. and Rolnik, S. (1996) *Micropolitica. Cartografias do Desejo*, 4th edn. Rio de Janeiro: Vozes.

Hall, S. (ed.) (1980) *Culture, Media, Language*. London and New York: Routledge.

Hall, S. and Jefferson, T. (eds) (1993) *Resistance through Rituals*. London and New York: Routledge.

Haraway, D. (1997) *Modest Witness@Second Millennium*. London and New York: Routledge.

Hardt, M. (1993) *Gilles Deleuze*. London: UCL Press.

Hardt, M. and Negri, A. (2000) *Empire*. Cambridge, MA and London: Harvard University Press.

Harris, J. (2001) *The New Art History: A Critical Introduction*. London: Routledge.

Hart, S. (1998) 'The future for brands', in S. Hart and J. Murphy (eds), *Brands: The New Wealth Creators*, Basingstoke and London: Macmillan Business, pp. 206–14.

Harvey, D. (1990) *The Condition of Postmodernity*. Oxford: Blackwell.

Hatfield, S. (2003) 'What makes Nike's advertising tick?', *Guardian*, 17 June.

Haug, W. F. (1986) *Critique of Commodity Aesthetics: Appearance, Sexuality and Advertising in Capitalist Society*. Cambridge: Polity.

Hayles, N. K. (1999) *How We Became Posthuman: Virtual Bodies in Cybernetics, Literature and Informatics*. Chicago: University of Chicago Press.

Hebdige, D. (1988) *Hiding in the Light: On Images and Things*. London: Comedia.

Hegel, G. W. F. (1998) *Lectures on the Philosophy of Religion*. Vol. III: *The Consummate Religion*. Berkeley, CA: University of California Press.

Heidegger, M. (1977) *The Question Concerning Technology*, trans. W. Lovitt. New York: Harper and Row.

Heidegger, M. (1994) 'Der Ursprung des Kunstwerkes', in *Holzwege*. Frankfurt: Klostermann, pp. 1–74.

Heller, A. (1984) *Everyday Life*. London and New York: Routledge.

Hesmondhalgh, D. (2002) *The Culture Industries: An Introduction*. London: Sage.

Hill, A. (2000) 'Sport couture', *Guardian*, 4 August.

Holloway, R. (1999) 'Levi Strauss: focus on the legend ... and record-breaking global sales', in F. Gilmore (ed.), *Brand Warriors: Corporate Leaders Share Their Winning Strategies*. London: HarperCollins Business, pp. 63–78.

Horkheimer, M. and Adorno, T. (1976) *Dialectic of Enlightenment*. New York: Continuum.

Horn, D. and Laing, D. (eds) (1990) *Popular Music 8:2 (Popular Music)*. Cambridge: Cambridge University Press.

Hosokawa, S. (1984) 'The walkman effect', in R. Middleton and D. Horn (eds), *Popular Music*. Vol. 4: *Performers and Audiences*. Cambridge: Cambridge University Press, pp. 165–80.

Huizinga, J. (1955) *Homo Ludens: A Study of the Play Element in Culture*. London: The Beacon Press.

Husserl, E. (1964) *Phenomenology of Internal Time Consciousness*. Bloomington: Indiana University Press.

Husserl, E. (1983) *Ideas Pertaining to a Pure Phenomenology and to a Phenomenological Philosophy: General Introduction to a Pure Phenomenology, Book 1*. Dordrecht: Kluwer.

Hvattum, M. (2004) *Gottfried Semper and the Problem of Historicism*. Cambridge: Cambridge University Press.

Interbrand et al. (eds) (1997) *Brand Valuation*. London: Premier Books.

Jameson, F. (1990) *Postmodernism, or, the Cultural Logic of Late Capitalism*. London: Verso.

Julier, G. (2000) *The Culture of Design*. London: Sage.

Kahlert, H., Muhe, R. and Brunner, G. L. (1986) *Wristwatches: History of a Century's Development*. West Chester, PA: Schiffer Publishing.

Kastner, J. (1995–6) 'Brilliant?', *Art Monthly* 192, pp. 10–15.

Katz, D. (1994) *Just Do It: The Nike Spirit in the Corporate World*. New York: Random House.

Keat, R. and Abercrombie, N. (eds) (1990) *Enterprise Culture*. London: Routledge.

Kittler, F. A. (1999) *Gramophone, Film, Typewriter*, trans. and with an introduction by G. Winthrop-Young and M. Wutz. Stanford: Stanford University Press.

Klein, N. (2000) *No Logo*. London: Flamingo.

Klein, N. M. (1993) *Seven Minutes: The Life and Death of the American Animated Cartoon*. London: Verso.

Klein, N. M. (2000) 'Animation and animorphs: a brief disappearing act', in V. Sobchack (ed.), *MetaMorphing: Visual Transformation and the Culture of Quick-Change*. Minneapolis and London: University of Minnesota Press, pp. 21–40.

Knorr Cetina, K. (1997) 'Sociality with objects: social relations in postsocial knowledge societies', *Theory, Culture and Society* 14/4, pp. 1–30.

Knorr Cetina, K. (2000) 'Post-social theory', in G. Ritzer and B. Smart (eds), *Handbook of Social Theory*. London: Sage.

Knorr Cetina, K. and Bruegger, U. (2002) 'Global microstructures: the virtual societies of financial markets', *American Journal of Sociology* 107/4 (January), pp. 905–50.

Knowles, C. and Sweetman, P. (eds) (2004) *Picturing the Social Landscape*. London: Routledge.

Koolhaas, R. (1977) *Delirious New York: A Retroactive Manifesto for Manhattan*. New York: Monicelli Press.

Koolhaas, R. (ed.) (2001) *The Harvard Guide to Shopping*. Cologne: Taschen.

Koolhaas, R. and Mau, B. (1995) 'The generic city', in Jennifer Sigler (ed.), *S, M, L, XL: Small, Medium, Large, Extra Large*. New York: Monacelli Press, pp. 1238–69.

Kopytoff, I. (1986) 'The cultural biography of things: commoditization as process', in A. Appadurai (ed.), *The Social Life of Things: Commodities in Cultural Perspective*. Cambridge: Cambridge University Press, pp. 64–94.

Kracauer, S. (1995) *The Mass Ornament: Weimar Essays*, trans., ed. and with an introduction by T. Y. Levin. Cambridge, MA, and London: Harvard University Press.

Krauss, R. (1986) 'Sculpture in the expanded field', in R. Krauss, *The Originality of the Avant-garde and Other Modernist Myths*. Cambridge, MA: MIT Press.

Krauss, R. (1999) 'A Voyage on the North Sea', *Art in the Age of the Post-Medium Condition*. London: Thames and Hudson.

Kristeva, J. (1982) *Powers of Horror: An Essay on Abjection*. New York: Columbia University Press.

Kwinter, S. (1998) 'The hammer and the song', *Tijdschrift voor architectuur OASE Architectual Journal* 48, pp. 31–43.

Kwinter, S. (2001) *Architectures of Time: Toward a Theory of the Event in Modernist Culture*. Cambridge, MA and London: MIT Press.

Lash, S. (2002) *Critique of Information*. London, Thousand Oaks and New Delhi: Sage.

Lash, S. (2005) 'Lebenssoziologie: Georg Simmel in the information age', *Theory, Culture & Society* 22/3, pp. 1–23.

Lash, S. and Urry, J. (1994) *Economies of Signs and Spaces*. London: Sage.

Lasseter, J. and Daly, S. (1996) *Toy Story: The Art and Making of the Animated Film*. New York: Hyperion.

Latour, B. (1987) *Science in Action*. Milton Keynes: Open University Press.

Latour, B. (1993) *We Have Never Been Modern*. New York: Prentice Hall.

Latour, B. (1996) 'On interobjectivity', *Mind, Culture and Activity* 3/4, pp. 228–45.

Latour, B. and Woolgar, S. (1986) *Laboratory Life: The Construction of Scientific Facts*, Princeton, NJ: Princeton University Press.

Law, J. (1984) *Organizing Modernity*. Oxford: Blackwell.

Law, J. (2002) *Aircraft Stories: Decentering the Object in Technoscience*. Durham, NC, and London: Duke University Press.

Lazzarato. M. (2002) *Puissances de l'invention: la psychologie économique de Gabriel Tarde contre l'économie politique*. Paris: Les Empecheurs de Penser en Rond.

Lee, B. and LiPuma, E. (2002) 'Cultures of circulation: the imaginations of modernity', *Public Culture*,14/1, pp. 191–213.

Lee, D. (1995) 'Damien Hirst: in profile', *Art Review* (June), pp. 6–10.

Lee, S. (1997) 'He's gotta have it', *Guardian Weekend*, 13 September.

Leibniz, G. W. (1992) *Monadology*. London: Routledge.

Leith, W. (1996) 'Existential angst of the sad, strange little man', *Observer Review*, 15 December.

Levin, T. (1995) Introduction to S. Kracauer, *The Mass Ornament*. Cambridge, MA: Harvard University Press.

Lévi-Strauss, C. (1999) *Structural Anthropology*. New York: Basic Books.

Lippard, L. (1997) *Six Years: The Dematerialization of the Art Object from 1966 to 1972*. Berkeley: University of California Press.

Lord, P. and Sibley, B. (1998) *Cracking Animation. The Aardman Book of 3-D Animation*. London: Thames and Hudson.

Luhmann, N. (1999) *Die Wirtschaft der Gesellschaft*. Frankfurt: Suhrkamp.

Lury, C. (1993) *Cultural Rights: Technology, Legality and Personality*. London: Routledge.

Lury, C. (1997) *Prosthetic Culture*. London and New York: Routledge.

Lury, C. (1999) 'Marking time with Nike: the illusion of the durable', *Public Culture* 11/3, pp. 499–526.

Lury, C. (2002) 'Portrait of the artist as a brand', in D. McClean and K. Schubert (eds), *Dear Images: Art, Copyright and Culture*. London: Ridinghouse, pp. 310–29.

Lury, C. (2004) *Brands: The Logos of the Global Economy*. London and New York: Routledge.

Lury, C. and Warde, A. (1996) 'Investments in the imaginary consumer: conjectures regarding power, knowledge and advertising', in M. Nava et al. (eds), *Buy This Book: Studies in Advertising and Consumption*. London: Routledge, pp. 87–102.

Lynch, K. (1960) *The Image of the City*. Cambridge MA: MIT Press.

Lyotard, J.-F. (1984) *The Postmodern Condition: A Report on Knowledge*, trans. G. Bennington and B. Massumi. Minneapolis: University of Minnesota Press.

Mackenzie, A. (2002) *Transductions: Bodies and Machines at Speed*. London and New York: Continuum.

Maharaj, S. (2001) *Work in Progress*. London: International Institute of Visual Arts.

Mahoney, E. (1999) 'Anya Gallacio, Tramway Corinthian, Glasgow', *Art Monthly* 226/5, pp. 31–3.

Malik, S. (2005) 'Information and knowledge', *Theory, Culture and Society* 22/1 (Special Issue): 'Inventive Life;, pp. 29–49.

Malinowski, B. (1984) *Argonauts of the Western Pacific*. Long Grove, IL: Waveland Press.

Maloney, M. (1995) 'Grunge corp: the class of '95'. *Artforum* (October), pp. 37–9.

Maloney, M. (1996) 'The Chapman Brothers: when will I be famous', *Flash Art* (January/February), pp. 64–7.

Manovich, L. (2001) *The Language of New Media*. Cambridge, MA: MIT Press.

Manovich, L. (2003) 'The poetics of augmented space: learning from Prada', <www.manovich.net>.

Manzini, E. (1989) *The Material of Invention*. London: Design Council.

Marcuse, H. (1991) *One-Dimensional Man*. Boston: Beacon.

Marks, L. U. (2000) 'Signs of the time: Deleuze, Peirce and the documentary image', in G. Flaxman (ed.), *The Brain is the Screen: Deleuze and the Philosophy of the Cinema*. Minneapolis and London: University of Minnesota Press, pp. 193–214.

Massumi, B. (1999) 'Notes on the translation and acknowledgements', in G. Deleuze and F. Guattari (eds), *A Thousand Plateaus: Capitalism and Schizophrenia*. London: Athlone Press.

Massumi, B. (2000) 'Too-blue: colour patch for an expanded empiricism', *Cultural Studies* 14/2, pp. 177–226.

Massumi, B. (2002) *Parables for the Virtual: Movement, Affect, Sensation*. Durham, NC, and London: Duke University Press.

Maturana, H. and Varela, F. (1979) *Autopoieisis and Cognition: The Realization of the Living*. Dordrecht: Kluwer.

Mauss, M. (1976) *The Gift*. New York: Norton.

McLuhan, M. (1997) *Understanding Media: The Extensions of Man*. London: Routledge.

McRobbie, A. (1998) *British Fashion Design: Rag Trade or Image Experience?* London and New York: Routledge.

McRobbie, A. (1999) *In the Culture Society: Art, Fashion and Popular Music*. London and New York: Routledge.

Merleau-Ponty, M. (1962) *Phenomenology of Perception*. London: Routledge.

Michael, M. (2000) *Reconnecting Culture, Technology and Nature*. London: Routledge.

Miege, B. (1989) *The Capitalization of Cultural Production*. New York: International General.

Miller, D. (1987) *Material Culture and Mass Consumption*. Oxford and Malden, MA: Blackwell.

Miller, D. (2000) 'The birth of value', in P. Jackson et al. (eds), *Commercial Cultures: Economies, Practices, Spaces*. Oxford: Berg.

Miller, D. (ed.) (2005) *Materiality*. Durham, NC, and London: Duke University Press.

Miller, P. (1998) 'The margins of accounting'. in M. Callon (ed.), *The Laws of the Markets*. Oxford and Malden, MA: Blackwell, pp. 174–93.

Moor, L. (2003) 'Branded spaces: the scope of "new marketing"', *Journal of Consumer Culture* 3/1, pp. 39–60.

Morris, R. (1995) *Continuous Process Altered Daily*. Cambridge, MA: MIT Press.

Morse, M. (1998) *Virtualities. Television, Media Art, and Cyberculture*. Bloomington and Indianapolis: Indiana University Press.

Multiplicity (2003) *Uncertain States of Europe*. Milan: Skira.

Myles, J. (1997) 'The field of art in England: a Bourdieuan analysis', PhD thesis. Lancaster University.

Negri, A. (2000) *The Savage Anomaly: The Power of Spinoza's Metaphysics and Politics*. Minneapolis: University of Minnesota Press.

Negroponte, N. (1996) *Being Digital*. London: Coronet Books.

Neidich, W. (2003) *Blow-Up: Photography, Cinema and the Brain*. New York: Zzdap Publishing.

O'Doherty, B. (2000) *Inside the White Cube: The Ideology of the Gallery Space*. Berkeley and London: University of California Press.

Osborne, P. (1999) 'Conceptual art and/as philosophy', in M. Newman and J. Bird (eds), *Rewriting Conceptual Art*. London: Reaktion, pp. 47–65.

Parameshwar Gaonkar, D. and Lee, B. (eds) (2002) 'New imaginaries', *Public Culture*

14/1 (Special Issue).

Parsons, T. (1955) *The Social System*. New York: Free Press.

Peirce, C. S. (1978) *The Philosophy of Peirce: Selected Writings*, ed. J. Buchler. London: Routledge.

Piers, G. (1953) *Shame and Guilt. A Psychoanalytic and a Cultural Study*. New York: Thomas.

Piper, A. (1999) *Out of Order, Out of Sight: Selected Essays in Art Criticism, 1967–92*, vol. 2. Cambridge, MA: MIT Press.

Plant, S. (1992) *The Most Radical Gesture: Situationist International in a Postmodern Age*. London: Routledge.

Poster, M. (1995) *The Second Media Age*. Cambridge: Polity.

Poster, M. (2001) *What's the Matter with the Internet?* Minneapolis and London: University of Minnesota Press.

Prigogine and Stengers, I. (1984) *Order out of Chaos. Man's Dialogue with Nature*. New York: Random House.

Propp, V. (1970) *Morphologie du conte*. Paris: Seuil.

Rickett, J. (2004) 'The bookseller', *Guardian Review*, 6 November.

Ricoeur, P. (1990) *Time and Narrative*. Chicago: University of Chicago Press.

Rodowick, D. N. (1997) *Gilles Deleuze's Time Machine*. Durham, NC, and London: Duke University Press.

Rodowick, D. N. (2001) *Reading the Figural, or, Philosophy after the New Media*. Durham, NC, and London: Duke University Press.

Rogoff, I. (2000) *Terra Infirma: Geography's Visual Culture*. London and New York: Routledge.

Rorimer, A. (1999) 'Siting the page: exhibiting works in publications. Some examples of conceptual art in the USA', in M. Newman and J. Bird (eds), *Rewriting Conceptua Art*. London: Reaktion Books, pp. 11–26,

Rushton, S. (2003) 'Nice and easy does it', *Independent on Sunday, The Sunday Review*, 28 September.

Saussure, F. de (1966) *Course in General Linguistics*. New York: McGraw-Hill.

Saussure, F. de (1983) *Course in General Linguistics*. London: Duckworth.

Semper, G. (2004) *Style in the Technical and Tectonic Arts: Or, Practical Aesthetics*. Los Angeles: Getty Publishing.

Serres, M. (1980) *Hermes. Critique*. Paris: Éditions de minuit.

Shields, R. (1997) 'Flow', *Space and Culture* 1, pp. 1–5.

Shields, R. (2003) *The Virtual*. London and New York: Routledge.

Sibley, B. (ed.) (1998) *Wallace and Gromit: The Wrong Trousers, Storyboard Collection*. London: BBC Worldwide Ltd.

Simmel, G. (1971) *On Individuality and Social Forms*. Chicago and London: The University of Chicago Press.

Simmel, G. (1990) *The Philosophy of Money*, ed. D. Frisby. London and New York: Routledge.

Simmel, G. (1995) 'Kant und Goethe'. *Gesamtausgabe Band 10*. Frankfurt: Suhrkamp, pp. 119–66.

Simmel, G. (1997) *Simmel on Culture. Selected Writings*. London: Sage.

Simondon, G. (1958) *Du mode d'existence des objets techniques*. Paris: Aubier.

Strathern, M. (1999) *Property, Substance and Effect: Anthropological Essays on Persons and Things*. London: Athlone Press.

Strathern, M. (2002) 'Externalities in comparative guise', *Economy and Society* 31/2 (May), pp. 250–67.

Taylor, L. (1994) (ed.) *Visualizing Theory. Selected Essays from V.A.R. 1990–1994*. New York and London: Routledge.

Taylor, W. (1993) 'Message and muscle: an interview with Swatch titan Nicolas Hayek', *Harvard Business Review* (March–April), pp. 98–110.

Terranova, T. (2004) *Network Culture. Politics for the Information Age*. London: Pluto Press.

Thomas, N. (1991) *Entangled Objects: Exchange, Material Culture and Colonialism in the Pacific*. Cambridge, MA: Harvard University Press.

Thompson, J. B. (1995) *Media and Modernity: A Social Theory of the Media*. Cambridge: Polity.

Thrift, N. (1997) 'The rise of soft capitalism', *Cultural Values* 1, pp. 29–57.

Thrift, N. (1998) 'Virtual capitalism: the globalization of reflexive business knowledge', in J. G. Carrier and D. Miller (eds), *Virtualism: A New Political Economy*. Oxford and New York: Berg, pp. 161–86.

Thrift, N. (2000) 'Performing cultures in the new economy', *Annals of the Association of American Geographers* 90/4, pp. 674–92.

Thrift, N. (2001) '"It's the romance, not the finance that makes the business worth pursuing": disclosing a new market culture', *Economy and Society* 30/4, pp. 412–32.

Thrift, N. (2004) *Knowing Capitalism*. London: Sage.

Troester, M. (1994) 'Swatch®', in J. Jorgensen (ed.), *Encyclopedia of Consumer Brands. Vol 2: Personal Products*. Detroit and London: St James Press, pp. 530–2.

Tschumi, B. (2005) *Event-Cities: Concept vs. Context vs. Content: No. 3*. Cambridge, MA: MIT Press.

Tsing, A. Lowenhaupt (2005) *Friction. An Ethnography of Global Connection*. Princeton and Oxford: Princeton University Press.

Tylor, E. (1964) *Researches into the Early History of Mankind and the Development of Civilization*. Chicago: University of Chicago Press.

Urry, J. (2000) *Sociology Beyond Societies: Mobilities for the Twenty-first Century*. London and New York: Routledge.

Urry, J. (2003) *Global Complexity*. Cambridge: Polity.

Valentine, J. (1999) 'Contemporary art and the political value of culture', *Critical Quarterly* 4, pp. 9–19.

Van Parys, B. (1996) 'Ewan McGregor', *US Magazine* (August).

Vancil, M. (1995) *I'm Back! More Rare Air*. San Francisco: HarperCollins Publishers.

Vanderbilt, T. (1998) *The Sneaker Book: Anatomy of an Industry and an Icon*. New York: The New Press.

Varela, F. et al. (1993) *The Embodied Mind*. Cambridge, MA: MIT Press.

Vattimo, G. (1994) *The Transparent Society*. Baltimore: Johns Hopkins University Press.

Venturi, R. (1977) *Complexity and Contradiction in Architecture*. New York: Museum of Modern Art.

Venturi, R., Scott Brown, D. and Izenour, S. (1977) *Learning From Las Vegas: The Forgotten Symbolism of Architectural Form*. Cambridge, MA: MIT Press.

Vergès, F. (1999) *Monsters and Revolutionaries*, Durham, NC: Duke University Press.

Virilio, P. (1994) *The Vision Machine: Perspectives*. Bloomington: Indiana University Press.

Warner. M. (1987) *Monuments and Maidens: The Allegory of the Female Form*. London: Picador.

Wells, P. (1998) *Understanding Animation*. London and New York: Routledge.

Whitehead, A. N. (1967) *Science and the Modern World*. New York: The Free Press.

Whitehead, A. N. (1970) *Nature and Life*. New York: Greenwood Publishing Group.

Whitehead, A. N. (1978) *Process and Reality: Corrected Edition*. New York: The Free Press.

Williams, G. (2000) 'The point of purchase', in J. Pavitt (ed.), *Brand.new*. London: V&A Publications, pp. 185–211.

Williams, J. (1989) *Hooligans Abroad. Behaviour and Control of English Fans in Continental Europe*. London: Routledge.

Williams, R. (1974) *Television: Technology and Cultural Form*. London: Fontana/Collins.

Williams, R. (1975) *Keywords: A Vocabulary of Culture and Society*. London: Fontana.

Willigan, G. (1992) 'High performance marketing: an interview with Nike's Phil Knight', *Harvard Business Review* (July–August), pp. 90–101.

Wilson, A. (1994) 'Out of control'. *Art Monthly* (June), pp. 3–9.

Winckelmann, K. (1996) 'Life/live. La scène artistique au Royaume-Uni en 1996', <www.jnwnklmnn.de/lifelive/htm>.

Wood, W. (1999) 'Still you ask for more': demand, display and "the new art"', in M. Newman and J. Bird (eds), *Rewriting Conceptual Art*. London: Reaktion, pp. 66–87.

Zizek, S. (1997) *The Plague of Fantasies*. London: Verso.

Index